Mary Colter
Architect of the Southwest

Mary Colter
Architect of the Southwest

Arnold Berke

COLOR PHOTOGRAPHS *by* ALEXANDER VERTIKOFF

Princeton Architectural Press
New York   2002

FOR JAKE

Princeton Architectural Press
37 East 7th Street
New York, NY 10003

For a free catalog of books
published by
Princeton Architectural Press,
call 1.800.722.6657
or visit www.papress.com

EDITOR: Jan Cigliano
COPY EDITOR: Heather Ewing
DESIGNER: Angela Voulangas

SPECIAL THANKS TO
Nettie Aljian, Ann Alter,
Amanda Atkins, Eugenia Bell,
Nicola Bednarek, Janet Behning,
Jane Garvie, Tom Hutten,
Clare Jacobson, Mark Lamster,
Linda Lee, Nancy Eklund Later,
Anne Nitschke, Evan Schoninger,
Lottchen Shivers, Jennifer
Thompson, and Deb Wood of
Princeton Architectural Press
—Kevin Lippert, PUBLISHER

ISBN 1-56898-295-X (hardcover)
ISBN 1-56898-345-X (paperback)

Library of Congress
Cataloging-in-Publication Data
Berke, Arnold (1945–
Includes bibliographical
references.

Printed in China

Drawn by the Desert:
"An Incomprehensible Woman in Pants"

ONE

SUNRISE AT DESERT VIEW ILLUMINES a boundless landscape as well as a curious round tower that pushes up boldly from its midst. Even as the canyon far below remains blue-brown and murky, its rippled layers and sharp peaks advancing sluggishly into the light, the sun rising from behind the mesa called Cedar Mountain models, warms, and tinges the rocky tower. Its oddly coursed bands of wide and narrow stone take on texture, and, high above the trees, the topmost windows start to shine in the sun. The monolith has become the dawning panorama's brightest feature. It is of earth, not sky, yet it is the first star of morning.

Spring is unfolding here at the eastern end of Arizona's Grand Canyon National Park. The "desert view" afforded from the tower, a National Park Service plaque explains, takes in not only vast stretches of the canyon—on whose rim the structure is perched—as well as the San Francisco Peaks to the south but also the Painted Desert far to the east. Because of the early hour and great and hazy distance, however, that famously gorgeous badland remains mostly monochrome. Close by, just below the

Sunrise at the Watchtower at Desert View, Grand Canyon National Park

tower, bits of snow still cling to the slopes, while at the bottom of the enormous chasm—almost a mile straight down—the drab and seemingly motionless Colorado River bends to the west as it flows from Marble Canyon. A cold wind whooshes up eerily from the void, sowing some of the spent night into the new day.

Over on the tower's still-unlit side, one catches sight of the jagged outline made against the morning sky by the structure's huge foundation boulders. This rough girdle forms the bottom of both the great tower itself and a large, also circular, but much lower structure that extends out from its base. Still deep in shadow a few feet west of the tower stands a roofless, semicircular assembly of stone walls that shelters a stack of firewood. It looks half-finished but also quite old; is it, perhaps, ages old? Is the entire tower ensemble, in fact, an ancient ruin? Was it abandoned long ago by the Native Americans who built it? Why was it created? For defense against an enemy tribe, for some unrevealed ceremony, to chart the sun and stars? Certainly there are enough peculiarities here to support any number of theories about origins and purposes: conspicuous cracks in the tower wall, a short row of triangular stones just under the jagged parapet, weathered rocks that protrude from the surface (one of them a snake-like grotesque), simple drawings pecked into certain stones, and door-like recesses filled with rocks and timbers that seem to have been walled in years after the tower was built.

Some of the animated, camera-laden tourists who begin to lumber onto the site from their cars and buses know the answers to the riddles here. Some of those who enter the low building, gaze out through its huge picture windows into the canyon, then climb up level by level through the tower's richly adorned chambers know, or will soon know, the true story of this stout eccentricity. They realize that it is in fact a fairly recent building (some seventy years old), that its designer was not a vanished people from antiquity but a twentieth-century woman who, taking her inspiration from real Indian towers in the region, consciously built into her tower all of its venerability and particularity. This woman, an architect, grew up in faraway Minnesota but was unusually attuned to the heritage of this region, especially its Native Americans and the splendors of their land. She possessed a special genius for interpreting the past to create new buildings and interiors that, with their striking forms and fanciful atmosphere, have enchanted generations of travelers crossing the American Southwest.

Yet the knowledge that the Watchtower at Desert View, as it is officially called, is a relatively new building does little to dispel its singular presence in a landscape that is already a triumph of singularity. The tower remains as engaging to gaze at and explore as if it had really risen a thousand years before. The story of its creator, Mary Colter, is just as compelling. It is a one-of-a-kind tale of talent and tenacity, played out against a backdrop of flourishing opportunity in a rugged region—telling of an exceptional person who pioneered both as an architect and as a woman.

Mary Elizabeth Jane Colter (1869–1958) was an architect and interior designer who spent virtually her entire career working simultaneously for the Fred Harvey Company and the Santa Fe Railway. The two companies worked in tandem, using Colter's innovative designs to help make the West pleasurably accessible to travelers for whom it was starkly but alluringly new. Beginning in the 1870s, as the Santa Fe built its way westward toward California, Fred Harvey dotted its route with dining establishments, hotels, and shops that became world-famous for their high standards of service as well as their fetching appearance. Working through most of the first half of the twentieth century, Colter designed hotels, train stations, shops, restaurants, and other touristic enticements, steeping them in the Native American and Hispanic history and art and the southwestern landscape that her employers promoted so ingeniously. Most of her structures, like the Watchtower, rose at the rim of the Grand Canyon, where Fred Harvey and the Santa Fe in association with the National Park Service produced one of the West's most popular tourist destinations.

Colter designed buildings not just to lodge, feed, or otherwise serve these travelers but also to entertain and engage them; she invariably sought to delight the eye and occupy the mind. Her works are beguiling stage sets rooted so masterfully in the history of the region that they seem to be genuine remnants of that history. Thus does the Watchtower often seduce people into thinking that it is a centuries-old Indian ruin preserved for the delight of the modern-day traveler. Thus does La Posada—a sprawling and ingeniously conceived hotel and railroad station finished in 1930 in Winslow, Arizona—pass so convincingly for the venerable hacienda of an aristocratic Spanish colonial. And thus does the quite oddly configured Hermit's Rest, built in 1914 at the western end of the Grand Canyon's south rim road, so cleverly evoke the retreat of a pioneer recluse with its seemingly offhand heaping of rocks, stones, and timbers.

Colter did not copy history but fashioned her environments from their essence, relying on her well-rounded artistic talents, practical bent, and sense of humor to work historical reference into buildings constructed with modern methods and materials. The results were often magical—but not hasty or effortless: Colter devoted considerable time to research, for example, trekking by car and plane to remote locations in the Southwest in search of Native American ruins and artifacts to study. She was an enthusiastic follower of Indian culture and an avid collector of Indian art (especially jewelry and baskets), making direct or derivative use of it in many of her designs. Hopi House at the Grand Canyon (1905) and the El Navajo hotel and train station in

Hopi House, Grand Canyon
National Park

The lounge of El Navajo Hotel,
Gallup, New Mexico, 1923

11

Gallup, New Mexico (1918–23), exemplify her exacting and ingenious use of Native American imagery. In some cases, she arranged for Indian artists to embellish the interiors of her buildings and to consecrate them with lavish ceremony upon their completion. She also traveled to Mexico to study its architecture and search for furnishings to either ship to or reproduce for projects like La Posada and the Bright Angel Lodge at Grand Canyon, a rustic hotel-and-cabin village that opened in 1935. Well-educated and employed as a teacher for years in her early adulthood, Colter remained a lifelong student of art history, natural history, and human civilization. Through her buildings she conveyed that learning, like a teacher, to the traveler.

Mimbreño china designed by Colter for the Santa Fe's 1937 Super Chief

"Nothing in her work, large or small, has escaped her careful study," marveled the celebrated Western writer Frank Waters in *Masked Gods*, his 1950 study of Indian life and ceremony. Taken by Colter's energy and skill, Waters wrote: "For years an incomprehensible woman in pants, she rode horseback through the Four Corners making sketches of prehistoric pueblo ruins, studying details of construction, the composition of adobes and washes. She could teach masons how to lay adobe bricks, plasterers how to mix washes, carpenters how to fit viga joints."[1]

Colter took great stock in materials and setting. She was a master of the properties and artistic use of stone and brick, wood and tile, iron and glass, and textiles—some of which were gleaned on-site and incorporated in their natural state into her projects. She chose materials indigenous to the region—Kaibab limestone and yellow pine, for example—to assemble and adorn her structures, juxtaposing contrasting materials in unusual ways. She treated structure and site as intertwined halves of a single composition, merging them with almost obsessive precision, yet

opposite: Mary Colter at Twin Towers ruin, Hovenweep National Monument, Utah, circa 1931

13

assuring that their synthesis appears far from contrived. It is an often-heard remark that Lookout Studio, perched right on the Grand Canyon's rim, looks as if it rose straight out of the earth, so closely does its layering of stonework mimic the texture, pattern, and color of the rock strata of the canyon wall below it. Above all, Colter was

Lookout Studio, Grand Canyon National Park

a thoroughgoing designer who took great pains to integrate architecture, interior decoration, and landscape design—and even, on occasion, tableware and waitresses' uniforms—into unified works of art.

Like many artists and architects at the turn of the twentieth century, Colter endorsed the use of American, rather than European, forms. Taste-makers during that time, abetted by the nation's centennial in 1876 and its industrialization and westward expansion, encouraged designers to break from European tradition in favor of developing designs that reflected the peoples and landscapes of their own continent. The dominance of European art and architecture, fed by the long-standing practice of traveling to Europe for education and cultural enrichment, began yielding to pride in the home-grown. "Is there any reason why American architects should not be something more than mere copyists of European models?" wrote Harold D. Mitchell in 1882 in *The California Architect and Building News*. "The time must come sooner or later (and why not now?), when an original *American style* must be born of the national genius."[2] The Prairie Style in architecture that was blazoned by Frank Lloyd Wright and his retinue of followers and the regionalism of painters like Thomas Moran were conspicuous assertions of this spreading confidence in American models. It was a progressive way of perceiving and affirming domestic idioms that would also find expression in the promotion of American Indian and Hispanic arts—both by artists like Colter and corporate patrons like the Santa Fe Railway and Fred Harvey Company, which used these arts in highly visible and notably successful campaigns to "see America first."

The aesthetic tastes of Colter and many of her contemporary American designers and consumers were also shaped by the Arts and Crafts movement, which in the late nineteenth century exerted a powerful influence on American design philosophies and their application to everyday life. The movement grew partly as a reaction to the spread of industrialization and the mass-produced goods it rained upon the public. The importance of sensitive handcrafting, of indigenous design, of simple and functional objects, and of the well-integrated bundling of the arts served as the movement's guiding principles. These began to be espoused in books, magazines, newspapers, and schools during the time when Colter was entering adulthood in St. Paul and then studying architecture in San Francisco in the late 1880s. This philosophy encouraged the development of an artistic setting for home life and a substantial role for women in promoting that environment. During this period, women began more frequently to study painting and the creation of art objects—pottery, jewelry, and textile art—and exhibited their works more often in public. Cultivating the home, women also began to associate more with one another, founding art and social-reform clubs that empowered them both as individuals and in concert. (Many of the great American art museums can trace their origins to that period and those women.)

An Arts and Crafts sensibility suffuses Colter's work for Fred Harvey—from her first paid commission, which was to concoct enticing museum and sales spaces in 1902 for the Indian Building at Albuquerque's Alvarado Hotel, to her last in 1949, when she designed a Mexican-themed cocktail lounge for La Fonda Hotel in Santa Fe. As a body her works are warm or even homey, playful, inviting, and unfailingly inventive. They are often woodsy or rustic. Steeped in authentic southwestern imagery, Colter's buildings are decked out with all manner of native furniture,

15

fixtures, paintings, and other craftwork—well synthesized with the architecture and with each other. Her buildings emerge effortlessly from their sites and, even when new, usually affected a look of age (achieved with great effort on her part, she was fond of pointing out). None of these qualities should come as a surprise, since Colter's enduring charge was to delight and comfort the traveling public. Even her most severe and abstract building, El Navajo Hotel, which exhibits close ties to international modernism, was at the same time a richly embellished and comfortable inn with an undeniable debt to Native American culture. "Skilled in architecture, landscape design, and decorative arts," wrote parks historian Linda Flint McClelland, "Colter was the quintessential practitioner of the Arts and Crafts movement."[3]

Colter made notable contributions to the growth of American architecture, helping assert its independence and confirm its individuality. Although she practiced outside the mainstream of the profession—as a woman in an overwhelmingly male field and because her output was relatively small and her buildings often remote from the centers of architectural production and study—she paralleled other architects in pursuing a new and very American path. Early in her career Colter began to strengthen the image of the Southwest through her buildings and interiors at the same time that she helped the Harvey Company and the Santa Fe wrest tourist architecture from its dependence on denatured Victorian revival motifs from the East and Europe. Her designs were also drawn from history, of course, but since it was regional history they were boldly novel for the period. Who would have dreamed, for instance, of as audacious a building as Hopi House? The notion of "transporting" a true Indian dwelling to the front yard of the El Tovar Hotel must have astounded travelers, who previously had viewed Indian art only in neoclassical museum buildings (or in Colter's own sales environments in the Mission Revival-style Alvarado) and Indian architecture hardly at all. But the rush to travel to what was promoted as a now safe-and-civilized West demanded a fresh new architecture to shelter that

A ground-floor salesroom at Hopi House, 1905

Entrance to Bright Angel Lodge,
Grand Canyon National Park

tourism. With her discerning interpretation of regional motifs, Colter cultivated and reinforced a comprehensive southwestern "style" with more scholarship and a freer imagination than most other designers of the period. And if one were to posit the separate existence down through the decades of a "travel architecture," then Colter would stand among its most successful innovators.

Colter's works were to have a special influence on architecture within the national parks, the growth of which paralleled the rise of the American travel industry. The federal government's preservation of huge expanses of western scenery as national parks or monuments was followed by the cultivation of these preserves for public visitation through the building of roads, hotels, and other improvements. But federal parks policy sought minimal disturbance of the natural environment, so these manmade enhancements were expected to harmonize with the land. At Lookout Studio, Hermit's Rest, and Phantom Ranch—a lodge and cabins constructed in 1922 at the bottom of the Grand Canyon—Colter carried out that intent with particular aplomb, avoiding formal, over-sophisticated designs that would have seemed inappropriate in such a grand domain. Instead, these buildings were small, simple, and rugged and were constructed of local, even on-site, materials; they rested with ease in their settings. Her Bright Angel Lodge and its gaggle of cabins was a later example of this approach, which subsequently came to be tagged "National Park Service rustic" architecture. Impressing other architects as well as park management, Colter's distinctive essays in this mode influenced the design of buildings that were to follow hers at the canyon and in other national parks. *Park and Recreation Structures*, the Park Service's landmark compendium of praiseworthy rustic structures built in the 1930s, lauded Bright Angel Lodge: "Inspired architecturally by surviving structures of stagecoach days, and motivated by a conviction that a group of low rambling structures is the only intrusion to be countenanced in a setting of such magnificence, the results are enormously successful."[4]

The story of Mary Colter is a particularly American one, a version of the "Go West, young man" theme that brought considerable success, in this case, to a woman. The western frontier, even as its rougher edges were being smoothed out, exerted a powerful attraction on this young woman from the Midwest, parts of which had just left their own frontier days. In her decision to travel to New Mexico for her first job with the Fred Harvey Company, Colter paralleled others who had yielded to the temptation of the West as a place to seek one's fortune. That she succeeded there as a woman can surely be ascribed to her particular talents and drive—and their fit with the work environment offered by her employer—but also, it seems, to the freedom that the West offered to both men and women to carve out unique careers, even to women in such a male bastion as architecture. Women in other cultures have broken into male-dominated professions, of course, but America has proved especially conducive to such breakthroughs. (Colter's own employer exemplified this faith through its training of the popular "Harvey Girls" into a disciplined corps of waitresses who formed the backbone of its famous restaurant service.) Colter was among the very first women in this country to enter and to successfully lead a career in architecture; that she flourished in it by espousing the distinctive qualities of the Southwest only heightens the very American character of her life.

Except for coverage in the local press in communities where she worked, as part of the great Fred Harvey enterprise, Colter did not achieve any measure of fame during her lifetime. She was not noticed by the popular national publications nor by the journals and magazines of the architectural world, even though her buildings and interiors, all of them open to the public, surely entertained more visitors than those of the big-name designers. After Colter died, she slipped out of sight, reduced to an obscure footnote, if that, in the story of twentieth-century architecture. The passenger-railroad culture had faded, and many of her creations were destroyed. Architectural and cultural tastes left her far behind. Starting slowly in the 1980s, however, and for an assortment of reasons, Colter's life and contributions have begun to receive the recognition that they always deserved but never enjoyed.

The relatively few people who knew Colter admired her for her intelligence, independence, and creativity. Many years after her death, our society tends to cherish and interpret extraordinary stories such as hers in broader contexts. As we rediscover Colter, we find ourselves fond of "reading" her life story for its significance in the history of the women's movement, for example, or the story of women in architecture. We assess her very thematic works for what they might tell us about the theme-driven vacation and entertainment architecture that has followed, and expanded enormously, since her day. We view her use of Indian art, the result of deeply sincere interest, through a lens that understandably has become much more cynical and untrusting, that sees much more pain and irony in the treatment of Native American culture. Even if occasionally we are prone to overanalyze, it is normal to deepen the appreciation of lives such as Colter's by seeking to understand their wider meanings and implications. After all, we are only placing her in history, including our own.

Mary Colter in 1939 at Awatovi
Pueblo site, Arizona

The Early Years and
the American Arts and Crafts

TWO

THE ST. PAUL TO WHICH MARY ELIZABETH JANE COLTER MOVED with her parents in 1880, when she was eleven, was a young and prosperous place. Minnesota had become a state only twenty-two years before, carved out of the Louisiana Purchase and the old Northwest Territory, and was enjoying a robust economy rooted in the development of lumber and flour milling, farming, iron-ore mining, and the railroads. Founded in 1841 on the banks of the Mississippi River and designated the capital of the new Minnesota Territory in 1849, St. Paul had grown to some 41,000 people by 1880 when the Colter family returned to the city.

Colter's parents were Irish immigrants who had previously lived in St. Paul, their first American home. The city had attracted a large Irish population, including relatives of her father, William Colter, who had preceded the Colters. But soon after Mary's older sister, Harriet, was born in 1863, the family moved to Pittsburgh, where Mary was born on April 4, 1869. William operated a clothing store there (he earlier had been in the furniture business); Mary's mother, Rebecca Crozier Colter, worked

Some of the furniture and objects made by Mechanic Arts High School students that won a Gold Medal at the 1904 St. Louis World's Fair

23

in the store as a milliner until Mary was born. The peripatetic Colters moved often—back to St. Paul when Mary was three, then on to Texas when she was seven and to Colorado when she was nine before resettling permanently in St. Paul.[1]

The Upper Mississippi Valley was part of what was considered the West in those years—more specifically, the Northwest—long before the region came to be known as the Midwest.[2] In Minnesota the recent frontier of exploration had been transformed into a land of expansion as its flourishing cities and farmlands swelled with immigration from the east (especially New England) and Europe (particularly Germany, Ireland, and Scandinavia). As was typical in such freshly booming and boastful states, residents were fond of stacking up their waxing indices of population, industry, finance, and culture against those of more established states to the east. Minnesota's bright future seemed limitless, and boosters rosily pictured the twin cities of St. Paul and Minneapolis, and even the Lake Superior port of Duluth, challenging Chicago for the title of gateway to the vast western hinterlands and the faraway Pacific Coast.[3] Enjoying the highest growth rate in the nation during the 1880s,[4] Minneapolis/St. Paul became the financial capital of Minnesota and the upper Northwest. Their expansion, proclaimed the *St. Paul Globe*, was "a tale of two cities that has no counterpart in history."[5]

These were still new cities, fresh with the accretions brought forth by unquestioned progress. Building booms enriched both of their downtowns and surrounding neighborhoods with imposing mercantile, residential, and public architecture, including numerous examples of that nationally popular style, Richardsonian Romanesque. Cass Gilbert, who was to go on to renown as the designer of New York City's soaring Woolworth Building (1913), first established himself in St. Paul in the mid-1880s, designing office buildings, retail stores, churches, and dozens of residences for the wealthy. He capped his career there with the elegant neoclassical Minnesota State Capitol, which opened in 1905 on a hill overlooking the city (not far from one of the houses where Mary Colter and her family had lived). Although architecture in the Twin Cities remained firmly rooted in the European-based revival styles that held sway nationwide, a restless spirit of progressivism was to be found in the region that grew as the turn of the century approached and agitation for American design—even for a single "national architecture"—gained credence nationwide. The area would soon prove receptive to the Prairie Style architecture conceived by such national luminaries as Frank Lloyd Wright as well as the local firm of Purcell and Elmslie.

By the time Mary Colter graduated from high school in 1883—at the age of only fourteen—cultural patronage and artistic aspiration were expanding beyond their limited base, finding outlets in the founding of museums like the Minneapolis Institute of Arts (1883) and schools like the St. Paul School of Fine Arts (1890). The Arts and Crafts movement began to bud locally soon after, in the 1890s, championed by artists and civic leaders—often women—who promoted the domestic and communal values of the movement as well as the craft works that it produced: ceramic and metal articles, leather work, jewelry, weaving, and graphic designs. The stage was set for the birth of two prominent associations of artists and supporters akin to organizations in other American cities: the Art Workers' Guild of St. Paul (1902) and the Handicraft Guild of Minneapolis (1904). Colter was later to become active in the former group during her years as a high school teacher.[6] The Guild sought "to encourage the worker in art. To forward the interest of art. To develop in the community a love of beauty in every form."[7] Women were also establishing civic groups like the New Century Club, which was founded in St. Paul in 1887 "for the literary and social culture of its members, the promotion of a higher acquaintance of women with each other, and the stimulation of intellectual development;[8] Colter later lectured there.

Drawings made in 1877–78 by Sioux prisoners from the Battle of the Little Bighorn, given to Colter when she was a child

Colter's own artistic development had been nurtured in the public schools, from elementary school through St. Paul High School, which offered art courses as part of a comprehensive curriculum.[9] She also developed an interest in Native American culture and arts; encouraged perhaps by the proximity of a large Sioux (or

Portrait of Mary Colter painted circa 1890 by her teacher Arthur Mathews

Dakota) population in Minnesota, which not so many years before had been the home territory for many of the Sioux tribes. Her enthusiasm for Indian life was also roused as a child when John Graham, a relative of her father, presented the Colter family with a number of Indian-made gifts, including a set of Sioux drawings, some of them whimsical or joking. The sketches had been drawn by Indian prisoners at Fort Keogh, people who had fought in the 1876 Battle of the Little Bighorn. When Mary's mother learned that smallpox had broken out on the reservation, however, she burned all of the articles. All, that is, except the drawings, which Mary hid under her mattress. "It was not until many years later that my mother learned I still had them," Colter wrote in a 1956 letter to the superintendent of the Custer (now Little Bighorn) Battlefield National Monument in Montana, to which she bequeathed the drawings. Although by that time Colter had amassed a large and impressive collection of Indian jewelry and other art, she had held on to the drawings ever since childhood, proclaiming them her "most priceless and precious possession."[10]

Colter had set her sights on a career in art but was too young to leave home in pursuit of the higher education that was key to that goal. Then, in 1886, her father died suddenly at the age of 53. Although William Colter's death left his family pressed for money, Mary was finally able to convince her mother to let her attend art school in San Francisco; in exchange, she promised to return to St. Paul afterwards and help support her mother and sister by teaching. Using funds left by her father, and accompanied by Rebecca and Harriet, Mary moved to Oakland, California, and in 1887 enrolled in the California School of Design across the bay in San Francisco.[11]

Young, prosperous, and immodestly proud of itself, San Francisco was in many respects similar to the Twin Cities. Thanks at first to breakneck growth induced by the 1849 Gold Rush and the Comstock Lode silver-mining boom of the late 1850s and later to the development of banking, shipping, and the railroads, the city boasted 234,000 residents by 1880, higher by far than the population of its nascent southern rival, Los Angeles. San Francisco had emerged as the financial capital of the West, replete with new fortunes and the desire by the families who had made them to raise the city's cultural profile by founding arts institutions. In one case, a group of civic leaders and artists banded together in 1871 to found the influential San Francisco Art Association. Buoyed by the success of a series of its paintings exhibitions, the association opened the California School of Design in 1874 at its headquarters at 313 Pine Street, offering its forty young students—most of them women—a well-rounded, four-year curriculum of painting and drawing.[12] To gain professional experience in architecture and to help support herself while she attended the design school, Mary worked as an apprentice in the office of a San Francisco architect.[13] She lived for part or all of her California period at 1066 10th Street in Oakland, on the city's west side near San Francisco Bay.

Among Colter's teachers at the school was Arthur Frank Mathews (1860–1945), a prominent illustrator, designer, and painter who was appointed their

director in 1890. Talented as both artist and administrator, Mathews evidently grew close to Colter, for in the early 1890s he painted her portrait, inscribing upon it: "To my very dear friend M. E. J. Colter, Arthur F. Mathews." In this earliest surviving, and surely the most arresting, likeness of Colter, the elegantly dressed and coiffed student gazes winsomely at (actually, slightly to the left of) the viewer. It is interesting that Mathews came from a family of architects—his father and two brothers were in the profession—and he apprenticed for four years as a draftsman in his father's office in Oakland. Moreover, he entered an elaborate design in the 1879 competition to complete the long-unfinished Washington Monument in Washington, D.C., and in 1880 he won first prize for his design of a model New York City public school building.[14] With such an expansive background, it is entirely possible that Mathews was influential in persuading Colter to pursue a career in architecture as well as art.[15]

Also teaching at the California School of Design was Bernard Maybeck (1862–1957), who through his residential and civic commissions in the Bay Area later gained fame as one of the West Coast's most innovative and eclectic architects. It is possible, but not known for certain, that Maybeck instructed Colter. Through their professional practice and teaching, starting in the late 1890s, Mathews and a round of other California architects and artists helped import the principles of the Arts and Crafts movement into California.[16] In applying his design talents to a range of products—including in later years furniture, picture frames, and decorative objects—Mathews came to exemplify the Arts and Crafts ideal of the seamless integration of the arts with one another and with daily life. Mathews worked closely in these pursuits with his wife, Lucia Kleinhans Mathews, a student at the design school whom he married in 1894.

Even before the period of Arts and Crafts influence, rebellious designers in the Bay Area and elsewhere in California during the 1880s were concerning themselves with the question of which architectural styles best suited the young, vigorous, and still provincial state—whose history, landscape, and climate were so different from those back east—and which materials and colors would best fit into its landscape. Some of them were reacting against the European-based Victorian and classical revival modes popular in so much of the nation, including California itself. No specific new Bay Area style emerged from this ferment, but by the 1890s practitioners like Maybeck, Willis Polk, and A.C. Schweinfurth—all immigrants from the East—were producing distinctive, progressive architecture that often employed native and rustic materials and forms.[17]

Architects in southern California followed a more conspicuous way out of the identity crisis by reviving and synthesizing forms from the state's Spanish colonial past to produce the so-called Mission or Mission Revival style. Buildings of this bent incorporated the stucco surfaces, red-tile roofs, bell towers, and long arcades that typified the late eighteenth- and early nineteenth-century mission compounds established from San Diego to Sonoma by the Franciscan padres. Not limiting themselves to churches, however, designers also fashioned houses, commercial structures, and public buildings in the style. The Santa Fe Railway, via the Fred Harvey Company, Colter's future employer, was to adopt the Mission Revival after the turn of the century for a number of its railroad stations and hotels in the Southwest. Another path, not entirely separate from the Mission Revival, led architects like the Pasadena-based Greene brothers, Charles Sumner and Henry Mather, to the Craftsman Style, designing expansive bungalows that drew upon the English Arts and Crafts tradition and oriental joinery. The national search for suitably American and regional design, which had set off the Georgian Revival in the east and the Prairie Style in the Midwest, was yielding another set of innovations in California. It was into this heady atmosphere of architectural philosophizing and designing—some of it beginning to flower, the rest just over the horizon—that Mary Colter graduated in 1890 from the School of Design.

As she had promised, the Colters returned to St. Paul after graduation. Her search for employment first bore fruit some sixty miles to the east in Menomonie, Wisconsin, where she landed a job in 1891 teaching drawing and architecture at the newly established Stout Manual Training School. She and the other teachers were hired at the behest of State Senator James H. Stout, a lumber baron and civic progressive who founded the school, which specialized in manual training as well as domestic science and which ultimately grew into the present-day University of Wisconsin–Stout.

In 1892 Colter was back in St. Paul, teaching at a manual training school that had been established a few years before as part of the Central High School. From this program sprang the Mechanic Arts High School, which debuted in 1895 in a new structure that was appended to an existing school building. Mechanic Arts was a four-year, co-educational school that combined the offerings of a traditional

academic high school with courses in shop (wood turning and cabinet-making, for instance, foundry work, and machine shop) and those in art (typically freehand and mechanical drawing). Colter taught the latter two subjects. It was not entirely an equal-opportunity system between shop and art students. An 1899 city board of education report noted that "the girls take instead of the shop work two additional terms in [clay] modeling, four additional terms in freehand drawing, and two additional terms in wood carving."[18] By most accounts, the school was organized along the lines of the technical high schools that were being established around that time in big cities nationwide.

Mechanic Arts began as a small school of "eight teachers, 150 pupils and a [sic] worse than indifferent equipment."[19] It endured some rather wobbly times, since it was an experiment that required not only students but the blessing of the school board. Some years later, after she had left St. Paul, Colter recalled that struggle in an essay she wrote for a student booklet published in memory of Mechanic Arts' first principal and driving force, George Weitbrecht. Describing a poem ("Lark," by Gelett Burgess) that he had read to the students in 1897, Colter wrote: "I shall never forget the tense high silence in which his 'children' filed out or the light in Whitey's eyes as he watched them go. Those were days when we felt things hard! The Mechanic Arts had to prove its right to live."[20]

Under Weitbrecht's direction the school slowly blossomed into a well-equipped and prestigious institution; in 1911 it moved into a large new Tudor Revival building with a capacity for 1,200 students that was constructed expressly for it.[21] But even early on, Mechanic Arts students were attracting local and even national attention. In 1893, prior to its establishment as an independent school, Weitbrecht's pupils put on an exhibit at the World's Columbian Exposition in Chicago "that astounded visitors and educators from all over the world" and won the Gold Medal.[22] One wonders if Colter took the train down to visit that celebrated fair, either with students or otherwise, to take in its global display of arts, crafts, and architecture and to appreciate, in a few cases, the new creative roles it offered women. The Women's Building, for example, was designed by architect Sophia Hayden, and that building's library was undertaken by designer and social reformer Candace Wheeler.

In 1904 Mechanic Arts students won another Gold Medal for an exhibit of works for the Minnesota Building at the St. Louis World's Fair (Louisiana Purchase Exposition) that they had both designed and made. Among the objects—some of which were brought back to be displayed proudly at the high school in January 1905 after the fair—were Mission Style furniture (settees, tables, chairs, and other pieces), pottery, statuary, freehand drawings, and machinery (including a ten-horsepower steam engine). Remarked one enthusiastic hometown newspaper: "The furniture on display lacked only the presence of rubicund friars to convince the onlooker that these ponderous chairs and tables, these rugged leather-cushioned settees, were appurtenances of a sixteenth-century monastery in a glowing California valley."[23] It is possible that Colter was involved in the production of some portion of the St. Louis exhibit. The drawings for the steam engine, for example, were made in the mechanical drawing classes.[24]

In addition to her classroom duties, Colter participated in the students' extracurricular events, chaperoning their dances, for one. The Mechanic Arts archives house a number of fetching publications crafted for these events—the dances as well as receptions, exhibitions, literary functions, and graduations—that were designed, illustrated, and probably printed by the pupils, often under her guidance. Colter also took a student, Arthur Larkin, under her wing, helping him design decorative boxes that he sold to pay his way through school. That relationship was the beginning of a close and enduring friendship with Larkin and his family.[25]

opposite, top: Mechanic Arts High School in St. Paul (building on right), where Colter taught for years

opposite, below: Graduation booklet, 1896, Mechanic Arts High School

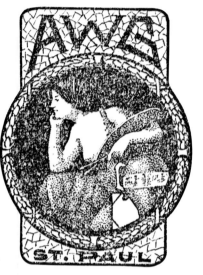

Colter was a member of the Art Workers' Guild of St. Paul.

During the years of her association with Mechanic Arts, which lasted until 1907, Colter continued on her own to study design, archaeology, world history, and architecture, a penchant for self-education that would persist throughout her life. She lectured on history and architecture to evening classes at the University of Minnesota extension school.[26] She also made her presence felt among other talented women who were becoming active in civic and arts clubs. As an artist herself, Colter joined the Art Workers' Guild of St. Paul, specializing in metalcrafting and design, and lectured there—in 1906, for instance, on metalwork and jewelry making.[27] A photograph of Colter taken in the early 1890s shows her staring intently at a metal bowl she is in the process of fashioning, hammers at the ready in her lap and at her side. She served in 1905 as a juror for the Minnesota State Art Society, an outgrowth of a St. Paul women's art and history club that sponsored exhibitions in the capital and statewide and promoted art in the schools.[28] Colter mentions in her autobiographic sketch that "during this period" she "also was Literary Editor for two years on [the] *St. Paul Globe*."[29] Those who have studied Colter have yet to pin down what that role entailed and when she performed it or to locate articles that she wrote or edited for the newspaper.[30]

In 1899 Colter also joined the New Century Club, a circle of women who met—first in private homes, then in rented rooms downtown—to discuss the social, political, and artistic topics of the day. A progressive group, the club in 1901 came out in favor of black women's organizations being admitted to the state and national federations of women's clubs. Guests and members gave lectures to the club on a wide range of topics, from "Ibsen and His Doll's House" to "Women as Bread-winners." Colter lectured there a number of times and even took to the road to give talks for the club in other Minnesota cities and in Iowa. In May 1900 she addressed the New Century Club on "The Utilitarian Basis of the Aesthetic," and in May 1907 she lectured on "The Red Craftsman," using a stereopticon to show images of Indian baskets and pottery.[31] By that year, she had already been to New Mexico and Arizona (in 1902 and 1904) to work on important decorating and architectural schemes for the Fred Harvey Company, so she was quite likely one of the most informed persons in the Twin Cities on Native American culture.

Mary Colter was making a name for herself in St. Paul. She designed temporary decorations for a convention in the Armory building not far from Mechanic Arts that were well received—moving a local newspaper to heap praise on the scheme as well as on Colter and to call for making the design permanent:

Mary Colter at age 23, circa 1892, crafting a metal bowl

WHEN THE CITY HAS PRODUCED A THING OF ADMIRABLE BEAUTY, THIS SHOULD NOT BE PERMITTED TO REMAIN AN EPISODE, BUT SHOULD BE PRESERVED AS AN ATTAINMENT AND AN INSPIRATION.

IT HAS SURPRISED EVEN ST. PAUL, WHICH HAS LEARNED TO THINK REASONABLY WELL OF ITSELF, THAT THE SCHEME AND EXECUTION OF THE DECORATIONS AT THE ARMORY HALL SHOULD HAVE BEEN OF SUCH UNIQUE, SUCH INDIVIDUAL QUALITY, SO PERFECTLY ADAPTED TO ITS USES IN SPACE AND PROPORTION, SO FINELY ADAPTED TOWARD A HIGHER USE IN RESTING EYE AND STIMULATING SPIRIT.... IT WAS SOMETHING MORE THAN MERE DECORATION; IT WAS THE CREATION OF AN INTEGRAL PART OF A BUILDING PLAN....

[IT] SHOULD NOT BE PERMITTED TO PASS WITH THE PASSING OF THE CONVENTION FOR WHICH IT DID SERVICE, BUT SHOULD BECOME A PERMANENT POSSESSION OF LASTING SERVICE TO THE CITY. MISS M. E. J. COLTER HAS CONTRIBUTED VERY DEFINITELY THROUGH HER WORK IN THE MECHANIC ARTS HIGH SCHOOL, TO THE ART AND CRAFT DEVELOPMENT OF THE CITY. SHE WAS ASSISTED IN THE MANIFESTING OF THIS SCHEME BY THE PUPILS OF THIS SCHOOL. IN ANOTHER COUNTRY, SAY, IN JAPAN, WHENCE SHE HAS DRAWN MUCH OF HER INSPIRATION, THIS DECORATION WOULD BE REWARDED WITH A PERMANENT PLACE....

MORE AND MORE IT IS FELT THAT A SMALL HALL FOR CLUB AND REHEARSAL PURPOSES SHOULD BE PROVIDED IN THE ARMORY. IF SUCH A HALL IS SET OFF, THERE COULD BE NO MORE APPROPRIATE PLACE TO ESTABLISH THIS DECORATIVE SCHEME OF THE ARMORY.... THERE HAS BEEN TOO WIDESPREAD [AN] APPRECIATION OF MISS COLTER'S DESIGNS FOR THE CITY TO LOSE WHAT THE COUNTRY HAS FOUND GOOD.[32]

This passage confirms that Colter was a well-known, much-appreciated artist and teacher and also suggests the influential role played by the Arts and Crafts movement at Mechanic Arts High and in the Twin Cities at large. The flattering reference to Japan reveals Colter's interest in and creative use of motifs from what was then called the Orient, a regard that was common among devotees of the Arts and Crafts. Decorative and architectural works inspired by Japan were especially popular in America during that period. Colter studied and collected Japanese and Chinese art objects and was fond of using them in the decoration of her own apartments and houses. She rarely displayed Asian arts in the Fred Harvey Company schemes in the Southwest that she was to create during the first half of the twentieth century, since they were inspired primarily by Native American and Hispanic cultures, but she did treat those spaces with an exoticism and simplicity that echo the oriental aesthetic.

During her later St. Paul years in the 1890s and early 1900s, Colter, her mother and sister moved a number of times. In 1893 they exited their 176 14th Street address at the northern edge of downtown in favor of 880 Lincoln Avenue to the west. By 1903 Colter was living in a graceful row of porch-fronted apartments that still stands, renovated but stripped of its balconies, on Selby Avenue. Nearby rises the huge Cathedral of St. Paul, whose long period of construction was begun in 1906, two years after Mary and her mother had moved farther out Selby to an apartment block called the Seville Flats. Lincoln and Selby were part of the grid of streets that was forming around Summit Avenue, a lengthy boulevard that was fast developing into St. Paul's most fashionable residential address. For Cass Gilbert and his architectural contemporaries, receiving a commission to design a house or a church on or near Summit was a mark of the highest prestige. Colter probably lived close to some of the wealthy women whom she knew as leaders in the New Century Club and the Art Workers' Guild. The Colters' own station in life, however, remained modest, and Mary continued to serve as the family's chief breadwinner.

Mary Colter circa 1892

Among the Colters' turn-of-the-century homes was this row of apartments on Selby Avenue west of St. Paul Cathedral.

(EAST FACADE, SHOWING ENTRANCE TO INDIAN BUILDING EXHIBITS)

H.4474—THE FRED HARVEY-ALVARADO HOTEL, ALBUQUERQUE, NEW MEXICO

Colter Meets Harvey

THREE

Fred Harvey, circa 1880

opposite: The Indian Building at the
Alvarado Hotel in Albuquerque,
New Mexico

THE PIVOTAL EVENT IN MARY COLTER'S CAREER was her encounter with
the Fred Harvey Company, the famously able purveyor of comfort, reliability, and
luxury to the American train traveler. In order to fully understand the significance of the Harvey connection to Colter, it is necessary to review the
phenomenal strides the Harvey organization had made by the time of her first
commission for the company, soon after the turn of the century.

The story of Fred Harvey himself is one in which observation sparks with
opportunity to generate an enterprise that ultimately captures both markets and the
imagination. Like so many of those stories, it begins with an immigrant. Frederick
Henry Harvey was an Englishman born in London in 1835 who sailed to the United
States in 1850 and bobbed about the country taking odd jobs, working in cafes,
opening (and shutting) his own restaurants, and working as a mail clerk on board a
train. In 1875, while living with his wife and children in Leavenworth, Kansas, and
already serving as a freight agent for the Chicago, Quincy, and Burlington Railroad
(not to mention working part-time as a newspaper ad salesman), Harvey opened two
railroad cafes for the Kansas Pacific Railroad, managing them from afar. That venture
convinced him that he could provide much better service than the low-grade food

and lodging he had endured riding the rails for his regular job. He devised a system of such upgraded restaurants and proposed the idea to his Burlington bosses, but they turned him down flat. Go to the Atchinson, Topeka and Santa Fe Railroad, they reportedly said, since that company "would try anything."[1]

Harvey did find a sympathetic ear in Charles F. Morse, the superintendent of the Santa Fe, and Thomas Nickerson, its president, and so in 1876 he opened his first establishment for them by taking over a lunchroom on the second floor of Santa Fe's Topeka depot. This he followed in 1878 with a hotel and restaurant in Florence, Kansas—luring a chef from Chicago's Palmer House to run the dining room—and by 1880 he had added eating establishments at Lakin, Coolidge, and Emporia, Kansas. In his second formal contract with the railroad, signed in 1889, Harvey secured the right to operate all restaurants and hotels on the Santa Fe line west of the Missouri River. (An 1893 contract gave him the rights to its dining-car service.) He was to supply the equipment, food, supplies, and management, and the railroad was to haul them and Harvey's employees for free. The profits were his.[2]

Harvey's corporate partner was born in 1859 as the Atchison and Topeka Railroad, chartered by promoter-politician Cyrus K. Holliday. The romantic and prophetic "Santa Fe" was tacked on to the name a few years later, but it was not until April 1869 (just weeks before the Golden Spike was hammered in Utah, at the completion of the first transcontinental railroad) that the fledgling line opened its initial seven miles of tracks, which ran southwest from Topeka. At a picnic celebrating that inauguration, Holliday delivered a grand oration, proclaiming "the coming tide of immigration will flow along these [railway] lines and, like an ocean wave, advance up the sides of the Rockies and dash their foamy crests down upon the Pacific."[3] The Santa Fe would be among those lines, Holliday was certain, and would one day stretch from Lake Michigan to the Pacific Ocean. He was right—but roadblocks thrown up by tough competition and tougher terrain made the race a harrowing and

Harvey opened his first restaurant for the Santa Fe Railroad in 1876 in the Topeka, Kansas, depot.

sometimes violent one. It was not until May 1887 that the first transcontinental Santa Fe train arrived in Los Angeles.[4]

The Santa Fe's westward path followed the historic Santa Fe Trail, a prospering but slow, tough, and limited way to transport goods. The contrast between the old route's restraints and the new railroad's speed, reliability, and vast capacity could hardly have been greater. Still, one deprivation of the bad old days lingered on: the inferior food and lodging that plagued travelers. The stories of vile meals and slovenly service were legion; meat was rancid, greasy, unyielding, and of indeterminate origin. According to one report, "the chops were generally as tough as hanks of whipcord and the knives as blunt as a bricklayer's trowel," and "chicken stew" was really prairie dog.[5] Coffee was cold, eggs were old, and the soda biscuits served with them were called "sinkers" by the patrons.[6] Those with time to eat them, that is, since train crews were known to conspire with lunchroom owners to pull the train out early, leaving the food paid for but untouched and ready to do double duty for the next trainload. The lunchrooms were likely to be dirty, noisy, and crowded, and insolent staff waited tables covered with dirty cloths and furnished with cracked dishes. Likewise, there were very few comfortable hotels—just shacks or rooms with cots. As passenger service grew into a prominent part of the western railway business, this state of affairs became intolerable, especially to travelers used to eastern trains and hotels. Fred Harvey seems to have walked on stage at just the right moment.

Harvey turned the Topeka lunchroom into a first-class restaurant. He and his manager cleaned the place, outfitted it with better napery and flatware, and overhauled the menu. "A typical breakfast consisted of steak with eggs, hashed brown potatoes, a six-high stack of pan-sized wheat cakes with maple syrup, and apple pie with coffee for dessert. The millennium had come!"[7] Soon Harvey was doing a brisk business feeding both railroad passengers and crew as well as local patrons, and the Santa Fe urged him to open more establishments along the line. His expansion followed the railroad's as it laid tracks across Kansas, Colorado, and into New Mexico on its westward path to the Pacific. By 1883 Fred Harvey ran seventeen dining places on the railroad's main line.[8] Kept under close watch by Harvey, who was fond of dropping in unannounced for lightning inspections, they garnered high praise for both the company and the Santa Fe. "Meals by Fred Harvey" became one of the railway's most seductive slogans.

Harvey's food was of the highest quality, much of it supplied by local farmers. The rest could come from farther afield—fruit and vegetables from California, beef from Texas, shellfish from the East Coast, and whitefish from the Great Lakes—since it was hauled by Santa Fe trains along with the ice to keep it fresh. Harvey ran his own dairies and brought in his own spring water so that his specially blended coffee would not be ruined by the brackish local liquid. In the 1880s, even at Harvey outlets in the middle of the desert, patrons could sit down to a full-course meal, from oysters on the half shell to homemade pie and coffee, for seventy-five cents. Menus were planned so they did not repeat during a train journey—no chicken hash two days in a row. Such zealous attention to the customer became the enduring hallmark of service at his burgeoning "Harvey House" chain of restaurants, hotels, shops, and tourist attractions, which continued to grow for decades after Harvey's death in 1901. Years later, railroad historian and boulevardier Lucius Beebe wrote: "Harvey imposed a rule of culinary benevolence over a region larger than any Roman province and richer than any single British dominion save India."[9]

A key ingredient in Harvey's success was the formidable corps of capable waitresses he began hiring in 1883 to add expert service and homey ambience to his establishments. The idea for the Harvey Girls, as they became known, was born at the Harvey House in Raton, New Mexico. On one of his inspections, Fred Harvey fired the manager and all-male staff after some of them had gotten into a fight, and the new manager suggested that he hire women as replacements.[10] The idea proved so

A group of Harvey Girls at the first Harvey House in Winslow, Arizona, circa 1910

44

popular with the townsfolk and Santa Fe passengers that Harvey decided to replace all the waiters on the line with waitresses. The Harvey Girls soon matured into a disciplined army emblematic of their boss' devotion to first-class service.

Recruited through newspaper ads in the East and Midwest that sought "young women, 18 to 30 years of age, of good character, attractive and intelligent," they exchanged their lives in small towns or farms for duty in the Harvey battalions. The "girls" were rigorously trained and then housed in group dorms or in Harvey hotels, in both cases closely monitored during off-hours by matrons. Dressed crisply and conservatively in black and white, they brought an air of cheery competence to mealtimes that had once been free-for-alls. The women and other staff ran the dining ritual on the Santa Fe line like a precision drill. Meal orders were taken on board the train and wired to the station. Upon arrival, a gong sounded and the manager ushered passengers into the spotless Harvey House dining room or lunch counter, where the Harvey Girls, warned in advance, were already standing at their stations and ready to serve the freshly cooked meal, which often went on for four courses. The whole exercise turned on split-second timing and lasted but thirty minutes, yet the polish and politeness of the Harvey Girls kept customers from feeling rushed. "Harvey made serving food in the West into a profession and joining the staff of a Harvey House into a way of life," wrote Harvey Girls historian Lesley Poling-Kempes.[11]

Of the approximately 100,000 women who heeded Harvey's call between 1883 and the 1950s, about half stayed on after their service.[12] Many of them married—which was prohibited during their Harvey stints—and raised families, contributing to the growth of southwestern communities, a great number of which had started as remote railroad outposts. "[T]he Harvey Girls could only have appeared in the West, where there was a new country in search of a new identity," wrote Poling-Kempes. "Harvey Girls and Harvey employees, along with Santa Fe railroadmen, were often the founding fathers, and mothers, of entire towns."[13] The women's reminiscences of working for Harvey have been woven into the social and economic history, and folklore, of the nineteenth- and twentieth-century West. And as one of the first groups of American women to strike out on their own, even if it was under the sheltering wing of Fred Harvey, they augured the entry of others into professional lives.

"The Harvey House was not only a haven in the wilderness, but an institution that had no parallel in America," wrote Frank Waters. "Perhaps more than any single organization, the Fred Harvey system introduced America to Americans."[14] The Fred Harvey Company and the Santa Fe Railway worked closely together to promote the wonders of the Southwest and make them accessible to the growing numbers of railroad passengers. Although California with its alluring ocean, exquisite climate, and thriving cities was the ultimate mind's-eye destination of many eastern travelers, the states or territories leading to it—especially Colorado, New Mexico, and Arizona—offered their own scenic and historic treasures. Reports and portraits of lofty mountain ranges and astounding canyons, trackless deserts, and ancient settlements, and that target of ever-mounting curiosity, the Native American, had flowed east, but few easterners had made the reverse trip to see for themselves. Not so many years since it had been acquired and "tamed," the region remained a mystery. What better way to unfurl that mystery than on the Santa Fe, whose very name was perfumed with the Southwest?

The time was ripe for such discovery. America was finding itself. Wresting its artistic soul from servility to Europe, it was only natural that the nation would turn inward—and westward—in its search for indigenous inspiration. Writers and publicists like the gifted and prolific Charles F. Lummis churned out books and tracts by the dozens that exalted the glories of the land and all but demanded that Americans get out there and see it. Lummis—who coined the slogan "See America First!"—had in fact done that himself, walking in 1892 from Cincinnati to Los Angeles and along the way reporting his adventures to eager readers.[15]

Guests out for a jaunt at the Montezuma Hotel near Las Vegas, New Mexico, circa 1883

45

In 1882, in their first joint venture off the main line, Harvey and the Santa Fe built the Montezuma Hotel at a hot spring six miles from Las Vegas, New Mexico. A huge 270-room building anchored with a massive cupola-topped tower—reportedly the largest frame structure in the country—the hotel was a distinct departure from the small utilitarian outlets from which the companies first operated together. Built (and promptly rebuilt, after two fires) in the Queen Anne style that was popular nationwide, the hotel proved an enormously popular resort in the grand European manner, featuring lavish mineral baths and the best of Harvey food and service. Four trains per day brought guests up the spur line built by the Santa Fe, which publicized the spa as "the Karlsbad of America." The Montezuma's success was fairly brief, however, and it closed in 1903, victim of a national economic depression and competition from hotels farther west; El Tovar, built by Santa Fe and Harvey in 1905 at the Grand Canyon—next door to which Mary Colter would work on her second job for Harvey—would assume the mantle of the favored resort hostelry.[16] The Santa Fe Railroad itself went into receivership in 1893, reemerging in 1895 after a reorganization.

The Montezuma set the tone for larger hotels situated deeper into the scenery that would invite longer stays in the region. The goal of luring more tourists was taken up with great enthusiasm in 1896 by the new president of the reorganized Santa Fe Railway, Edward P. Ripley. One of the leaders in developing the recent World's Columbian Exposition in Chicago, Ripley modernized and ratcheted up the company's publicity for the Harvey chain and the railway, with heavy emphasis on the scenic, historic, and ethnic glories of the Southwest. The company had already made an auspicious start in marketing tourism. In 1892 it plugged California and the Grand Canyon for the debut of its first luxury train, the California Limited. That same year it paid celebrated painter Thomas Moran's transportation and lodging for a trip to the Grand Canyon, in exchange for the rights to one of the paintings he would

opposite: "The Grand Canyon of the Colorado," painted by Thomas Moran in 1892 for the Santa Fe Railroad

One of the Santa Fe advertisements for the California Limited, from a 1902 issue of *Harper's Magazine*

47

An early view of the Castañeda Hotel in Las Vegas, New Mexico

create of that marvel. The choice of the work was up to the company. It picked "The Grand Canyon of the Colorado," which it copied and reprinted as a color lithograph, framed, then distributed by the thousands to offices, schools, hotels, and railroad stations.[17] Moran's magnificent oil was the first of many paintings, drawings, and written works that the railroad commissioned from professional artists, writers, and designers over the years to adorn advertisements, brochures, posters, postcards, calendars, menus, books, and other publications about the Southwest. "I think that we were the first road to take art seriously, as a valuable advertising adjunct," William Haskell Simpson, the Santa Fe's masterful advertising chief, is claimed to have said.[18]

The companies also began to design new Harvey Houses more fittingly for the Southwest. Gone were the old Victorian revival modes. Instead, styles emanating from the region's Spanish colonial or Native American history and harmonizing with its landscape became the order of the day, both for exterior and interior designs. The very names of these hotels, their restaurants, and trains and railroad cars were redolent: El Otero, El Ortiz, Alvarado, Casa del Desierto, El Navajo, Gran Quivira, El Capitan, Mimbres Gap, and others rolled off the tongue as if read from a conquistador's map. One of the first of the new line was the Castañeda in Las Vegas, New Mexico. Replacing a small-frame Harvey House lunchroom, the U-shaped, stucco-clad hotel opened next to the depot in 1899, offering forty guest rooms and lavish dining and entertaining spaces. The Castañeda was designed by California architect Frederick Roehrig as a typical Mission Revival-style composition with bell tower, red-tile roof, and long arched arcades. Although the Mission Revival style was imported by the Santa Fe and Harvey from California, it proved an enduringly popular style for this region, too.

If the Harvey Company and the Santa Fe "introduced America to Americans," they also presented Americans to other Americans. During this period the companies were taking advantage of passengers' growing interest in Indians and their art. For years it had been customary to see Native Americans selling pottery, jewelry, baskets, and blankets to travelers directly from the side of the tracks. Travelers prized the Indian objects, not just as souvenirs of an exotic new land but for their value in decorating parlors and dens back home. A Navajo rug, a Pomo basket, or a pottery vessel from one of the pueblos was the perfect embellishment for the Arts and Crafts interior deemed ideal in the late Victorian era. Handmade, indigenous, unique, and, of course, colorful and beautiful, they were a departure from the mass-produced goods that had crowded into homes in less artistically philosophical times. Although this form of contact, for the simplest of transactions, was but one of many impacts that the railroads were having on Indian life, both negative and positive, it would lead to considerable good fortune for the Harvey Company and the Santa Fe.

It was a time when the study of the continent's native peoples, past and present, was becoming something of an industry. Their paths paved by the country's subjugation of the region, archeologists, anthropologists, ethnographers, and self-taught amateurs were heading Southwest to investigate the ruins of ancient settlements and the lives and folkways of living Indians. Working for museums, the government, companies (like the Santa Fe), or independently, they brought back both knowledge, in the form of scholarly treatises, and objects—artifacts and

This advertisement for a mail-order house that sold Indian art appeared in George Wharton James' *Indian Basketry* (1902).

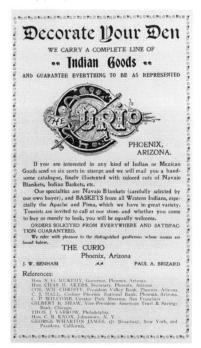

49

artworks for further study, display, or sale to private collectors. Among the most prominent of these investigators were Adolph Bandelier, Jesse Walter Fewkes, George Dorsey, and H. R. Voth, the latter two of whom would work at times for the Harvey Company. Americans' interest had already been piqued by reading accounts of southwestern exploration in books and newspapers and by viewing exhibits at major fairs. One such popular display was the exhibit at the 1893 Chicago fair of artifacts from the cliff dwellings at Mesa Verde in southwestern Colorado, which had just been discovered in 1888. At some of these shows the Indians themselves were brought in to "live" in exhibits and demonstrate the making of blankets, jewelry, or pottery. The first American fair to do this was the Chicago, where an encampment of Indians next to the Anthropological Building included a group of Navajos living in a small hogan and where Pueblo Indians moved onto the Midway to inhabit a plaster mock-up of their southwestern home.[19] The folks back east were not only seeing America first, they were seeing the first Americans.

The Santa Fe and the Harvey Company picked up on this budding curiosity in a most thorough way. Together or separately they published a multitude of books and guidebooks on the Southwest—ranging from George Dorsey's monumental study, *Indians of the Southwest* (1903), to short pamphlets and brochures. With superb typography, layout, and art—tinted photographs and full-color copies of paintings and drawings—the publications were designed to lure travelers to the Southwest, educate them on the region's landscape and culture, and guide them to specific sites. The series started in 1892 with Santa Fe assistant passenger agent C. A. Higgins's *Grand Cañon of the Colorado River*, and lasted well into the 1930s; some titles enjoyed frequent reprints and revisions, like the dazzling 1911 album of multi-toned photographs, *The Great Southwest Along the Santa Fe*. As a whole, the publications established the companies' wide-ranging authority on the Southwest.[20]

In an oft-repeated scene, Pueblo residents sell pottery and food to Santa Fe passengers.

The cover of *The Great Southwest Along the Santa Fe*, above, depicted Indians watching a train passing in the distance.

Herman Schweizer, the Harvey Company's virtuoso collector and merchant of Native American art

The publications also spurred sales of Native American arts and crafts, a business that seeded many careers at the Fred Harvey Company, including Mary Colter's. The founding genius of Harvey's Indian trade was Herman Schweizer, an immigrant like Harvey and a career-long employee of the company like Colter. Schweizer, a son of German Jews, sailed to New York City in 1885 and worked for a time as a "butcher boy" (newsboy) on a Santa Fe subsidiary line. Hired by the Harvey Company, which sent him to its Coolidge, Kansas, restaurant to improve service, Schweizer soon began to buy Navajo blankets and jewelry for resale to railroad passengers. It was not long before he was commissioning native silversmiths to make jewelry, supplying them with turquoise and silver and requesting pieces small enough to appeal to travelers. "He had that gift of the gods, a sure taste for the authentic and beautiful," wrote Erna Fergusson.[21] This was the beginning of a network of ties among Native American craftsmen, traders, tourists, and collectors that would make him famous throughout the Southwest and beyond. Soon Schweizer's small but growing venture came to the attention of Fred Harvey's daughter Minnie, wife of Harvey executive John F. Huckel and also an enthusiastic student of Indian arts. It was Minnie's idea to start the company's Indian Department and in 1901 to appoint Schweizer its manager, a post he held until his death in 1943.[22]

The department aimed to increase and coordinate the company's buying and selling of Indian arts, to house and display them as appealing tourist attractions—as a draw, often having Native Americans craft their artworks on-site—and to publish pamphlets and other tourist materials. The operation would later spread through the Harvey system, but it first met the public in Albuquerque at the new Alvarado Hotel. This was no ordinary inn but the largest new star of the Santa Fe-Harvey combine. With its debut in May 1902, a rough-stuccoed Spanish mission, tower-studded and arcaded to a fare-the-well, took a prominent position along the tracks in the center of

town. Composed of an interconnected hotel, railroad station, and curio (Indian Department) building, the Alvarado was the work of the Santa Fe's chief architect, Charles F. Whittlesey. The hotel offered eighty-eight guest rooms, all the service and entertainment facilities required of a world-class establishment, and the fanciful fountains and gardens expected of an idyllic Spanish hideaway.[23] It opened, reported a local newspaper, "in a burst of rhetoric, a flow of red carpet and the glow of myriad brilliant electric lights" (electricity was still a novelty), with hopes that it "would attract the wealthier classes to stop in Albuquerque on their travels to the west."[24] Like so many Harvey Houses, the Alvarado became the dusty little city's window on the world and its enduring social heart. Albuquerque residents fought its razing in 1970 with a passion akin to that of the New Yorkers who tried to save Pennsylvania Station in the mid-1960s. Neither group was to prevail.[25]

"The Indian and Mexican Building and Museum," as it was first called, was cleverly positioned along the shady arcade between the depot, where passengers disembarked, and the hotel and all of its attractions. It also fronted onto the tracks, where a large circular plaque painted with a spread-winged figure that the Santa Fe identified as the Zuni god of war[26] beckoned them inside to richly festooned rooms,

The Alvarado Hotel complex, shown here circa 1908, stretched from the railroad station, far left, to the hotel, right.

53

as novel to them as they were experimental to the Harvey Company and the Santa Fe. Just as new to the scene was Mary Colter, the gifted young midwesterner who had traveled here to decorate the building. This was her initiation into a long and very fruitful association with both companies. ⊡

How did Colter first come in contact with the Fred Harvey Company? The record has not been entirely clear on this. The pioneering biography by Virginia Grattan states that Colter, vacationing in San Francisco with a friend who worked in a Harvey gift shop, told the shop's manager of her interest in working for the company. Later, in Minnesota, she received a telegram from them offering her a position.[27] More recent research by documentary-film producer Karen Bartlett indicates that the crucial link was Minnie Harvey Huckel, who had likely met Colter through art circles in St. Paul, or another midwestern city, and called her husband's attention to the young designer. Stewart Harvey, the company founder's great-grandson, told Bartlett that, as stated in one paraphrased source, "Minnie became Colter's benefactor and must have been very persuasive to have convinced her husband to bring a single woman to Albuquerque in 1902."[28] In either case, Colter was sure to have communicated her mastery of design and Native American culture convincingly enough to have persuaded the Harvey Company, which "needed a decorator who knew Indian things and had imagination,"[29] to pick her for the job.

Passengers inspecting Indian wares in front of the Alvarado's Indian Building, circa 1912

opposite: One of the alluring Indian Building rooms that Colter decorated with a profusion of wares

The Indian Building comprised a series of rooms devoted to museum, demonstration, and sales space, which visitors were encouraged to sample in that order so that, as they proceeded, they would gather up ideas for home decoration. Thus did a promotional publication say of the Navajo Room that its "blanketed walls and decorations of pottery and basketry furnish an admirable idea for a luxurious home 'den.'" One could also wander through the Spanish and Mexican Room and even one that represented the South Seas. In the "cunningly wrought" Navajo Summer Hogan Room, "patient Navajo squaws" sat at their looms around a large rug, weaving blankets while a silversmith hammered out jewelry. Indians from Acoma fashioned pottery, while other Pueblo people wove baskets. The Navajo weaver Elle of Ganado became a major attraction herself when she wove blankets at the Indian Building, while her husband Tom greeted visitors and helped in sales. Harvey and the Santa Fe made Elle into one of the most famous Native American artists and, in addition to featuring her in person, used her name and image in countless promotional publications for both the Alvarado and the Harvey/Santa Fe system in general.[30]

As a whole, "the harmony of colors . . . is marked [and] the goods . . . so artistically arranged and grouped that one first sees only the beautiful, symmetrical whole."[31] Here we have high (if official company) praise for the anonymous decorator. Colter worked hard at achieving an appealing informality by artfully spreading out, clustering, and hanging all manner and sizes of wares—rugs and blankets, pots and baskets—in home-like spaces with inviting and cozy little nooks. The rooms were encased almost entirely in wood and furnished with sturdy tables, low benches, shelves, and fireplaces to showcase the merchandise, and decorative extras like masks, elk heads, hand tools, and even feathers were affixed in eye-catching positions from floor to ceiling. Visitors were encouraged to touch, pick up, and closely inspect the merchandise. In this warm environment, tourists could buy items similar to those they had just seen being crafted or on exhibit in the museum. "The room was a textbook lesson in a Southwest rendering of an arts and crafts interior," wrote Leah Dilworth of one room on which Colter worked.[32] In 1902 the Indian Building's shops were a far cry from the typical store in which merchandise was kept under glass or beyond a sales counter on a shelf. It was an unusual way to sell but a pioneering one that would work very well for Harvey over a long period of time.

In the museum section were displayed many of the art works, ancient and modern, that Schweizer and J. F. Huckel had spent some years gathering. The treasures were arranged by, and in part bought from, noted ethnographer and Mennonite missionary H. R. Voth, reinforcing the sense that Harvey was an authority in the field. These works, and a larger number stored in the vault next door, formed the nucleus of the Fred Harvey collection of Indian and other art that Schweizer would enlarge over the years, traveling all over the Southwest to befriend Indians, traders, and other collectors. Often tagged "the Harvey anthropologist" for his thorough knowledge of Indian life and art, Schweizer earned a reputation for acquiring and selling only the finest pieces. Ethnographers, natural history museums, and wealthy collectors came to him for guidance; for years he transacted business with newspaper czar William Randolph Hearst, visiting him at his San Simeon "castle" in California.[33] The Indian Department grew with the Harvey system, and many of his finds were displayed or offered for sale in new Harvey Houses and other tourist venues in settings modeled after those in the Alvarado building. The extensive collection that Schweizer amassed, later known as the Fred Harvey Fine Arts Collection, was ultimately loaned to the Heard Museum in Phoenix. Schweizer's interest in Native American culture paralleled that of Colter, and the two would later find themselves working together on other Harvey projects—for example, the Watchtower at the Grand Canyon, which Colter designed. The pair formed a long-lasting professional bond and fond friendship.

The Santa Fe built the first rail line to the Grand Canyon; the first passenger train is shown arriving on September 17, 1901.

After the Indian Building opened to the public—a few months after the hotel did—her summer design job came to an end, so Colter returned to St. Paul and resumed teaching at Mechanic Arts High School. But the Harvey Company people were not through with her. If they were impressed with her knowledge and talents before she went to work, the performance Colter gave on the job in Albuquerque delighted them even more. In fact, during that time she had already begun work with Whittlesey on a similar concept at the Grand Canyon, a hotel (El Tovar) and a building that would display Native American art (Hopi House). Two years later, in 1904, she was back in the Southwest and back on their payroll to help carry out that scheme. There, at the onset of the scenic wonder's rise to tourist popularity, Colter would collaborate with Harvey and the railroad on the first of a highly unusual set of buildings.

Spanish explorers were the first Europeans to see the Grand Canyon. That was in 1540, but the canyon was essentially forgotten or dismissed for the next three centuries, until the United States completed its acquisition of the West and started to explore and settle the region. The canyon began to permeate the public's consciousness, abetted by engaging portrayals in words and oil. Americans were enthralled with Major John Wesley Powell, the one-armed Civil War veteran who reported in *Scribner's* magazine on his voyages through the canyon down the Colorado River in 1869 and 1871–72. The Smithsonian Institution published his accounts in 1875. Powell brought Thomas Moran to the canyon in 1873, where, in the growing vogue of artists taking on the American wilderness, he painted *Chasm of the Colorado*. This was the first of many canyon Morans and a work that, with its companion painting, *Grand Canyon of the Yellowstone*,[34] was viewed by the crowds at the 1876 Centennial Exhibition in Philadelphia.[35] Many more like narratives and images ensued. But tourist trips to the exalted panorama itself remained few, given its remote location, the lack of comfortable means of transport—hardened travelers

With the El Tovar Hotel, shown here circa 1905, the Santa Fe and Fred Harvey launched an auspicious tourist enterprise at the Grand Canyon.

could choose to bounce through a seventy-mile, eleven-hour stagecoach ride from Flagstaff—and a scarcity of visitor comforts at the journey's end. The path remained unbeaten until the Santa Fe Railway, accompanied by its own flood of words and pictures, built a railway line to the very rim.

A fortuitous event sped the way for this line—in 1899 the newly organized Santa Fe and Grand Canyon Railroad launched a project to link Williams, Arizona, which was located on the Santa Fe's main line, to the canyon rim. The company, using track and other supplies purchased from the Santa Fe, constructed most of the line—sixty-three miles to a copper mine the company was developing—but went bankrupt when the copper lode quickly fizzled out. Seizing the opportunity, Santa Fe President Ripley set up a subsidiary called the Grand Canyon Railway, which bought the defunct railway and finished the job. The first passenger train to the canyon arrived at the rim on September 17, 1901.[36]

The Santa Fe and Fred Harvey Company eyed the canyon as a powerful tourist draw that they were resolved to play the most prominent role in molding. With lodging first on their agenda, even before the construction of a train depot, they soon were laying plans to build a first-class resort hotel to accommodate the crowds that the railroad line was sure to attract. The inn field was occupied mainly by the Bright Angel Hotel, which perched on the rim not far from the train, a small and shabby structure that sheltered travelers at the end of the old stagecoach line. The companies sought something far grander, a suitable replacement for their first, and now fading, resort, the Montezuma Hotel in New Mexico. Railroad access to the canyon offered

another chance to enhance their line of
premium hotels, this time just steps away
from one of the most wondrous sights on
the continent. Once again they hired
architect Charles F. Whittlesey, who had
designed the Alvarado Hotel in
Albuquerque.

El Tovar's main lobby, the
Rendezvous, was publicized as a
place for "ladies to read and
gossip" and "gentlemen to smoke
and tell of their latest adventures."

The new hotel was named El Tovar,
after the Spanish explorer Pedro Álvarez
de Tovar, who had never actually seen the
canyon but dispatched the advance party
that did.[37] Harvey and the railroad wanted
the hotel to defer to the mighty scenery
yet, like the Alvarado, express a regional
feeling both inside and out. The precedent
for such a hotel in scenic surroundings
had been set in 1903, when the Northern
Pacific Railroad opened the Old Faithful
Inn in Yellowstone National Park.[38] For El Tovar, Whittlesey followed suit, giving
them a dark-wooded, long and rather low building that proclaimed no distinct
architectural style yet, according to the inaugural Santa Fe brochure, "combined in
admirable proportions the Swiss châlet and the Norway villa." From a rough limestone base, the structure rose through a log-clad first floor and planked second to a
third that was set into a mansard roof, a vestige of the Victorian architecture that the
Santa Fe and others of a naturalistic bent were trying to leave behind. A low tower
rose from the roof, topped with an amiable hat-like turret, and porches and balconies
afforded relaxing places from which to gaze out over the canyon. The interior was a

Hopi House, opened in 1905, was Mary Colter's first building, an unusual edifice that evoked historic dwellings she had visited in the ancient village of Oraibi, Arizona.

Shown below in an early view, the structure was fashioned from local stone and wood. The generous terraces, ladders, and upper doors reinforce its residential character.

opposite: Hopi House today

lumberman's dream, with peeled logs from Oregon used for ceilings, walls, beams, and columns and planks filling in elsewhere, all assembled with simple joinery. "El Tovar is probably the most expensively constructed and appointed log house in America," commented *The Hotel Monthly*.[39] Plain wooden furniture and fireplaces sustained the rusticity, while an abundance of "Indian curios and trophies of the chase" reminded visitors that they were in the Southwest. High Harvey service was the rule throughout, from the Norway Dining Room to the guest quarters, and the company bragged about the pains it took to coddle guests: "Extra pure spring water is brought from Del Rio, Ariz., 120 miles distant." Yet the managers wanted guests to relax in this "big country clubhouse" and find "freedom from ultra fashionable restrictions."[40]

Directly across from El Tovar stood a startling sight for this vacation venue, a craggy building with tiny windows, terraced and irregular roof, and wooden ladders propped up against its jagged stone walls. Contrasting starkly with the politely rustic hotel, the structure seemed intensely southwestern and also very old. Only the former was true, however, since the place had opened on New Year's Day 1905, two weeks before El Tovar did. This was Hopi House, Mary Colter's second commission for the Harvey Company and her architectural debut. Here, from the ground up, was Colter's most literal evocation of Native American architecture.

Like the Indian Building in Albuquerque, Hopi House was built by the Harvey Company to showcase native Americana but, unlike the earlier structure, it was a freestanding building. What is more, it completely departed from its predecessor's Spanish revivalism to assume the guise of an Indian pueblo—an actual one, in fact, since Colter imitated Hopi dwellings she had visited at Oraibi, a village in northeastern Arizona that dates to 1100 and is said to be the oldest inhabited community in the nation. Colter reproduced the size, proportions, and materials of the prototype, using local Kaibab limestone for the structure, Coconino sandstone for the facing, and peeled, local logs for the floor and roof supports, although she relied on sections of Santa Fe rails to span some of the wider openings. As in the original, ladders and doors on the stepped-back upper levels indicated access from roof terraces to separate living units, some of which temporarily housed the Hopis who worked on the building, laying up its stone courses with mud mortar made of fine sand and clay. Chimneys were crafted from stacked pottery water jars with broken bottoms.[41] The chief difference from an original Hopi building was that Hopi House needed a first-floor entrance; traditionally, for defense purposes, access was made via an opening in the roof. The result was a building that could not fail to draw visitors and then, once they spotted the Harvey Company sign, encourage them to step inside.

Harvey's principal display and selling center at the canyon for Native American arts and crafts, "Hopi House symbolized the partnership between commercialism and romanticism that typified so much of Fred Harvey architecture," states one study of parks architecture.[42] As with the Indian Building, it was divided into a set of profusely decorated museum, demonstration, and sales spaces through which visitors were invited to meander. To the extent that it was possible with a public facility, Colter treated the interior as authentically as the exterior, using cement floors that resembled mud, irregularly shaped plaster walls that looked like adobe, and ceilings with vigas (log beams) that held up two layers of smaller branches. All wooden members were left as crooked as nature left them, heightening the sense of age and authenticity—a technique that would become a Colter hallmark. She scattered southwestern Indian artworks—Navajo rugs and blankets, baskets, and pottery—through the low-ceilinged rooms. She also provided a museum room for Northwest Coastal Indian art and attended to Hispanic culture with a Spanish-Mexican room, which she trimmed with relics ranging from carved bultos (religious figures) and rifles to a sombrero, a wooden plow, and an aged leather chest.[43] Once again, by gathering a bounty of hand-made artworks and showing them off with calculated informality,

Native artisans, shown here on a rooftop, lived and worked at Hopi House.

65

Colter proved herself a consummate disciple of the Arts and Crafts. In his 1910 book, *The Grand Canyon of Arizona: How to See It*, George Wharton James wrote: "[O]ne will come away with a keen appreciation of the incomparable ethnological advantages [Hopi House] affords him, and he will not grudge any purchase, however large, the attractiveness of the display has led him to indulge in."[44]

Colter planned the three-story building to allow Hopi families to live there and demonstrate their crafts. Visitors enjoyed stopping by the workspace to watch them weave blankets and fashion other items for sale. The Harvey Company bolstered this attraction in 1905 when J. F. Huckel brought the famous Hopi potter Nampeyo to live and demonstrate her art for a few months with her family. She arrived shortly after the building opened in January 1905. When she soon ran out of her accustomed potting clay, Herman Schweizer, who had been buying Nampeyo's pottery since 1901, arranged for more to be collected near her home at Hano and shipped to her. She stayed until April and also returned for a period in 1907. Much as Elle of Ganado was revered at the Alvarado's Indian Building, Nampeyo, who is credited with reviving older forms of pottery during a period of their decline, became the star at Hopi House. Also like Elle, Nampeyo was pictured in many Harvey/Santa Fe publications, even on a set of its playing cards. Nampeyo's sons and husband performed Hopi dances as part of the song and ritual dance shows that became popular with tourists.[45]

In describing Hopi House, the Harvey Company and Santa Fe Railway literature often portrayed Native Americans with a paternalism that seems offensive to

Colter made Hopi House look ages old, enhancing its displays of Native American and Hispanic artistry.

Demonstrations of rug weaving, basket making, and other crafts added to the sense of authenticity displayed by the interior.

many of today's readers but which played on then-prevalent public assumptions of racial inferiority. The brochures and other publications showed great interest in Indian culture and high praise for their art but, in attempting to make the people as colorful as their products, belittled them at the same time that they romanticized them. In its first brochure for El Tovar and Hopi House, for example, William Haskell Simpson, from 1900 to 1933 the Santa Fe's brilliant advertising manager, describes Hopis as "the most primitive Indians in America" and pictures the "tall, taciturn Navajos—smooth-faced, keen-eyed Bedouins—who live in adjacent 'hogans.' The Navajo women weave fine wool blankets. The men cunningly fashion silver ornaments."[46] In its long-lived brochure, *The Great Southwest Along the Santa Fe*, the Harvey Company stated that "[t]he Hopi cling tenaciously to their crude way of living."[47] Even as many writers, artists, and other observers of Indian life expressed the desire simply to understand and not exploit native culture, assumptions of white superiority persisted down through the decades. They became less marked, perhaps, but still required to one degree or another that the Indian remain a model of the primitive, a notion that was essential to casting the region for tourists as rugged, unspoiled, and uncivilized. In 1929 Grand Canyon National Park Superintendent Miner Tillotson described the park region as "one of the very few areas in the United States where the 'red' man still lives in his native state, primitive but happy, contented, unchanged by the white man's civilization."[48]

Although Colter was not free of the presumptions of her times, she held Native American culture, art, and architecture in great esteem all through her life. She possessed accurate and comprehensive knowledge of Indian art works and symbolism and incorporated them sensitively into her buildings and interiors. Among the few surviving examples of Colter's writing, most notably the *Manual for Drivers and Guides* that she wrote about the Watchtower at the Grand Canyon (see Chapter VI), she displayed great admiration for the peoples and the individuals who created that culture. But a larger question looms as to the impact of Harvey/Santa Fe architecture and mercantilism on the Indians themselves. On the one hand, the companies' enterprise allowed the Indians a stake, albeit small, in the opening of the Southwest to tourism. On the other hand, it was inevitable that commercial and social interchange with the tourist market would expose ancient traditions and religious practices to scrutiny and possible exploitation, both cultural and economic. The Harvey Company obviously saw this as a fair deal. Some others were not so sure, especially later in the twentieth century, from the vantage point of history. From all evidence Mary Colter fully supported this exchange as necessary for her employer and for her professional growth, and together with company officials like John F. Huckel and Herman Schweizer did her part to keep the goods flowing and the sales brisk.

Although Colter was Hopi House's inspiration and architect, she collaborated on its creation with ethnographer H.R. Voth, who oversaw its construction and museum presentation.[49] Voth had amassed many of the museum artifacts shown on the second floor, including collections of Hopi artifacts and old Navajo blankets that had won grand prizes for the Harvey Company at the 1904 Louisiana Purchase Exposition in St. Louis. A Pomo basket collection, another fair winner, was also on display. Similar to what he had done in the Alvarado's Indian Building, in 1913 Voth installed in Hopi House a reproduction he had made of two Hopi altars. They were controversial among the Hopis, however, who demanded the return of a mask they felt should not have been included; it was removed and returned.[50] Hopi House was a direct outgrowth of the popular "anthropological" exhibits of Native Americans, complete with dwellings, that Harvey and others had set up at world's fairs and other expositions of the day and would continue to do. In this case, however, the "exhibit" was permanent and over the years would grow into of the most-visited sites at the Grand Canyon. ⊡

With the Hopi House project finished, Colter, not yet a permanent Fred Harvey employee, moved back to St. Paul to resume her teaching career at Mechanic Arts High School. The longing to create her own designs, however, whetted so acutely by her Harvey Company commissions in Albuquerque and at the Grand Canyon, induced her to look elsewhere for fulfillment. In 1908 she accepted a visual merchandising job at the Frederick and Nelson department store in Seattle, moving to that booming city—which reached 237,000 people by 1910—with her sister and mother. They lived at 2626 10th Avenue North. Founded in 1890, Frederick and Nelson became the city's most prestigious department store and the predecessor of a large regional chain. Like some of its siblings in other big cities, the store was a retail pioneer, diversifying its stock and devising new and clever ways to sell it—offering ready-to-wear apparel, for example, modernizing store layout and merchandise display, and expanding customer services. Frederick's had recently completed a series of major expansions of its Second Avenue location when Colter was hired to develop its decoration and display department.[51]

Frederick and Nelson, shown here circa 1908, was growing into a leading department store when Colter was hired to develop its display department.

opposite: John Bradstreet's atmospheric Craftshouse in Minneapolis pioneered the merchandising of home furnishings from around the world.

70

The growth of department and furnishings stores during that period reflected not only prosperity and its encouragement of consumer-goods purchasing, both oiled by the ability of the railroads to ship more goods and faster, but also American society's increased emphasis on improving the appearance and functioning of the home. As the notion of the home as a haven for art and a place in which to live artfully took hold, encouraged philosophically by the Arts and Crafts movement and practically by stores' ability to obtain wares world-wide,[52] the need to sell such goods in an artistic and compelling manner also grew. One notable instance of this was enfolding back in the Twin Cities, where interior designer John Scott Bradstreet had opened his Craftshouse in 1904 in Minneapolis. Bradstreet sold his own hand-crafted furnishings, adroitly displayed with a range of antique and modern goods he brought back from Europe and the Far East, in spacious wood-framed galleries that were themselves works of art. His innovative casual-but-studied approach to the display of his wares encouraged curious customers to explore all the corners of his store.[53] The Craftshouse became such a popular attraction that Colter could not have failed to notice the enterprise, before or after her Seattle period, and learn from it. Of course, she had already demonstrated her own acumen in marketing via design, when she laid out the retail spaces at the Alvarado's Indian Building and at Hopi House. There were marked similarities of approach between those romantic and alluring rooms and the selling departments and store windows of progressive retailers of the day.[54]

Colter's Seattle career was cut short, however, in December of the following year when her mother, Rebecca Colter, died. Mary and her sister Harriet buried their mother in St. Paul at the Oakland Cemetery in the family plot next to their father.[55] 🗔

The Fred Harvey Company hired Mary Colter on a permanent basis in 1910, and she moved to Kansas City to work at Harvey headquarters as its architect and interior designer. The city would be both home and work base for many years, but she was only sporadically to be found there, since the job demanded that she be out riding the rails in service to a touristic empire. Harvey was her official employer, but given its exceptionally close corporate bond with the Santa Fe Railway on most of its undertakings, the latter agreed to pay part of her salary. The Harvey Company at that time was headed by Ford F. Harvey, one of the founder's two sons, but J. F. Huckel, vice president and general manager, was her immediate boss. Over the years Colter would work closely, and sometimes combatively, with him on developing project concepts and implementing them in all their details.

Colter was not a registered architect. She had graduated from design school before California required such, and early in her career architects were rarely registered in any event. She apparently never pursued an architectural license, but her rather unusual working circumstances did not require that ranking. Her charge was to create general concepts for buildings, both exterior and interior, and then to draw floor plans, building elevations, and perspectives from which Santa Fe's licensed architects and engineers would create and sign the working drawings. One of the Santa Fe architects with whom she worked for years was E. A. Harrison, and it is his name that was to be found on many of the official drawings for her buildings. The railway was in charge of the entire construction process for Harvey facilities, mustering its considerable resources as a builder of railroads, and it owned the land and buildings where Fred Harvey hotels and restaurants were installed. Harvey owned only the furnishings and contents inside. Needless to say, this situation complicated the process of design and construction.[56]

opposite: Louis Curtiss's El Ortiz in
Lamy, New Mexico, mingled Spanish
Pueblo and other styles.

The view left shows the "little
fellow of the Harvey system"
before it was enlarged.

Colter had entered a small but growing sorority. In 1890 the U.S. Census listed twenty-two women architects, a number that increased nearly five times by 1900. These women were trained either in academic programs or, like Colter, in offices; the latter education was more unusual. (It is interesting to note that traditionally architects were trained by their predecessors in an apprentice situation; university degrees took hold only late in the nineteenth century and, in fact, helped open the profession to women.) Typically they practiced alone or in partnership with other women. A celebrated exception was Colter's contemporary, Julia Morgan, who headed a large office in San Francisco.[57] Colter's situation, working within the architecture and design office of a major hotel/restaurant company, was rare if not unique. It provided her shelter from the stormy realities of keeping a lone practice or a firm afloat—often a problem for new architects but certainly more so for early women in the field. It also helped her to practice architecture. "Many women, white and black, were shunted away from architecture into allied fields like drafting but also interior design and landscape architecture, decoration and gardens being considered appropriately feminine spheres," notes Mary N. Woods in her study of the profession.[58] Colter also practiced interior and landscape design, of course, not grudgingly but with great enthusiasm, for she considered those pursuits indispensable to the creation of a total package, complete as art as well as history.

The patio reinforced the notion that El Ortiz was "unquestionably the most romantic" of the early twentieth-century Harvey hotels.

Colter's first project as a permanent Fred Harvey Company employee took her in 1910 to one of the more remote points on the Santa Fe line, the tiny town of Lamy, New Mexico. The railway was constructing a new hotel there, called El Ortiz, and it was her job to design its interior.

Lamy was established in 1880 as the junction between the railroad's main east-west line and Santa Fe, the state capital, located some eighteen miles to the northwest.[59] Owing to the barrier created by difficult mountain terrain or, according to another explanation, to the city having once supported a rival railway, the Santa Fe in its early years decided to bypass its namesake. A spur line of the railway carried passengers into Santa Fe. Lamy, which also housed the crews who serviced the steam engines used to push trains over the Glorieta Pass to the east, grew into a thriving settlement.[60]

Replacing a prior wooden depot hotel that had burned, the railway in 1909 began construction of a new station, a simple stucco structure roofed in red tiles and topped with a low tower. To its east rose the remarkable, and quite different, El Ortiz Hotel. Its architect was Louis Curtiss, a prolific and eccentric Canadian-born man from Kansas City who had already worked for Harvey and the Santa Fe in Kansas, designing the El Bisonte Hotel in Hutchinson in 1906 and depots and Harvey Houses in Emporia, Syracuse, and Wellington in 1907. During his career, Curtiss (1865–1924) produced depots for other railroads as well, including the union station in Wichita, and was responsible for the Bolley Building in Kansas City, said to be the first glass-and-metal curtain-wall building in the country.

Continuing along the path established by the Alvarado Hotel and other evocative Santa Fe/Harvey buildings, Curtiss created El Ortiz as an essay in the Old Southwest mode but in a highly individual manner that combined elements of the Spanish Pueblo style with echoes of the Mission Revival and even the Vienna Secession. The latter trait is not surprising, since the Secession exerted a strong influence on Curtiss's later work, including a number of stations, hotels, and other railroad buildings that he designed in a more forthrightly geometric manner shortly after El Ortiz.[61]

The small hotel was a one-story flat-roofed structure finished in stucco—except for the sides, which were exposed adobe—and lined with long deep porches facing the railroad tracks. That facade was dominated on one end by a protruding barrel-roofed bay affixed with Santa Fe's famous round corporate symbol. The roof beams are thought to have come from a northern pueblo church, and after the hotel was razed, were reused to build a ranch.[62] Rows of projecting vigas led the eye to the capped-parapet main entrance bay on the other end, above which "El Ortiz" was spelled out ornately in raised Old Spanish script. The hotel was named after an old New Mexico family.[63] In his consideration of the early twentieth-century Harvey hotels, architectural historian David Gebhard deemed El Ortiz "unquestionably the most romantic and in certain ways the most eclectic," yet emphasized also that, as part of the group, it also was "an aspect of the early modernist movement in American architecture."[64]

Inside, ten guest rooms opened onto a completely enclosed patio centered on a fountain, "whose perimeter in the growing season was a verdant scene of hanging vines and split-log planter boxes."[65] The containers were no doubt the product of Colter's studied consideration, as she went about decorating the rooms and public spaces, following a Mexican theme enhanced with Indian motifs. For the main lounge—also known, fittingly, as the "living room"—Colter placed sturdy carved tables and chairs atop Navajo rugs and adorned the walls with Spanish religious paintings, other artwork, and light fixtures. According to Byron Harvey III, the rugs were "almost certainly obtained" by Herman Schweizer.[66] She constructed the ceiling with dark viga logs, actually sections of old telephone poles. She arranged hammered copper pieces above the raised fireplace, weaving an Indian motif into its

Colter enhanced her scheme for the El Ortiz lounge with an alcove centered on a large fireplace adorned with patterned brickwork.

surrounding brickwork. This generously arched cavity, set with Arts and Crafts sensibility into an alcove, presaged the massive hearths of later Colter buildings like Hermit's Rest and the Bright Angel Lodge.

William F. Cody ("Buffalo Bill") "toasted his booted toes at the huge fireplace," reportedly saying that "this little hotel would have made a nice little ranch house."[67] Indeed, El Ortiz' oasis of atmosphere won the little hotel a wide and affectionate following among desert-weary travelers and locals alike. After staying there for a week in 1922, writer Owen Wister, author of *The Virginian*, was moved to vivid appreciation. "As a result of [the Santa Fe's] intelligent perceptions it has created a little flower of art at the lonely junction in New Mexico," Wister wrote in recollection in 1922.[68]

It is interesting that Wister also wrote: "The circumstances of [El Ortiz'] growth were laid bare [to him] by two who had much to do with it." Although he did not name these persons, he referred to one as "a lady, whose father's rare and imaginative ability had passed into her." The father was Fred Harvey and the woman his daughter Minnie Harvey Huckel, who, with her husband and Harvey Company executive, John F. Huckel, inspired and shepherded many of the Harvey projects. A later article describes the Huckels: "It was before the turn of the century, when the end of the Santa Fe railroad line was at Lamy, that she and her husband conceived the idea for a 'dream hotel' in the tiny New Mexico village. They directed the building of El Ortiz, that still stands at Lamy, a miniature hotel, perfect in every detail. . . . The works of art that make the 'little fellow' of the Harvey system so delightful were selected by them for the hotel from the Harvey collection that at that time was already growing into one of major importance to the Spanish history of the Southwest."[69]

Minnie also was Colter's mentor from the beginning of the designer's association with Harvey. A 1943 obituary noted: "She had been closely associated with her late husband in linking Indian lore with [the] rail eating system. . . . Theirs was the support that enabled Miss Mary E. J. Colter to transpose the Spanish and Indian culture to the modern buildings of the Harvey system."

The Grand Canyon Period

FOUR

IN 1913, IN THE FIRST OF A CAREER-LONG SERIES of big-city railroad-station assignments, Colter began work on decorating the Fred Harvey restaurants and shops for the immense new Kansas City Union Station, which opened in October of the following year. Designed by Jarvis Hunt of Chicago, a nephew of famous architect Richard Morris Hunt, this grand Beaux Arts-style edifice with its broad plaza—the third-largest station ever built in America—marked the culmination of development of the city's renowned City Beautiful system of parks and boulevards. "This mighty structure will be a schoolroom of beauty for the thousands who will enter it," exclaimed one speaker at the opening banquet.[1]

Mary Colter worked in Kansas City at Fred Harvey headquarters, which moved into Union Station soon after it opened in 1914.

The station today, opposite

Colter is shown, above, first row center with her Harvey colleagues, circa 1916.

In probably the first instance of her name in public print, *The Santa Fe Magazine* reported that "[t]he credit for the decorative scheme throughout [the station] goes to Miss Mary E. J. Coulter [sic], Fred Harvey's official decorator."[2] The Harvey lunchroom, a tall classically decorated box painted gray and pink and outfitted with a huge marble-topped counter, was attended by the famous corps of

83

The largest of the Harvey spaces that Colter designed at the station were the dining room, above, and lunchroom, opposite.

Harvey Girls in their black-and-white frocks. Waiters in black trousers and white jackets served in the more formal dining room, a large hall seating 152 people that Colter colored mulberry, cream, white, and gold. Large baskets of white and yellow chrysanthemums were placed along the walls. Both became popular places for local socializing. The Harvey Company was the exclusive retailer for the station, which was a showcase for the company; in addition to the restaurants, it also operated a bookstore, a toy store, a candy store, and the largest drugstore in town.[3] Upon completion of the station, Ford Harvey moved the company's headquarters to the building, where Colter would work for more than two decades.[4]

"From Miss Colter's studio came the designs for the beautiful Roman urns made by Tiffany in gold and silver for the soda fountain in the new Union Station," wrote the *Kansas City Star*, taking the occasion of the station's debut to inform its readers that the designer whose work they had seen at the Grand Canyon and other western venues lived and worked in town, "where she makes designs for new feature houses along the Santa Fe." The article also recounted a charming and revealing tale from Hopi House:

MISS COLTER DESCRIBES HER SEARCH FOR AN IDEA FOR THE FURNITURE OF HOPI HOUSE AS RATHER DISCOURAGING UNTIL SHE CHANCED UPON A CURIOUS OLD BENCH IN A HOUSE OF THE HOPIS. IT WAS HEWN OUT OF A LOG AND HAD BECOME BEAUTIFULLY WEATHERED WITH TIME. TABLES AND MANY KINDS OF SEATS WERE DEVISED FROM THIS MODEL, AND THE ARTIST WAS MUCH AMUSED ONE DAY TO OVERHEAR THE FOREMAN OF THE WORKMEN TELLING A VISITOR THAT THIS—POINTING TO ONE OF THE IMITATIONS—WAS THE ORIGINAL SEAT, AND THIS—PLACING HAND ON THE ORIGINAL—[WAS] A MIGHTY GOOD COPY.[5]

By this point in her career with the Harvey Company, Colter had demonstrated that she could decorate and design original interior spaces, as well as a complete building (Hopi House), that would both cater to and delight the traveler. Her work was helping bring distinction—and profits—to the company as it expanded its hotel/restaurant/retail empire along the Santa Fe Railway line. It must have become clear to Colter also that her future lay with the Harveys and with the West.

Yet she had not severed ties with St. Paul. After all, her sister, Harriet, still lived there as did colleagues from her prior career as a teacher at Mechanic Art High School. She maintained ties with the school as well as with her prize pupil there, Arthur Larkin, who had graduated from the University of Minnesota as a civil engineer, married, and started a family in Minneapolis. In January 1913 Larkin and his wife, Lou, named their first child Mary Colter Larkin. The next month Colter sent the baby a Valentine telegram:

TO MY OWN VALENTINE: IF YOU EVER LOVE ME AS I NOW YOU OUR BONDS WILL BE STRONGER THAN LEPAGE'S GLUE. I COULD NOT BE SURE THAT MINE WOULD BE YOUR FIRST VALENTINE, BUT AM HOPING IT WILL BE YOUR FIRST TELEGRAM. GIVE VALENTINE LOVE TO YOUR FAMILY, FROM MARY COLTER[6]

In October that year, Colter sent little Mary a note while her parents were on vacation: "If they keep this sort of thing up you just better come and live with me—you know you're part mine anyway!"[7] For the rest of her life, "Aunt Mary" would remain close to her namesake, doting on her, sending her gifts, and even helping finance her college education. Colter visited the Larkins often, which could prove trying to Lou Larkin. Colter would stay in her room, waited on by Lou, who would bring meals up to her. (Colter was used to staying in hotels.) There she would remain until Arthur came home from work. "And it drove my mother crazy because she smoked. . . . She was so generous to my father, so we didn't care," recalled Mary

Colter Larkin Smith. Although she was devoted to Smith, "she really loved men, and not so much women," Smith observed.[8] That perception does not mean that Colter was innately prejudiced against women but reflects the fact that her professional life then, which was essentially her entire life, was lived almost entirely with men. Colter enjoyed very much meeting and working with her intellectual equals, and at that time the opportunity to do such was presented mostly by men. This would change in later years.

Even children, to whom Colter could be most affectionate, had not really "graduated" until they were old enough to carry on an intelligent conversation with her. And at that point, while they were still young, the teacher in Colter came out. She enjoyed eliciting their observations. Patricia Smyth, whose mother knew Mary and Mary's sister, Harriet, in Kansas City and to whom Colter was also "Aunt Mary," recalled visiting her in the 1950s after college, during Colter's retirement years in Santa Fe. "There were two questions she'd always ask me," says Smyth. "She'd say, 'What have you bought?' And then she sent me into a huge storage room but didn't say why. When I came out, she said, 'What did you see?' And I knew that was the acid test, and I had picked out the right thing. I said I'd never seen a Chinese lacquer screen that tall. And she nodded, pleased."[9]

Even before she had finished her Kansas City station project, Mary Colter was drafting designs for another building at the Grand Cãnyon, one of a pair of rocky roosts that the Harvey Company would open in 1914 on the south rim. In a third undertaking a few years later, she would tuck a group of buildings into the bottom of the canyon near the Colorado River. All three assignments declare Colter's fascination with natural materials and her gift for adapting a building to its surrounding landscape. Moreover, they would strongly influence the architecture of subsequent park buildings, both at the Grand Canyon and at other western parks.

As the public became more aware of the canyon's unique splendor, sentiment grew for the protection of the chasm and its surroundings as a national park. Although that would not come to pass for a few more years, the federal government was edging toward that end. Indiana Senator Benjamin Harrison introduced a bill for park designation. It was defeated, but as president in 1893 he designated the area a forest reserve, and in 1897 it came under the supervision of the Department of the Interior. It took that celebrated outdoorsman and naturalist, Theodore Roosevelt, to popularize and accelerate the protection process. His first visit to the Grand Canyon in May 1903 moved President Roosevelt to comment on this "absolutely unparalleled" sight: "Leave it as it is. You cannot improve on it. The ages have been at work on it, and man can only mar it. What you can do is keep it for . . . all who come after you."[10] In 1906 Roosevelt proclaimed the Grand Canyon Game Reserve, and in 1908, enabled by the 1906 Act for the Preservation of American Antiquities and by the discovery of ruins in the reserve, he established the Grand Canyon National Monument. Political pressure for national park designation continued to mount, especially after Arizona became a state in 1912.

Rooseveltian passion notwithstanding, the Fred Harvey Company and the Santa Fe Railway felt that they certainly could "improve on" the canyon by studding its edge, and possibly the gorge itself, with tourist attractions. As they had hoped, the 1901 rail connection to the canyon was boosting visitation there, and they needed to accommodate the new crowds. Exploration and then prospecting and mining had first attracted people to the canyon and rim, but tourism was rapidly taking over as the area's chief economic activity. "The rails brought the canyon into the realm of industrial tourism," comments historian Stephen Pyne on this shift. "The visitor replaced the explorer, the Kodak snapshot the grand canvas, the inscribed overlook the monographs, atlases, and personal narratives of its bold creators."[11]

A sprinkling of buildings, which would later constitute Grand Canyon Village, began to accumulate in the vicinity of El Tovar Hotel, Hopi House, and earlier structures built before the turn of the century. Chief among the latter was the small wood-frame Bright Angel Hotel (1896), which incorporated a log cabin built by financier William "Buckey" O'Neill. Close by was the Cameron Hotel, a tiny inn that began as a log cabin sixteen miles to the south, then was moved to a site near the original Santa Fe railroad terminus. The cabin was expanded with a second story. Harvey took over the Bright Angel Hotel, renaming it Bright Angel Camp, and the Cameron eventually closed. Colter admired the indigenous qualities of the older buildings and fought successfully in the 1930s to incorporate both structures into the sprawling Bright Angel Lodge and Cabins that she was designing.

The Santa Fe depot at Grand Canyon opened in 1909 near El Tovar.

Some of the new growth was in Harvey facilities, like the mule barn, livery stable, and blacksmith shop built in 1906 to house animals and equipment for canyon mule rides and horse-drawn vehicles. In 1909 Harvey's railway partner built a terminal just down the slope from El Tovar, a log chalet-style depot with Craftsman style flavor that was modeled after the hotel by Santa Barbara architect Francis Wilson. He also had converted the Bright Angel Hotel/O'Neill cabin complex into Harvey's Bright Angel Camp, an inn and campground more modestly priced than El Tovar. The new depot—the only such station inside a national park—turned arrival at the Grand Canyon into a more memorable rite, one akin to alighting at the Alvarado or other imposing train stations on the main line. The terminal also was several hundred feet east of the old terminus near

Colter conceived Hermit's Rest, built at the west end of the new rim road, as the former retreat of a recluse who had made the building of materials found around him. A log loggia shelters the entrance.

At Hermit's Rest, timber meets
stone to forge a rough-hewn union.

the competing Cameron Hotel. Other rival concessionaires muscled in, most notably John Verkamp, who built a curio store near Hopi House in 1905, and the illustrious Kolb Brothers, Ellsworth and Emery, adventurer/photographers who in 1904 perched a house-studio on the rim near the head of Bright Angel Trail; there they launched a nearly seven-decade run of taking pictures of hikers descending into the gorge.[12] Struggles for control of Grand Canyon trade between the Santa Fe/Harvey combine and other commercial or land interests would drag on for years, but the Harvey organization eventually came to control all of the tourist accommodations and vending on the south rim.

Grand Canyon Village was the first service node along the lengthy rim, but the Harvey Company wanted to open other areas for tourist enjoyment and, with that, increase profits. Between 1910–1912 the Santa Fe constructed the Hermit Rim Road eight miles westward from the village. Now Harvey could offer open-topped, horse-drawn carriages (later the famous Harveycars) that offered sightseers comfortable transportation to formerly distant panoramic points. A rest and viewing station was a must for the end of the long leisurely ride. Charged with planning this facility, Colter was immediately faced with a challenging design decision. Should the new building emulate the proto-European chalet represented by El Tovar? Would the more indigenous pueblo style exemplified by Hopi House better fit this rugged terrain? Or was something more innovative and daring needed? She chose this last direction and, fortunately for her career and architectural experimentation, was able to win over her Harvey bosses. Hermit's Rest, as the structure was named, became one of the most remarkable and memorable park buildings anywhere.

The site was Colter's muse—both historically and physically. The "hermit" represented by the new rim road was Louis D. Boucher, a reclusive Canadian who around 1890 had established a nearby camp at the head of what became known as Hermit Canyon. Boucher also built a trail to Long Canyon, where he set up a camp that lodged tourists riding into the main canyon on horseback. The hermit story offered Colter the perfect name for her new building and a theme for its design. As she would do many times, Colter reached into history to guide her art. In her imaginary architectural tale, the structure was the remote dwelling of an old-time prospector who had cobbled it together with materials he found around him. The old place had somehow survived long enough to welcome a new type of sojourner, the weary tourist. "Like her other designs, Hermit's Rest housed a vague dream world, a material point of departure for visions of rustic frontier life and nature as a sanctuary from civilization."[13]

Hermit's Rest was Colter's most original design to date and firmly demonstrated her skill in architectural design and site planning. If Hopi House was a striking sight, surely this new building was even more so. Built into a low hill at the edge of the canyon, it looks like an undulating pile of boulders and timber ready to tumble into the abyss. Sprouting from one end of its uneven roofline is an uneasily stacked chimney, and extending from the canyon side of the structure is a log-framed porch roof, held up by log columns, a pier of piled-up rock, and a barkless tree trunk studded with the stubs of branches and hung with bear traps. The cool recess of this loggia contrasts with the bright landscape, and the timbers frame views of the yawning canyon almost as paintings. Here and elsewhere the junctions of stone with wood are treated simply, but in some cases—the double logs over the east and west clerestory windows, for instance—they seem over-designed, just as an amateur architect worried about the place holding up might have created them.

From the road turnaround, where carriage visitors were dropped, not much is evident. One originally approached Hermit's Rest through a quaint gravity-defying arch of massive boulders that Colter whimsically adorned with a rusty cracked bell that she had found on one of her many antiques hunting trips, possibly in Santa Fe. The gravel path rose, then slowly descended and curved through the trees toward the

Tourists in 1920 pose under the bell at the entrance arch at Hermit's Rest.

93

building, a visual trick that emphasized the way the structure nestled into the hill and reduced its apparent size. One's first view was of the "pile of rocks," which only took form as a real building as the path flowed into the loggia. Overall, Hermit's Rest seems like it simply happened, accreting randomly through the years. Of course, none of it did; the apparent lack of contrivance masks Colter's exacting artifice.

Inside, a surprisingly lofty hall centers on an enormous arched fireplace alcove, as enticing to wayfarers as the canyon that looms through the window wall at their backs. The large stones that line the half-domed recess are blackened with soot, an effect that Colter specified to lend the hall instant age. The alcove, sort of a super-scaled inglenook, is stepped up above the rest of the room, subtly emphasizing its individuality. Here and in most of her other buildings, Colter lavished special attention on the design and placement of fireplaces, anchoring public rooms visually and at the same time imparting feelings of sheltering welcome and domestic serenity. This main fireplace—another heats a subsidiary room—was the sort that, George Wharton James suggested, "must have warmed the toes of the giant Vikings when they reached Valhalla."[14] Rows of Prairie Style clerestory windows under the timber-framed ceiling admit daylight into the room without competing with framed views of the canyon through the lower windows. The hall was originally furnished with sturdy tables and chairs, some of the latter hollowed out from tree trunks, and was trimmed with wrought iron light fixtures. A bearskin rug lay in front of the fireplace, gaping back open-jawed at visitors. To James the space was "one vast cave." Indeed, the story is told that Colter was teased about the building's dark and rustic look. In response to the question, " 'Why don't you clean up this place?' Colter laughed, 'You can't imagine what it cost to make it look this old.' "[15]

Colter worked Hermit's Rest ingeniously into the site by burrowing it partly into the bluff—which actually was heaped up expressly for this project—and giving it an erratic profile. Right angles and geometric perfection were banished to the

opposite: An enormous fireplace alcove dominates the main hall at Hermit's Rest, beckoning visitors to linger under its generous arch.

above: A period postcard reveals the outdoor stairs descending from the loggia.

95

The fireplace alcove at Hermit's
Rest in an early view

Picture and clerestory windows in the main hall brighten views of the canyon to the left.

An early view of Lookout Studio, which opened the same year as Hermit's Rest

opposite: Colter designed the Lookout Studio to look as if it grew out of the canyon ledge.

The walls and terraces of Lookout, left, mimic the myriad strata of the canyon wall below them.

The lower portion of Lookout, above, was crafted from rock rubble that merges into the landscape.

interior. She used stone that seems like it could have been found right in the neighborhood or nearby from some canyon ledge and hauled into place with little if any treatment. The stone walls' highly irregular coursing accentuates the building's ad hoc, unstudied appearance. The wood is left similarly rough-hewn, some of it looking like fallen logs encountered by chance. To further merge the building into the hill, the roof was originally covered with earth and planted as an extension of the adjoining landscape. As with most of Colter's Grand Canyon buildings, she made no attempt to design or formalize the natural surroundings; no yard or garden sphere mediates between structure and landscape.

Hermit's Rest would be Colter's first essay in her unique style—site-driven, irregular, and, in the precise sense of the term, fantastic. (Two decades later, the Watchtower at Desert View at the opposite end of the park, would be her last.) The building was a new and remarkable departure, but the Fred Harvey/Santa Fe advertising operatives were equal to the task of portraying the rewards of a visit. In its *California and the Grand Canyon of Arizona* booklet, Harvey stated, with slight inaccuracy: "The site was dug out of the solid rock. The resthouse itself extends out to the rim of the Canyon, from which point can be observed the ever shifting lights and shadows of the Canyon's gorge. Inside it is furnished with a view to comfort and rest."[16]

Viewed from some angles or in certain lighting, Hermit's Rest seems more like a landform than a building. The same is true of Lookout Studio, the second sightseeing attraction on the canyon rim that Colter designed in 1914. The Harvey Company conceived the little structure as an all-weather port from which to take in framed views of the canyon. Its location on a promontory ensured that people strolling along the canyon's edge from El Tovar Hotel would quickly notice it, although they might not immediately make it out as man-made, so deftly did Colter layer the structure with its terraces into the canyon wall. The building looks like it

grows out of the ledge—or even as if the erosion of centuries had created it as it created the canyon.

Lookout Studio is a low, horizontal construction of rough-cut Kaibab limestone walls—the same stone as that of the upper canyon wall—that rise to an uneven parapet at the roof. A square tower anchors the far end like a diminutive rampart, enclosing space for canyon-gazing and exits that lead down to a series of crisscrossing staircases and terraces that descend a bit of the perpendicular canyon wall. The slightly sloping roof hoods a long bank of windows that floods the interior with eastern light. Unlike Hermit's Rest, none of the walls are buried. Colter fitted outsized stones into the walls here and there, especially at the bottom, and piled up rock rubble for the massive base of the chimney. Before parts of the building were later reconstructed into slightly more regular form, this was the building's roughest feature. Colter, of course, designed it that way and was probably on the job inspecting the placement of each boulder, given her reputation for perfectionism. As an added touch of the plain and genuine, she specified that small native plants sprout from among the stones.

A visit to the Lookout takes one along a low, curving stone wall that springs off the main promenade and at the entrance melts gracefully into the building's facade. Within, the building's structure was left exposed with stone walls, timber-framed ceiling, and scored-concrete floor but was trimmed with wooden window frames, cabinets, and room dividers. The interior exudes a domestic feeling, heightened by an arched stone fireplace in an alcove, less prominent than the one at Hermit's Rest. Originally, Indian rugs lay on the floor, topographic maps of the canyon hung on the walls, and portfolios of photographs rested on the tables. Half-story changes of level take one up to the viewing gallery and porch, where tourists would peer into the canyon through a powerful binocular telescope, and down to a vestibule that opens to the outside and its descending terraces. There tourists do what they have always done: wander with tentative steps a bit closer and down into the canyon, gulp and gasp at the sight, and finally take photos of each other with the great gorge as backdrop.

"A tiny rustic club is The Lookout with its bright hued Navaho rugs, electric lights, cozy fireplace and many easy chairs," reads an early Harvey brochure.[17] Indeed, the space was first furnished comfortably, encouraging one to tarry by contemplating the canyon or simply relaxing; one photo in the brochure shows a woman writing postcards or a letter and a man reading a book, sitting next to windows that gave them a sweeping view of the chasm. "One may sit through the long, quiet, still days, and rest and read and watch the changes caused by sun and shadow upon the panorama spread below." At night the Lookout allowed people to watch the "rise and wane" of the "unnaturally bright" stars and planets viewable in the region. The ambiance has changed dramatically over the years, as the Lookout Studio—and Hermit's Rest—has taken on the role of a standard-issue souvenir shop; its rooms are crowded and the relaxing and contemplative atmosphere that Colter carefully fashioned has largely been lost.

Harvey built the structure to compete with the Kolb Studio, located not far west on the rim trail. The Kolb brothers had refused to sell out to the Santa Fe, so the railway decided to out-do them, offering even better views of the canyon and likenesses of it for sale—photos, postcards, and paintings. When the building first opened, it was known simply as the Lookout; "studio" was added to enhance its

The main room of the Lookout Studio includes a rustic stone fireplace.

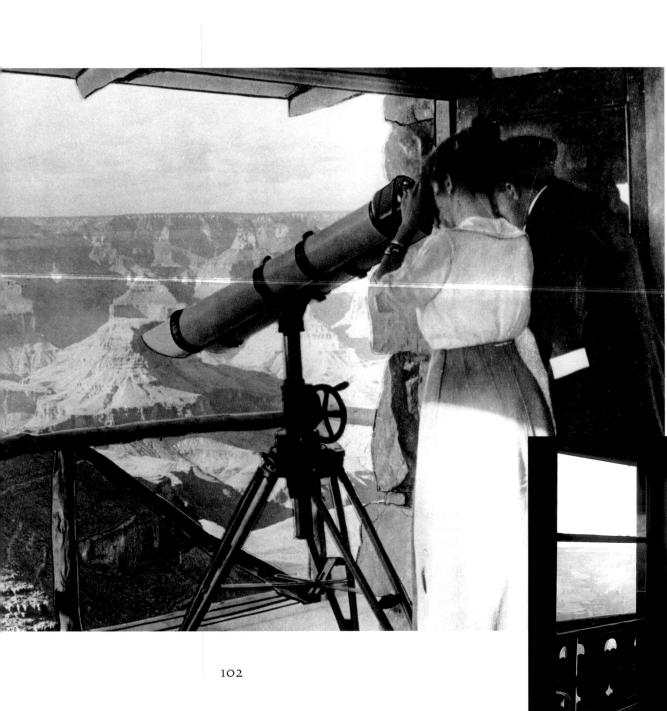

A telescope in the upper gallery of Lookout Studio enabled early visitors to gaze deep into the sun and shadow of the canyon.

The upper gallery today, below

competitive edge in 1937 after the photography studio at El Tovar was eliminated. In response to the opening of the Lookout, the Kolbs expanded their studio and showed the first motion picture of the Grand Canyon, which they had filmed on a 1911 river trip.[18]

Both Hermit's Rest and Lookout Studio are suggestive of follies, buildings that were popular in eighteenth- and nineteenth-century Europe, one-of-a-kind structures that adorned estates or parks with their eccentric shapes, materials, and placement. Follies were intended to enhance a view or create a picturesque effect. Some exhibited tricks of scale and materials, effects that Colter also employed. At times, they were designed purposely as ruins, usually gothic or classical, a description not inappropriate for the two Colter buildings with their built-in age and somewhat tumbledown demeanor. The imaginative observer might even see them as reduced—or ruined—versions of structures that were once more formal. One difference stands out, however. Follies were rarely planned with specific uses in mind. The Colter buildings were. ▣

With Hermit's Rest and Lookout Studio, Colter departed from the ethnographic approach that she had used for Hopi House. She returned to a Native American theme when asked to collaborate on the design of a southwestern Indian life exhibit for the 1915 San Diego exposition. The impetus for the fair was the opening of the Panama Canal, which in greatly shortening the journey from the east coast to the west augured wealth for California's port cities. After San Francisco was chosen to host the official world celebration of the event (the Panama-Pacific Exposition), San Diego, its chief but much less populous rival, decided to put on its own show. For its smaller Panama-California Exposition, the southern city chose to trumpet the scenic, economic, and cultural splendors of the American Southwest.

The Santa Fe Railway exhibited at each fair, enticing its passengers to visit both by taking advantage of a special offer that advertised "two fairs for one fare." The railroad and the Fred Harvey Company were as keenly interested as ever in promoting both the golden region at the end of its line, California, and the exotic landscapes and Native American life the traveler would encounter along the way. The companies were well versed in the profitable display of authentic Indian wares and performances, having already exhibited such at the world's fairs in Chicago (1893) and St. Louis (1904) as well as at the Alvarado Hotel's Indian Building and the Grand Canyon's Hopi House.[19]

Colter's task was to prepare a model of the Painted Desert Exhibit, as it was to be called, based on a painting of an Indian village commissioned by J. F. Huckel and plans by Herman Schweizer.[20] Her own knowledge of Indian habitations, honed by the research and site visits she had conducted to design Hopi House, also guided her hand. As part of the fair promoters' publicity in the year before the opening, Colter's plaster model, which she cast from her wax original, was shipped to San Diego in March 1914 and displayed in the window of the Santa Fe offices in the U.S. Grant Hotel. "The little model is an artistic triumph in itself," stated a front-page newspaper article. "[It] was made by Miss Mary E. J. Colter of Kansas City, who does a great deal of art work and decoration for the Fred Harvey system, from an outline and preliminary plan by Herman Schweizer of the news and curio department." Copies of the model were to be displayed at Santa Fe offices throughout the country.[21]

Well-known New York architect Bertram Goodhue laid out the San Diego exposition, hewing to a Spanish Colonial Baroque theme for most of its prominent buildings. He designed the centerpiece California Building, a church in form with a typically Goodhue-tiled tower and dome, while his associate Carlton Winslow was responsible for the rest. All were decked out in highly modeled *churrigueresque* embellishments derived from Mexican examples and arranged along the spine avenue, El

Prado, or on the Plaza de Panama. Located at the northern end of a long amusement midway—aptly titled "the Isthmus" and featuring such exotica as a Chinatown complete with an "opium den" and a "War of the Worlds" multimedia show that depicted the destruction of New York City by alien armies in the year 2000—the ten-acre Painted Desert Exhibit was dominated by buildings made to resemble the Taos and Zuni pueblos of New Mexico on opposite sides of a plaza. Navajo hogans, Apache tipis, a small Hopi village, and a trading post filled out the "mesa," which also boasted two kivas. The village stood in ironic and perhaps intended contrast to the weighty official buildings of the fair, which embodied the triumph both of the natives' first colonial masters, the Spaniards, as well as of their American successors.

As in prior Harvey displays, the accent was on authenticity. Many of the materials (willow, cedar, sandstone), furnishings, and art objects were bought from Indians in Arizona and New Mexico, and the village was built mostly by them, using adobe made on site.[22] "Everything that the Indian possesses in his own home and haunts will be there," the article claimed.[23] Nothing was more authentic, of course, than real Indians, so the exhibit was peopled with some 300 members of various tribes, who crafted artworks, cooked meals, performed rituals, and otherwise lived their daily lives in full view of the crowds. "[They] are not idle and not in white man's clothes, but are living just as they have lived and their ancestors have lived for centuries."[24] Among the artists in residence were Maria Martinez and her husband Julian from San Ildefonso Pueblo, who in later years would become two of the most famous twentieth-century southwestern Indian potters. The desire for accuracy, however, stretched only so far; the village's name was chosen more for romantic appeal than complete realism, since Arizona's Painted Desert lay at some distance from many of the villages and peoples represented in the exhibit. ⊡

opposite: The Santa Fe and Fred Harvey used the San Diego exposition to proclaim the scenic wonders of California and the Southwest.

The Painted Desert Exhibit that grew out of Mary Colter's model included pueblos in the Taos, above, and Zuni, below, fashion—authentic in design, materials, and inhabitants.

Tourism to the Grand Canyon, which was already rising, surged even more as a result of Santa Fe/Fred Harvey promotions at the 1915 fairs. Annual visitation, which had numbered less than 1,000 prior to the railroad's arrival in 1901, topped 100,000 in 1915—6,000 more than the combined total of visits that year to Yellowstone, Yosemite, and Glacier national parks.[25] As a result, Grand Canyon Village became increasingly dotted with utilitarian structures that did not harmonize with either the natural landscape or the major visitor attractions. The influx over-taxed roads and trails as well as sanitary and water-supply systems. As pressure mounted for even more construction, the Forest Service stepped into the picture to attempt to coordinate the disparate building activities of concessionaires like the Harvey Company, other private parties, and the government itself.

The agency had drafted a plan for the village in 1910, but its 1917 Grand Canyon Working Plan was the first official statement. Written by Forest Supervisor Don P. Johnson and Aldo Leopold, a forest examiner who later gained fame as a pioneer of the environmental movement, the document made a case for orderly development more than it set forth a blueprint for action, but it did evaluate existing architecture in light of what was appropriate to the scenic setting. While buildings nearest to the rim, the report stated, "will naturally have to comply with a higher standard of appearance than elsewhere, no permit for an unnecessarily ugly or objec-tionable building should be issued anywhere for any purpose." The plan also proposed to zone development—into areas for accommodations, for example, camping, staff housing, and commercial functions—so as to keep the more utili-tarian structures in the background. Another plan, in 1918, mapped a rather formalistic village complete with a half-mile-long mall terminating at the canyon's edge. Although the specifics of these plans were not implemented, two of their concepts were: zoning by use and regulation of architectural styles. In the meantime, the National Park Service was created in 1916; and finally, in 1919, Grand Canyon National Park was established, placing it under the control of the Park Service.[26]

Among the few surviving drawings signed by Mary Colter are these 1916 sketches and plans for lodging at Indian Garden, opposite and overleaf, a project that was not built.

No 7

· FLOOR PLANS OF LODGE COTTAGES ·
· PROPOSED FOR GRAND CANYON ·

STYLE #E. — Accommodating 2 Persons

STYLE #5 — Accommodating 2 Persons

CABIN ACCOMMODATING 2 PERSONS
KITCHEN ELEVATION FACING ROAD
= SLAB CONSTRUCTION =

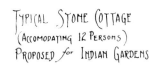

Typical Stone Cottage
(Accomodating 12 Persons)
Proposed for Indian Gardens

The Harvey Company/Santa Fe interests began working with the planners early on. Among the proposals that Harvey drafted in 1917 in response to the Working Plan were two schemes for tourist lodging, both devised by Colter. The first was at Bright Angel Camp, which the company had taken over a decade before to provide more modest lodging than that available at El Tovar. That facility was sprawling into a huge complex that included dozens of cottages and tents placed cheek by jowl behind the hotel itself, which was a simple everyday building. The companies wanted to replace the camp, well located at the head of Bright Angel Trail, with a more modern hotel and cottages, grouped as an agreeable village, that would better evoke the environment of rim and canyon.

The second Colter scheme was for a group of cottages at Indian Garden, an oasis halfway down the Bright Angel Trail (4.6 miles from the rim) that was a popular stopping point for hikers descending to the Colorado River.[27] Situated on a broad plateau, the pleasant stand of cottonwood trees boasts the only natural spring on the trail, which had once attracted the Havasupai Indians to raise corn, squash, and beans there. For the Harvey Company, this was the ideal spot to construct its first visitor accommodations within, not on the rim of, the Grand Canyon. In late 1916 Colter prepared a series of perspective sketches and floor plans for a group of variously sized cottages and a larger inn. Aside from a few of the drawings that Colter made in the 1930s for the redevelopment of Bright Angel Camp, some of these renderings for the Indian Garden buildings are the only signed drawings that have surfaced from her long career.

One sketch depicts a cabin for two persons, a chalet-like cottage with vertical siding in the gables, which are adorned with undulating and pierced barge-boards. A planter box hangs beneath a double window. A screen porch leads off the main chamber. The sketch states "slab construction" but shows log, or perhaps wide clap-board, siding. Another illustration depicts a "typical stone cottage" for twelve persons. Heavy stone walls in front and back rise to stepped parapets, sandwiching between them a gabled roof upon which are laid long slender logs that cross at the rooftop and continue down beyond the eaves. Vigas protrude above the main and rear doors, an effect that Colter somewhat optimistically labeled on the plan as "pergolas." Entry is through planked wooden doors crossed by strap hinges. The proposal blends Mission Revival and Pueblo Revival traits into a distinctly southwestern building that bears traces of Hermit's Rest and the Lookout Studio. The pueblo style also marks the main guesthouse, portrayed in Colter's rough drawing as a two-story, rather cubic structure standing at the bottom of soaring canyon walls, smoke curling romantically from its chimney. That Colter styled in both the chalet and the southwestern manner reflected the lingering uncertainty among parks officials and architects over which route architecture at the Grand Canyon, and other national parks for that matter, should take—the stylized and somewhat Euro-American or the indigenous and heavily rustic that was finding increasing support at that time.

In this case it did not matter, because the Indian Garden project was never built. Different explanations have been given for its being shelved. One theory is that war, with its attendant economic uncertainties, was on the horizon. The following April, in fact, the United States entered World War I, and the rail system was nationalized.[28] Another more immediately practical explanation is that the right to build at that location had long remained in doubt. For years the Santa Fe Railway had tussled with Ralph Cameron, who had opened the Cameron Hotel near the company's tracks, over land claims he established that stymied the expansion of the Santa Fe/Harvey dominion. He also built the Bright Angel Trail over the original Indian path, charging a toll for its use, and established questionable mining claims at Indian Garden that he did not relinquish to the National Park Service until around 1925. Under the circumstances, Harvey and the Santa Fe probably felt it wise to hold off on Colter's little village. The Park Service later built a caretaker's cabin and shelters at the site. The Bright Angel project was also dropped, but only for the time being; during the early 1930s, it was revived and constructed to designs by Colter that she based on her earlier conception. ⊡

Colter remained as busy as ever, both on and off the job. During the time when she was working on plans and sketches for Indian Garden and Bright Angel Camp, for example, she delivered a lecture on Native American art at the art museum in Kansas City. As reported in a newspaper there: "Miss M. E. Colter of Albuquerque, N. M., an authority on Indian handicraft, will talk at 10:30 o'clock this morning at the Fine Arts Institute on the exhibition now at the institute, which belongs to the collections of Mrs. Ford Harvey [Josephine, a daughter-in-law of the founder] and Mr. John F. Huckel."[29] The citation of Albuquerque as her base was either a mistake, since Colter lived officially in Kansas City, or a confirmation of the peripatetic life she led, riding the Santa Fe to spend extended intervals at jobs along the line. In either case, this shows that Mary Colter the designer, occupied as always with buildings and interiors, never left behind Mary Colter the scholar and teacher.

Also in 1916 Colter bought a house in Altadena, California, an unincorporated section of Los Angeles County in the foothills of the San Gabriel Mountains. The town, just north of Pasadena, was being developed from estates and farms into housing. Colter furnished the small stucco-clad house and moved her sister, Harriet, into it from wintry St. Paul, often staying there herself when on buying trips to California. The salubrious climate at that location may have appealed to her as a good choice for Harriet, who never enjoyed Mary's robust health. Indeed, the Pasadena area had become a fashionable winter resort for easterners. Many hotels were built there, including the Huntington, designed in 1906 by Charles Whittlesey, Colter's colleague from her Alvarado and El Tovar days. The area was also gaining renown for its artistic and architectural aspirations, especially in the Arts and Crafts, or Craftsman, mode exercised by the celebrated Greene brothers, who designed three houses in Altadena that were built before Colter acquired hers. The Colter residence, which remained in her possession until she retired in the late 1940s, also would have been convenient to the Santa Fe railroad depot in Pasadena.[30]

During this period, she also busied herself in the design of a major new hotel/railroad station complex in Gallup, New Mexico, to be named El Navajo. That project would show Colter taking a major stylistic detour from the architectural route she had been taking, creating designs that directly referenced southwestern landscape and history, to explore a new and more modern voice.

The Grand Canyon National Park Administration Building (1921) shows ties to the architecture of Colter, including her Phantom Ranch, in design at that time.

Tourism to the Grand Canyon surged again following World War I. But now the National Park Service was in charge of planning and development. One of the first policies of the new agency was articulated in 1918 by its first director, Stephen T. Mather: "In the construction of roads, trails, buildings, and other improvements, particular attention must be devoted always to the harmonizing of these improvements with the landscape."[31] Uncontrolled growth, it was clear, would no longer be tolerated. The Park Service wanted to launch a new comprehensive plan for Grand Canyon Village and elsewhere on the south rim. So did the Santa Fe, which had already constructed many of the park's prominent buildings, so the two parties and the Harvey Company collaborated on the document. At about this time the Harvey Company was selected as the park's chief concessionaire. Among the participants in plan preparation were Chicago architects

Graham, Anderson, Probst, and White, designers of a number of big-city railroad stations and consultants to the Santa Fe; park engineer Miner Tillotson, who advanced to park superintendent in 1927 and who later became a close colleague and friend of Mary Colter; and very likely Colter herself, representing her supervisor, Harvey vice president J. F. Huckel. In her position as the company's chief designer, Colter previously met in 1919 with the Park Service's first landscape engineer, Charles P. Punchard Jr., to review Harvey's proposals for tourist facilities in the new national park.[32] The comprehensive plan specified the location for new structures and grouped all buildings according to their functional affinities— ranging from rim accommodations to residential areas and utility zones—and in relation to topographical features. The plan also laid out a curvilinear system of roads and footpaths, including a village loop road, and reserved naturally landscaped areas as buffers. Officially adopted in 1924, the plan would govern development in the park for nearly two decades, a period that was a kind of golden age of cooperation between the Park Service and the Santa Fe/Harvey interests.[33]

Since several prominent Santa Fe and Fred Harvey buildings already stood in the village, it was obvious that new Park Service construction would have to respect its elders, at least in some basic fashion. The regard turned out to be more than just a nod, however, for the agency admired buildings like the El Tovar Hotel and especially Colter's Hopi House, Hermit's Rest, and Lookout Studio, deeming them particularly apt for the canyon setting; by 1922 they would also have her Phantom Ranch at the bottom of the canyon to commend. Park planners had already praised Colter in the 1917 Working Plan: "As long as the [Fred Harvey] Company's work is passed upon to Miss Colter, its present architect, its appropriateness can be considered assured."[34] At his meeting with Colter, "Punchard could not help but have taken note of the rustic stone structures Colter had designed

115

for the south rim."[35] Her preference for using locally obtained materials, in their natural state and in clever juxtaposition, and the modest impact the buildings had on their surroundings became the referentially rustic approach that they wanted for their own buildings. The agency's first major structure was the Grand Canyon National Park Administration Building, finished in 1921 to the design of Daniel R. Hull, who succeeded Punchard as landscape engineer in 1920. Sited at the foot of the road leading up to El Tovar and Hopi House and set into the slope, the building emulated precedents set by Colter in its use of massive randomly coursed stone piers, board-and-batten and other wood wall treatments, and a low-pitched gable roof with deep overhangs. This simple, strong-lined composition—which owes a special debt to Phantom Ranch, then in design stage—would be repeated in other agency buildings in the village, including the second administration building (1929). Hull, who joined in the preparation of the 1924 comprehensive plan, spent two weeks in 1923 collaborating with Colter on building proposals that would fit both Park Service needs and existing development.[36]

Colter's influence was also felt in the first interpretive facility in the park, the Yavapai Point Observation Building, which was finished in 1928 at a site two miles east of the village. It was the work of Herbert Maier, a young architect and museum designer whose portfolio would expand to include numerous notable park buildings and whose later pronouncements on appropriate architecture would become Park Service canon. Colter's mark is unmistakable in the pueblo style of the native-stone structure with its flat roof, ground-hugging profile, small and irregularly shaped window and door openings, and bristle of viga logs. Maier mirrored Colter by shying away from the regularity of right angles and straight lines, as the uneven and uncapped roof-line shows. Also, much like Hermit's Rest and Lookout Studio the museum hugs the edge of the canyon.

Maier's building and Colter's architecture would influence Sinnott Memorial (1929) at Crater Lake National Park, a boulder-clad museum built into the steep slope above the water. From Hopi House through her 1930s Bright Angel Lodge and Desert View Watchtower, Colter's work had a significant influence on the design of national and state park structures.[37] Her touch has also been detected in the lodge at Palo Duro State Park in Texas, the refectory at Longhorn Caverns State Park in Texas, and the administration building at South Mountain State Park in Phoenix—all built under Maier's direction in the 1930s. Although the Park Service came to favor buildings derived from the natural, as opposed to the cultural, landscape, all of Colter's Grand Canyon structures, even the overtly culture-based like Hopi House and the later Watchtower, were skillfully implanted into their settings. Colter deserves standing as a pioneer practitioner of the architecture that came to be known as "National Park Service rustic," a mode that would dominate construction in the parks until the early 1940s. ⌗

The Yavapai Point Observation Station, designed by Herbert Maier in 1928, is a rugged structure that owes much to Colter buildings like Hermit's Rest and Lookout Studio.

Since the daring explorations of the nineteenth century, encountering the Grand Canyon meant viewing the chasm from the rim as well as trekking down through it. The vast majority of visitors, however, were initially restricted to the former, owing to a lack of adequate trails, transportation, and lodging; the difficulty of construction in many areas; and controversies as to how accessible the canyon should be. In 1921 the Park Service began improving the Kaibab Trail from its origin east of the village some seven miles down to the Colorado River, where it constructed a swinging suspension bridge over the river. The agency also asked the Harvey Company to build new lodging on a flat expanse next to Bright Angel Creek, about a quarter mile above where it flowed into the Colorado and not far from the site of a

The lodge at Phantom Ranch (1922), part of the first set of buildings designed there by Colter

camp that David Rust had set up for hunters and tourists. In 1907 Rust had also built a cable car to haul mules—and brave mule riders—across the river near the bottom of the present Kaibab Trail.

Harvey wanted to offer a more commodious welcome to those descending the mile-deep canyon. Using some of the architectural and planning ideas she had conceived for the Indian Garden project, Colter designed the lodging, which she named Phantom Ranch, as a cluster of four two-person cabins, one for a caretaker, and a lodge that included a kitchen and dining hall. Hewing closely to her philosophy, and to the Park Service policy, that improvements should harmonize with the landscape, she devised modest stone and frame buildings that made use of rock gathered from the site. Wood for framing, doors and windows, and decorative purposes had to be hauled in by mule.[38] The stone, starting with larger boulders at the bottom, was laid up in random fashion and with deep mortar joints to form walls, corner piers, and chimneys, and the buildings were topped with low-pitched gable roofs. Wood was stained muted earth tones, the roofs were green, and the stone was of a reddish cast. Brighter colors of blue, red, and yellow were used inside. With the canyon walls looming behind and the boulder-strewn landscape all about, the little village intruded but

A 1924 postcard showing Colter's original Phantom Ranch, deep in the canyon next to Bright Angel Creek

minimally into the ancient scene. In true Colter fashion, each simply-furnished cabin boasted a fireplace and on the concrete-tile floor an Indian rug—a thunderbird pattern for the rooms done in a blue scheme and a sun shield for the ones in red.[39]

In the afterword to his 1923 book on the Colorado River, writer Lewis R. Freeman praised the architect:

> THE COMMISSION FOR THE WORK WAS GIVEN TO MISS MARY E. J. COLTER, ALREADY WELL KNOWN FOR HER NOTABLE ARTISTIC SUCCESSES....WORKING WITH THE NATIVE RED SUPAI SANDSTONE OF THE CANYON WALLS FOR BUILDING MATERIAL, MISS COLTER ACCOMPLISHED SOMETHING THAT IN MY OWN EXPERIENCE IS RIVALLED [SIC] IN ITS PERFECT FITNESS TO ITS SURROUNDINGS ONLY BY THE MOUNTAIN VILLAGES OF JAPAN AND THE HIMALAYAN FRONTIERS OF INDIA.... PHANTOM RANCH MAY BE CONSIDERED AS A MICROCOSM OF WHAT IS TO BE STRIVEN FOR ON A GRAND SCALE—SOMETHING THAT FITS AS NEARLY AS THE WIT AND IMAGINATION OF MAN CAN DEVISE INTO THE GREATER SCHEME OF NATURE; SOMETHING THAT "BELONGS."[40]

Colter did not conjure up a special "history" for this project, as she so often did with her buildings, perhaps because the ranch served such a practical purpose or because it was difficult to indulge in architectural flights of fancy at such an inaccessible site. She did choose a fanciful name, however, calling it Phantom Ranch after

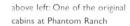

above left: One of the original
cabins at Phantom Ranch

above right: For her later
structures, Colter varied the roof
and wall treatments.

left: Colter and Phantom Ranch
guests enjoy tea outdoors.

nearby Phantom Creek and Canyon, which were so called because early cartographers found the canyon so narrow that it would appear and disappear from their view.[41] Other more romantic theories allude to ghostly figures, a favorite being that of explorer John Wesley Powell, or to strange mists that formed at the canyon's mouth. None of these tales kept the ever tireless Colter from visiting the site often during construction or even coaxing her ailing sister, Harriet, to join the mule trip down for the grand opening on November 9, 1922. The name Phantom Ranch would also have appealed to Colter and her bosses as a lure to travelers, for descending into the canyon had not yet become a popular trek. During its early years, in fact, the ranch was a rather exclusive place, attracting the wealthy and famous—Hollywood actors and other celebrities—to play at "dudes" roughing it in the great outdoors and journalists to file gossipy stories in their wake. After World War II it drew more diverse company.

Phantom Ranch has been expanded a number of times over the years. In 1927–28 eight more guest cabins were added, the dining hall was enlarged, and a recreation building was constructed, all under Colter's supervision and following her original designs, although she inserted board-and-batten panels in among the stone walls. Soon after, a replacement suspension bridge was installed over the Colorado. An orchard and vegetable garden were planted early on to help augment the food supply. Later additions include a swimming pool built by the Civilian Conservation Corps (CCC) in 1933–34 in a curving naturalistic pond shape edged with stream boulders. One of a number of CCC improvements to the camp and nearby trails, the pool later failed to meet water-quality regulations and was filled in 1972. Over the years, the cottonwood trees that had been planted in the 1920s grew tall, shading and softening the original desert setting. Initially built only for those arriving on mule-back, the ranch was later augmented to lodge hikers as well. From a handful of guests in 1922, the ranch grew to accommodate ninety-two people by 1977. Colter

was not done with Phantom Ranch, however. In 1946, close to retirement, she designed a laundry room addition at the ranch.

Returning years later to remodel or expand projects like Phantom Ranch was a staple of Colter's career, especially in her role as Harvey's chief "decorator," as she was often called. The same year that the ranch opened, she was back in Albuquerque working on the Alvarado Hotel. As is the case with all tourist accommodations, refurbishment appears on the menu sooner or later, and at the Alvarado it had been almost twenty years since the place had opened, so the hotel was both expanded and modernized, its public spaces as well as the guest quarters. The project gave the hotel 120 rooms, making the Alvarado the largest hotel in the Harvey system; private baths were installed in the many original guest rooms that lacked them. Outside, the courtyards were dressed with fountains and ponds, and the setting of lawns, flower gardens, shrubs, and shade trees was profusely landscaped by Paul Thiene, who had designed the grounds for the San Diego exposition. This luxuriant new density heightened passengers' delighted comparison of Alvarado the oasis to the boundless high-desert country that they had viewed from their train.[42]

Colter concentrated on enlarging the main lobby and the lounge, brightening dark walls and replacing heavy black furniture with pieces that, according to an observer, were "copies from the Coronado residence." She laid a tile floor in the lounge, placing upon it wooden tables and chairs with leather seats, some of them of the X-framed type. A rectilinear, rather modern sofa faced the large and formal fireplace, "in which was burning pinion wood" and above the mantel of which there was a carved noble crest. A floral rug and iron torchieres rounded out the updated Spanish baronial bearing of the room, in which "the ladies" might partake in tea parties served by "girls in Spanish costume."[43] Colter may well have designed their uniforms, too, for she was known for an eye so thorough that even employees' garb was brought into a treatment. She redecorated the lunchroom, where patrons enjoying the fifty-cent lunch at the lengthy double-horseshoe of countertop could admire her installation of shiny black onyx-like Belgian glass. Columns and walls were attired in tiles supplied by the Batchelder Tile Company of Los Angeles, whose founder, Ernest Batchelder, had directed the Handicraft Guild of Minneapolis' summer school from 1905 to 1909, when Colter was still living in St. Paul.[44] Colter also outfitted the dining room in a Spanish motif—one of a number of Harvey restaurants over the years that she Hispanicized. Guests dined on mission oak furniture atop a maple floor and viewed a prominent double-arched fireplace. The observer concluded his report by the tracks: "We saw more Indians on the platform at Albuquerque than at any other station, and the curio shop is one of the largest and, we should say, the best patronized, judging from the number of passengers who were buying."[45]

Decorating and redecorating brought out Colter the collector, the ardent hunter of furniture, fabrics, wall art, and other accouterments with which to clothe her rooms and amuse their occupants. She seemed to be always hitting the road or firing off letters or telegrams trying to track down just the right items—a tall oaken farm chair to round out a fireplace setting or a wrought-iron Mexican chandelier to dangle from a heavily beamed ceiling. Sometimes she bought by the lot, scattering her loot throughout a hotel, shop, or restaurant. Years later, writer Erna Fergusson summed up the phenomenon: "She has ravaged antique shops and bid at auctions from New York to Mexico, and she has shipped in or had copied furniture and rugs, curtains, dishes, iron lanterns, tiled friezes, and porcelain cocks. She has bought the work of Southwestern artists, and used rare examples of Mexican or Indian pottery and of hand-carved saints in the bedrooms."[46] Colter's unusual, one-of-a-kind finds deepened the sense of authentic history and culture and the feeling of age that she craved for her designs. Even when her role was that of architect, Colter was always the interior designer, also. The ultimate success of her buildings depended on that capability.

Hotel Architect

FIVE

THE 1920S SAW MARY COLTER devoting most of her energies to the design of hotels. Aside from Phantom Ranch, minor interior work, and plans for later buildings, these hotel projects took her away from the Grand Canyon. She had begun drawing the first of these inns, which was also the first hotel building that she ever designed, in 1916 before the United States entered World War I. The war brought the construction of most new Harvey establishments to a halt, but planning continued, since the company and the Santa Fe were eager to expand their line of first-class accommodations.

Gallup, New Mexico, provided a choice location for such a hotel. An established railroad and coal mining town on the Santa Fe's main line, Gallup offered easy access to a variety of tourist attractions—geologic and ethnographic wonders like Canyon de Chelly, Mesa Verde, Inscription Rock, and the Painted Desert—and to a large population of Native Americans. Not far from the Arizona border, the city had essentially been created by the Santa Fe Railway back in the 1880s and had grown into a regional trading center for both new settlers and Indians—the Navajo, Zuni,

top: An early sketch of El Navajo, thought to be by Colter

above: El Navajo as first opened in 1918

and western pueblo tribes. By this stage in the evolution of their collaboration, Harvey and the Santa Fe realized that a prosperous future for their station hotels lay in cultivating a lasting hotel-based tourist trade, not in the serving of quick meals to through passengers. The development of the train dining car, offering essentially the same level of service as the Harvey Houses, was already reducing the need for many of the meal stops along the line. The companies hoped that an attractive hotel like the one they were planning for Gallup, although it would still provide dining service for train passengers, would also encourage them to tarry, using the hotel as a convenient hub from which to explore the countryside.

For the new hotel-train station Colter returned to a Native American theme, in both architecture and interior design. The inn was named El Navajo, in tribute to the culture of the people whose large and populous homeland lay north and west of Gallup, but the inspiration for the hotel's designs was not exclusively Navajo. This was the first time since the Montezuma in 1882 that Harvey affixed a Native American name to a major hotel, although tacking on the Spanish article "El" assured that the place would conform in romantic spirit with the company's collection of Spanish-fantasy hotels. (Interestingly, the railway had since 1915 run a Chicago-to-Los Angeles train called The Navajo.) It was more than a decade since Colter had finished Hopi House, and she was eager to design another building with a Native American theme. "I have always longed to carry out the true Indian idea, to plan a hotel strictly Indian with none of the conventionalized modern motifs," she said in a news article in 1923 on the day of El Navajo's festive dedication.[1]

By "modern" Colter may have been referring to the prevalent use of diluted and commercialized Indian imagery in advertising or perhaps to the growing ranks of unremarkable tourist hotels. In the architectural historical sense of the word, however, her building was quite modern, the most modern of her career. It was a crisp-edged and flat-roofed, rather cubist ensemble of rectangular volumes arrayed

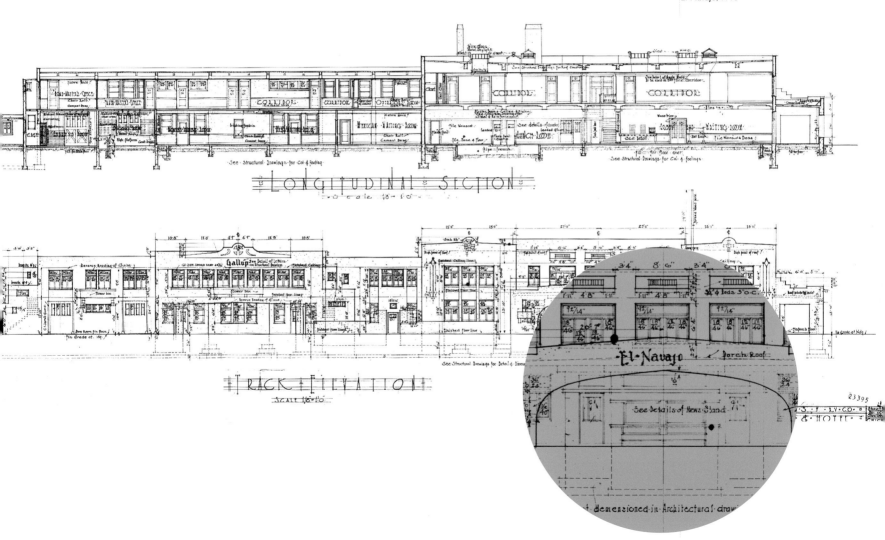

Section and track-side elevation of
El Navajo, 1918

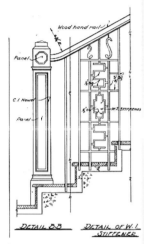

A stairway railing detail

along the tracks, projecting and receding so as to give somewhat the effect of a large pueblo Indian dwelling. The blankness of the walls was relieved by windows ganged in horizontal rows, some of them also set in deeply recessed two-story panels. Navajo references could be found in the arch of the main entrance, which resembled the roofline of a hogan, and the stair-step blocks used as ground-hugging buttresses and at the meeting of building segments, recalling a motif found in Navajo rugs.[2] Colter kept ornamentation to a minimum—chiefly two vertical wrought-iron lighting fixtures that in their elongation recalled the linear figures in Navajo sand paintings (a motif that reappeared, much smaller, in the lunchroom's lights), discreetly applied lettering for "El Navajo" and "Gallup," and small circular forms at the parapet that represented the Santa Fe corporate badge and the Zia Indian sun symbol.

Nearly forty years after it opened, *New Mexico Architect* magazine called El Navajo "the most vigorous modern statement" of the Harvey hotels of the first two decades of the century. "One discovers horizontal and vertical grouping of windows, 'cubistic' handling of walls and projecting balconies, the three-tassled pairs of lights attached to the main block of the building, all of which were design motifs which had become the vocabulary of the early modern movements in European and American architecture."[3] Speaking of the originality of the group of Harvey hotels, the writer, architectural historian David Gebhard, invoked the architecture of Europeans Adolf Loos and Josef Hoffmann and Californian Irving Gill, all of them contemporaries of Colter.

Harvey and the Santa Fe saw El Navajo as an oasis for travelers, but Colter provided no beckoning courtyards with splashing fountains nor a mantle of lushly landscaped grounds. After all, this was not a moist and shady retreat in the Spanish Colonial style, like the Alvarado or the missions upon which that hotel was based. El Navajo was Indian-inspired, a paean to native America, so its aesthetic was more severe and contained and the building a more abrupt feature on the land. If anything, the structure descended not from colonial Spain but from the pueblos that sat starkly atop the high-desert mesas. For Hopi House, Colter had referenced the rough textures and free-form silhouette of an actual pueblo dwelling. In El Navajo she showed equal skill in integrating Indian forms and colors into a sophisticated modernist composition that did not cede its sense of historical place.

This marriage of modernism and regionalism was carried off just as nimbly inside. In designing and furnishing the interior, Colter pursued the same goals she always had—originality, comfort, and visual and intellectual delight—but broke new ground by achieving them through a fresh artistic language. The restaurant, although a white-cloth facility in the full-service Harvey tradition, was a fairly plain room trimmed with linear designs that echoed sand paintings and hung with simple boxy chandeliers that echoed the building's cubist mien. The hotel's other public rooms, consisting mainly of a writing room to the left of the track-side entrance and a stair hall and lounge to the right, were spare, simply furnished spaces unified by a rigorously rectilinear geometry exhibited at a range of scales. The walls and ceilings were mostly smooth-finished or plastered concrete, including the ceiling beams, the primary ones of which ran in long, very gentle arches. Soft-red quarry tile covered the floors, and sections

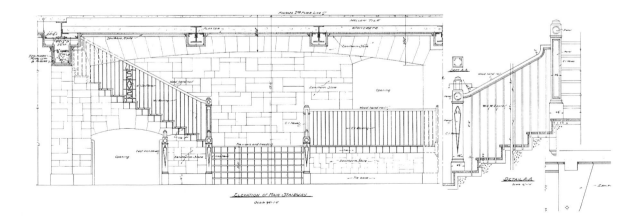

Elevation of the reception desk and office enclosure, and of the main staircase, below

Centered on a fireplace below the sand painting called "The Man Who Killed Fear," the lounge at El Navajo was a clean-lined but comfortable showcase for Indian-inspired art.

opposite: The main staircase provided an excellent niche to display the sand painting known as "The Ascension of the Holy One."

of other square tile wainscoted the walls. As always with Colter, an enticing fireplace dominated the main lounge. The hearth's surround was as large as ever— and superbly faced in a crosshatch of the same wall tiles—but its aperture was a much diminished rectangle in keeping with the hotel's modernist theme, not the yawning arch typical of earlier Colter buildings. On each side stood a tall wrought-iron torchiere composed of a zigzag motif that rose to a five-light-bulb candelabra; this Navajo design, representing lightning and clouds, was mimicked by wall fixtures next to the main staircase. Wood appeared only mini-mally in El Navajo, in some of the furniture and in the front lobby's paneled reception enclosure. Resting their feet on rugs of Navajo manufacture, guests relaxed in sofas covered in pale fringed buckskin, chairs with leather seats, or wicker settees colored brightly, as were the drapes, in hues similar to those the Navajos derived from natural materials. The guest rooms, decorated in orange and blue, also displayed Navajo rugs as well as pottery and baskets.

"Navajo colors, as a rule, are not restful," commented one newspaper article, "but Miss Colter has achieved both truth and repose in her designing."[4] She arranged for some of the wrought-iron decoration to be crafted by students at the Fort Wingate Indian School, a federal Bureau of Indian Affairs school located just east of Gallup.[5] Colter "evolved a scheme of decoration for El Navajo that is unique in hoteldom," stated another contemporary account.[6] The *piece-de-resistance* of that scheme was the authentic Navajo sand-painting reproductions that hung on the inte-

rior walls of the hotel. Colter originated the idea of using the paintings in this way, collaborating in its implementation with her Harvey Company boss, J. F. Huckel, with whom she shared a serious and abiding interest in collecting Indian art. The paintings had never before been employed as decoration for a building, let alone a public one such as this.

The intricate art of sand painting—which some experts prefer to call "dry painting"—had been traditionally used by the Navajos for sacred, private purposes only—to cure illnesses, for example, ward off evil, or beseech blessings. Composed of different colors of sand but also of cornmeal, charcoal, pollen, and powdered flower petals, the paintings are painstakingly created on the ground and take many hours to prepare under the supervision of Navajo ritual medicine men known as "singers." Incorporating highly stylized images of people, plants, or natural objects, the paintings are created according to prescribed methods that have been passed down in memory from generation to generation. Some 500 different types of sand paintings, associated with fifty different rituals, are said to exist. Because Navajos believe them to be the temporary residence of holy spirits, their creation must be accompanied by appropriate ritual as part of ceremonies, or "sings," that can last for days. In the curing ceremony, for example, the sick person sits on the completed painting and parts of it are applied to him, transferring the painting's sacred curative powers to the patient. Most surprising to those who think in decorative instead of ritualistic terms, the paintings are not permanent; immediately after use, they are swept away, erased by the singer in the opposite order from which they were fashioned.[7]

The execution of Colter's concept of decorating with sand paintings unfolded as a sometimes touchy cultural ballet. The search for paintings that would accurately represent the Navajo ritual works led her and Huckel to Sam Day, Jr., a well-known Indian trader in St. Michaels, Arizona, who had developed a close and knowledgeable relationship with the Navajos. Day supplied them with eighty-four watercolors of

Najavo elders Hash-kay Yashi and Haquali Yashi, who participated in the opening-day ceremonies, stand below the sand painting titled "The Day."

sand paintings made by four Navajo singers from 1902 to 1905. From these, Harvey Company artist Fred Geary, aided by prominent Navajo medicine man Miguelito, who had worked for Harvey at the 1915 San Diego and San Francisco expositions, painted large copies of twelve of the sand paintings on El Navajo's walls.[8]

Each sand painting was associated with a particular rite. The painting over the main fireplace, for instance, belonged to the shooting chant or ceremony. It depicted "Nayenezgani" (The Man Who Killed Fear) in four figures, two male and two female, the former armed with thunderbolts and the latter with rainbows. He is the great war god, a slayer of monsters and even fear. To the right of the fireplace hung a square painting with rounded corners called "The Day," which was used in the buffalo chant. It represented the twenty-four-hour course of the sun through heavens decorated with moons and other lights and also includes the four plants sacred to the Navajos. Other paintings depicted the Sky Man and Earth Mother, the Eagle Trap, the Clouds, and the Ascension of the Holy One.[9] After the hotel opened, Huckel commissioned Day to prepare more paintings for his collection as well as explanatory legends to go with them. As usual, the process was a difficult one for Day, for he obtained the information by keeping in close touch with the Navajos— attending sand-painting ceremonies and working often at considerable length, and with diplomatic tact, with medicine men. Huckel's collection grew over the years, however, and after his death in 1943 was donated to the Colorado Springs Fine Arts Center. [10]

The notion of using sand paintings as a basis for permanent decoration in the hotel proved unsettling to several of the Navajo leaders. Secular use of the paintings had occurred before El Navajo, but this was the boldest appropriation. According to Frank Waters, "Miss Colter was 'brought to trial' by several Navajo singers."[11] What that entailed is not clear, but the Harvey Company reacted by ordering the immediate removal of the paintings. The Navajos apparently were impressed by that reaction, for they then agreed to allow the paintings to remain provided they conduct a ritual that would purge the works of evil spirits, rendering them acceptable to the Navajo gods.[12] From this agreement evolved an opening-day ceremony held in May 1923 to bless the hotel as well as the paintings.

In truth, El Navajo had already opened. It is not well known that the structure was built in two stages, the first of which debuted in 1918. The second was appended in 1923 to the western end of the first, which was partly reconfigured and incorporated into the more lavishly appointed new structure. At both stages, wings— providing sixty-five guest rooms in 1923—extended at right angles from the rear, although the original building housed mainly railroad workers. "When completed the

THE SAND PAINTINGS OF THE NAVAJO

The meaning and purpose of the sacred art of the Medicine Men as exemplified by authentic reproductions on the walls of

EL NAVAJO
SANTA FE HOTEL
GALLUP, NEW MEXICO

With a brief description of "The Blessing-of-the-House" Ceremony of May 25, 1923

Published by
FRED HARVEY
KANSAS CITY, MISSOURI

Preparation of the sand painting was part of an elaborate and well-publicized ceremony that also included a solemn procession around and through the building. A brochure explained the ritual of sand painting and the works that adorned the walls of El Navajo.

138

entire building will present one structure as tho [*sic*] built at the same time," ran a 1922 newspaper account.[13] Most later descriptions of the hotel and station ignore the phasing, stating that El Navajo was built or finished in 1923. Completion of the original building has been mostly overshadowed by attention paid to the design of the final structure's interior, with its remarkable sand-paintings, and to the ceremony that opened the building. That El Navajo first opened during World War I may also help explain the oversight, since Harvey and the Santa Fe may have thought it improper to herald their new facility during wartime.

The hotel's resplendent debut on May 25, 1923, more than made up for the earlier "soft" opening. Colter, Huckel, and Herman Schweizer worked closely on the ceremony, ironing out differences over its staging. "Miss Colter . . . does not see how it can be given unless inside of the hotel," Huckel wrote to Schweizer two weeks before the event. But Huckel worried that "[i]f it is all to be held inside the hotel, I can't see we can get any moving picture[s], and the people of Gallup or other spectators see the ceremony." He added, however, that "Miss Colter is perfectly agreeable to having the ceremony carried out outside, or partly so, if it can be done suitably." What finally transpired on opening day was just that: an indoor-outdoor event. In attendance were Santa Fe and Harvey officials, Gallup residents and leaders, visitors—including those who had driven from Albuquerque on the half-finished Route 66—writers and artists, and some 2,000 Native Americans, including fifteen Navajo medicine men. Among the latter were Hash-kay Yashi, head of the shooting chant—said to have been more than 100 years old—and Hosteen Bi-nen-m, head of the wind ceremony. The only white persons to take direct part in the "blessing of the house" or "hogan bigi'n" were Sam Day, Jr., and his wife, who represented the owners. In a ritual invoking blessing upon the building, the Days were placed on two actual sand paintings on pavement in front of the hotel, carefully repeating the prayers uttered by the singers, who then sprinkled them with sacred pollen. In another highlight of the elaborate two-hour ceremony, a procession led by the medicine men encircled the building, then passed through it, anointing its rooms and specially blessing each sand painting.[14]

"The ceremony was profoundly solemn, an earnest, impressive ritual." But it occurred "to the accompaniment of clicking movie cameras."[15] The house-blessing served a purpose larger than just the showering of good spirits and fortune upon El Navajo and its sand paintings, helpful though that sanction was in launching the new hotel. Well publicized in newspapers, newsreels, and magazines nationwide, the ceremony in effect also helped bless the Fred Harvey/Santa Fe system, especially in its association with Native Americans—showing or strongly implying that all was well between the two. Further validating the companies' endeavors in the eyes of the American public, the ceremony painted a benign gloss over an entire touristic dominion.

If Mary Colter had any qualms about using sand-painting imagery as decoration for commercial purposes, she apparently kept them to herself (or off the record). She was by now one of the most knowledgeable professionals about Indian cultural ways and artifacts, and she had shrewdly and insistently built a superior personal collection of baskets, jewelry, and pottery. There is no doubt that she genuinely loved and admired Indian art and craft and understood the religious connections as well as any non-Indian. She was for years a regular visitor to pueblos and ceremonial gatherings. It is possible that she discounted the religious and private aspects of sand painting in order to exploit the artistic aspects she admired and so appreciated for their supporting role in the context of El Navajo. Moreover, she may have rationalized that exposure of this art so prominently could really help the Indians. The destruction of the hotel portion of El Navajo in 1957 and the loss of the sand paintings she had worked so hard to obtain must have hurt Colter deeply.

The summer before the opening, the first Inter-Tribal Indian Ceremonial was held in Gallup. Organized to showcase the supposedly vanishing arts and crafts of tribes in the region and beyond, the gathering grew into a well-known event that is still held every August, featuring ceremonial dances, games, storytelling sessions, a rodeo, and an arts exhibition. Attending the Ceremonial became a must for Colter, an earnest and lifelong devotee of Indian art and ritual; starting in 1924, she showed up every year. At the 1948 event her friends George Babbitt, Jr., a prominent Flagstaff businessman, and his wife, Ruth Babbitt, presented her with a booklet entitled "Arizona Place Names," which George inscribed: "To Mary Colter on the occasion of her 25th anniversary attendance at Inter Tribal Ceremonies." Ruth added: "To Mary Jane Colter. There is only one!!! It's you!" George finished off with: "I coincide."[16]

El Navajo was a bold new statement for Colter, perhaps her boldest, if one considers the building's place in the progression of international modernism. In this country, it was one of the earliest modernist structures of its kind. Yet with its distinct cultural base and regional consciousness it was still Colter, and Harvey, through and through. Speaking of El Navajo in the context of a number of Harvey hotels, David Gebhard wrote in his *New Mexico Architect* article:

THE REAL FASCINATION OF EITHER THE EL ORTIZ (THE LAMY, NEW MEXICO, INN WHOSE INTERIOR COLTER HAD DESIGNED IN 1910) OR THE EL NAVAJO, OR FOR THAT MATTER THE ALVARADO IN ALBUQUERQUE, IS THE IMPRESSION ONE COMES AWAY WITH THAT THESE BUILDINGS ARE NEITHER FULLY COMMITTED TO AN ECLECTIC OR MODERN POINT OF VIEW. INSTEAD THE GOVERNING FEATURES SEEM TO HAVE BEEN A CONCERN FOR HUMAN-ORIENTED SCALE, A DEEP FEELING FOR NATURAL TEXTURES AND MATERIALS, AND A DESIRE ORGANICALLY TO INTEGRATE THE BUILDING TO ITS NATURAL AND HISTORICAL ENVIRONMENT; FEATURES WHICH ARE ALL TOO OFTEN MISSING IN OUR PRESENT ARCHITECTURAL SCENE.

This is one of the very few instances in which a professional journal commented on Colter's work, during or soon after her life. It is quite telling, however, that Gebhard failed to even mention Colter by name, crediting the building's design instead to the Santa Fe's chief architect, E. A. Harrison. Since Harrison officially signed off on practically all of Colter's work, the omission is understandable, if regrettable. Similar misattributions have occurred before and since. Also, Colter had fallen into such obscurity by the time the article was written in 1962 that it is possible that Gebhard had never heard of her—and probable that no one noticed his error. Yet his admiration for the building and insights into the human and historical qualities of El Navajo and the other Harvey hotels are unmistakable and right on the mark. The attributes that earned Gebhard's esteem for these buildings are the same ones that ultimately won Colter a revival in public notice and scholarly esteem.

The Franciscan Hotel in Albuquerque, shown here in 1926, may have been influenced by the design of El Navajo.

Colter's El Navajo was built at a time when Indian-based architecture was beginning to flower in the Southwest. Buildings derived from the forms, materials, and finishes of pueblo structures were gaining in popularity, especially in New Mexico and particularly in Santa Fe. Admitted to the union in 1912, the state paraded itself to the nation in 1915 at the Panama-California Exposition in San Diego with a building designed in a mish-mash of Pueblo and Spanish Colonial traditions. (Standing nearby was the more purely Pueblo-style Painted Desert Exhibit that Colter designed.) The Spanish inheritance influenced both exterior and interior designs as well as the floor layouts of this evolving southwestern style. The exposition structure was effectively duplicated and elaborated upon back in Santa Fe, capital of the old Mexican province and then of the new state, by construction in 1916 of the Fine Arts Museum. Also, the 1610 Palace of the Governors on Santa Fe's Plaza had recently been slipcovered in a Spanish-Pueblo manner. "These two public buildings . . . appear to have turned the tide in favor of the Santa Fe style, as the Spanish-Pueblo revival was known in the early days," wrote architectural historian Bainbridge Bunting in his biography of John Gaw Meem, who, launching his practice in Santa Fe at the time, became an avid practitioner and promoter of the new style.[17] A few years after finishing El Navajo, Colter would be working with Meem on his first major commission in Santa Fe, the expansion of the La Fonda Hotel.

Prominently located along a great east-west transportation corridor, El Navajo was in step with, if not ahead of, this Spanish-Pueblo Revival. In her analysis of Colter's architecture, Clair Shepherd-Lanier has suggested that El Navajo influenced the design of two Albuquerque buildings built shortly after it. The Franciscan Hotel (opened December 1923), designed by well-known El Paso architects Trost and Trost, recalls Colter's building through its accumulation of rectangular massing, smooth stucco walls with deep window and door recesses, light color, and dearth of ornamentation. Some of the windows were separated vertically by recessed panels. The building also displays stylized *vigas* and *canales* (drainspouts), and some of its exterior recesses for doors and windows and its interior arches were tapered at the top. The architects differed from El Navajo in a major sense, however, by molding a vertical composition that rises ziggurat-like to a massive central block and in a minor one by attaching to the structure in an almost offhand manner tiny corner domes, imported from the Mission Revival style. The Franciscan bears an intriguing kinship also to La Fonda and some of Meem's later structures. The other related building is the KiMo Theater (1927), designed by Carl and Robert Boller in a Pueblo Revival style but much more heavily festooned with Indian motifs on its facade and inside than was Colter's structure.[18] Colter's pioneering use of sand paintings as building decoration was also picked up by others, including their use in 1937 in an Arizona public building as part of a Works Progress Administration (WPA) project. The first-class cocktail lounge of the *S.S. United States* was decorated in 1952 with highly stylized sand-painting motifs.[19]

As in all of the more elaborate and atmospheric Harvey Houses, the company's public relations corps used the historic or ethnic theme embodied by the hotel in promotional materials, menus, and other printed matter. The result was often inspired in both text and graphics and, if not always culturally sensitive to Native Americans or Hispanics, could be cleverly humorous. The cover of an El Navajo wine list, for instance, undated but obviously printed after the demise of Prohibition in 1933, sports a colorful drawing of masked Indian figures dancing around a champagne bottle; the art is titled "Mudheads—the clown dancers of certain southwestern Indian tribes." Inside the folder, the beverage list is labeled "El Navajo, Lodge of the Four Smokes," in reference to the fires used in Navajo ceremonies that represent the four compass directions. Libations are grouped into facetious categories: "Big Medicine" (cocktails), "Snake Bite Medicine" (bourbon, rye, scotch, and Canadian), "Son of the Sun's Medicine" (liqueurs), "The Earth Mother's Medicine" (wine), "Bitter Root Medicine" (beer), "Frog's Medicine" (sparkling water), and "Pale Face Medicine" (soft drinks). The cover of another booklet, from Colter's personal collection, spells out "El Navajo" in lively stylized letters, which echo Navajo weavings, placed above a drawing of a native woman weaving at her loom, a small pottery jug at her feet. A small dinner folder from 1927 features a drawing on its cover of "Navajos making sand painting." ⊡

Later that year, Mary's sister, Harriet Colter, died at the age of sixty. She had been living at the house Mary had purchased for her in Altadena, California. Colter arranged for the funeral to be held back in St. Paul[20] and burial in that city's Oakland Cemetery in the Colter family plot. Mary, at fifty-four, was now the only surviving member of her immediate family.

Before her next hotel project, at the La Fonda Hotel in Santa Fe, Harvey assigned Colter to design and decorate its shops and restaurants in the new Union Station in Chicago. As was the case in Kansas City, the opening of the railway station

The Chicago Union Station circa 1925. In front stood the concourse building (since demolished) and behind it the station proper.

Colter's designs for dining encompassed, clockwise from right, the dining room, a luxurious club-like chamber; the lunchroom, a large hall that could serve masses of people with style and efficiency; and the whimsically styled Little Restaurant.

in July 1925 was a major architectural and civic event for the city. Designed by architects Graham, Anderson, Probst, and White (successors to the firm headed by the famous Chicagoan, Daniel H. Burnham) in a weighty neoclassical style often used for midwestern and eastern stations, the monumental building with its lofty concourse extended over the tracks just west of the Chicago River and the Loop. It was a spacious structure designed to meet the needs of four of the railroads (not including the Santa Fe) that served Chicago, the hub of the nation's passenger railroad system. The Harvey Company's branching out into retail shops, which had proved so successful at the Kansas City station a decade before, blossomed further in Chicago, where Harvey opened restaurants and newsstands as well as a bookstore, drugstore, barber and beauty shops, and other stores conveniently grouped and located to take advantage of the streams of train passengers, both transcontinental and commuter. As at Kansas City, Harvey moved its offices into the new station.

As it had done at Kansas City, the Chicago project showed Colter working with ease outside of the southwestern themes that she had been developing at the Grand Canyon and along the Santa Fe Railway. The most elegant of her treatments at the station was carried out in its dining room. Entered from the main waiting room, the restaurant was a big and tall space with a coffered ceiling, divided by two huge stop-fluted columns and wainscoted with walnut paneling nearly halfway up the walls. Light poured in through large windows in the west wall. Colter furnished the white-tablecloth room with round tables set with Windsor chairs, long rectangular tables supplied with upholstered arm and high-back chairs, and elaborately carved sideboards. Tasteful and restful, the chamber, ran a contemporary account, "bespeaks the luxurious club, where the patron may enjoy his meal leisurely, in comfort, and have specially prepared epicurean dishes served by trained waiters selected for proficiency in their art."[21] She lined the restaurant's unusually long entrance foyer with wing chairs, low tables, and tall settees—one of the latter a carved Chinese piece—

and guarded its entrance with a pair of ceramic elephants topped with tall vases. At a curve in the foyer wall, she strategically situated a marble-topped pier table garnished with an ornate clock in front of a tall mirror. "The clock," praised the same report, "is an antique discovered by Miss Colter, and forms the most striking feature of this furnishment."[22]

The lunchroom next door was an immense hall that could serve 5,000 meals a day. Occupying one side of the room was a mezzanine, while in the center, wrapping around another set of fluted columns, was a lunch counter composed of three U-shaped segments, all topped in green marble. Its stools, equipped with leather seats with backs, swung out to accommodate patrons. Colter also arrayed round and rectangular metal tables at either end of the room, topping them with white marble; she finished tables on the mezzanine with richly variegated green marble, chosen no doubt to harmonize with the lunch counter below. She specified a checkered pattern of rubber tile for the mezzanine's floor and rose drapes to trim its long bank of windows. The lunchroom's model style and service a la Harvey were buttressed by an elaborate battery of the latest equipment for the storage, preparation, transport, and serving of food.

At the other end of the station, just off the lofty iron-columned concourse, Colter decorated the Little Restaurant, which served breakfast, lunch, and afternoon tea. She lined the room with colorful art tile that she obtained from the Batchelder Tile Company in Los Angeles—squares of different sizes on the walls, echoing the pattern at El Navajo, and hexagonal tiles on the floor. She had two large birds painted over the tiles and furnished the room simply with small delicate-looking tables and stylish curved-back chairs. In a thoroughness typical of both Colter and her employer, she designed the uniforms for the waitresses as well as those of the clerks in the Minute Shops—a multipurpose space off the concourse that included a book shop, soda fountain, drug store, and other convenience shops—and of its larger sibling, the Shoppers' Mart, located off the main waiting room. The latter, boasted Harvey, contained the nation's largest drugstore. Both shopping marts made ample use of walnut, tile, marble, mirrors, and plate glass.

New Mexico beckoned again for the Harvey Company and the Santa Fe Railway, and thus for Mary Colter. The Santa Fe had nothing to do with creating its namesake city, which had been founded in 1610 as a northern provincial capital of Spanish colonial Mexico, but much to do with promoting it as a tourist center, even though it took some years for the company to establish a solid presence there through the development of a Harvey House. That opportunity came in 1926, when the Santa Fe purchased the failed La Fonda Hotel, situated at the southeastern corner of the historic Plaza. This site had been occupied for years by a much-remodeled and variously named hostelry last called the Exchange Hotel, an adobe building that had been ceremoniously razed in 1919.[23]

The original La Fonda Hotel, one of the first buildings in the new-old Santa Fe style, was acquired and expanded by the Santa Fe Railway.

By that year—in response to vigorous promotion by the town fathers, who wanted to revive Santa Fe's fast-disappearing indigenous architecture as well as its sagging tourist trade—Spanish-Pueblo (or Pueblo-Spanish or Santa Fe) style architecture was taking hold for both the design of new structures and the remodeling of existing ones. Edgar Lee Hewitt, an ardent leader of this architectural revival who helped direct the 1912 city planning effort that defined the new style, reported that between 1912 and 1917 half of the new houses and some ninety percent of the remodeled ones took on the Santa Fe mode.[24] Hewitt was a prominent archaeologist who had worked with Colter and others on the design of the Painted Desert Exhibit at the 1915 San Diego exposition. The style-masters determined early on that the new look should be specifically regional; the ever-popular Mission Revival with its roots in California would not do. For a 1913 local chamber-of-commerce competition to design a "New-Old Santa Fe" style house, participants were "warned to keep away from this style, which has been appropriated by Southern California. Nothing can retard the development of Santa Fe style more than to confuse it with the California Mission Style."[25] The Santa Fe Railway, of course, had largely introduced the Mission Revival style to New Mexico at the turn of the century with its Castañeda and Alvarado hotels.

The Couriers helped the Indian Detours run with both charm and grit.

The new La Fonda Hotel, built by a group of investors, was one of the first public buildings in the nascent Santa Fe style. It was the work of architects Rapp, Rapp, and Hendrickson, which had recently earned praise for its Spanish-Pueblo style Fine Arts Museum (1916) on the opposite corner of the Plaza.[26] The hotel was named La Fonda (Spanish for "inn"), validating the nickname, "the American fonda," that had long clung to the prior hostelry. La Fonda deftly displayed the picturesque form and appointments that the promoters of the new-old Santa Fe mode craved. Its exterior expressed the Pueblo style with Spanish touches and its interior the Spanish (or Mexican) style with Pueblo touches. Uniformly surfaced with stucco that imitated adobe and studded with rows of wood vigas, the three-story building rose from the street in a series of deep setbacks. Capping this formation was a bell-tower on one end offset by a mission-style parapet on the other. It was an essay in the purposely informal; crisp right angles, axial geometry, and regularity in any form were all but banished. Recessed balconies, undulating rooflines, and a host of window shapes and locations further animated the composition, resulting in a structure that, as far as keeping the eye engaged was concerned, may have outdone

The poster-like cover of the November 1930 Indian Detours brochure lured travelers with the majesty of the land and the magic of Native American culture.

anything to be found at a genuine pueblo. The interior, arrayed around a rectangular patio just off the lobby, ushered the visitor into an old Mexico of dark-beamed ceilings, tiled floors, stuccoed walls, and chunky wooden furniture. The original La Fonda was not built as a Harvey hotel, but when it came to immersing the traveler in scrupulously tuned history, it measured up favorably to the most imaginative of the Harvey Houses.

Indeed, La Fonda was well received by both the town and travelers. Financial difficulties facing the stock company that owned it, however, forced its closing in 1924. Two years later, a subsidiary of the Santa Fe Railway bought the building and set about expanding it. A major incentive for the expansion was to enable the hotel to better accommodate the Harvey Company's popular sightseeing service known as the Indian Detours. Of the many chapters in the long biography of the company, few offer as intriguing a tale of southwestern travel as these motoring excursions. A blend of Harvey's famous first-rate service with a touch of backroads adventure, the detours allowed tourists to get much closer to the scenery and history of the region than they could through the windows of a train. And this was the intent of Harvey and the Santa Fe. With travel *through* the Southwest booming, they reasoned, why not take the tourists *into* the Southwest?

The Indian Detours were the brainchild of Major R. Hunter Clarkson, a native of Scotland who was in charge of Harvey's transportation services at the Grand Canyon. Clarkson sold his boss, Fred Harvey's son Ford, on the idea of a break in the transcontinental train trip—a three-day sightseeing jaunt via comfortable motorcoach between the Santa Fe depots at Las Vegas, New Mexico, and Albuquerque as well as in the opposite direction. The excursion would escort train passengers to Santa Fe and the Indian pueblos while showing off the rugged countryside, most of it still a daunting trip for private motorists. As an early company brochure put it: "It is 3 days and 300 miles of sunshine and relaxation and mountain air, in a land of unique human contrasts and natural grandeur."[27]

Key to much of the pleasure offered on the Harveycoaches or smaller Harveycars, as the tour vehicles were named, were the Couriers. These guides, young women dressed comfortably for the road in simple skirts and Navajo-style blouses but often heavily bedecked in Indian jewelry (including the ubiquitous squash-blossom necklace), kept the tours running smoothly while they charmed the passengers with their sunny dispositions and impressed them with their detailed knowledge of the sights and Indian culture. As rigorously trained as any of the Harvey Girls, the Couriers were touted as trusted mediators between the tourist and the mysteries of the Southwest. They could explain Indian jewelry-making and sacred dances, recite the history of Santa Fe, and discourse on the geology and botany of the desert. They were concierges-on-the-go, handling all of the arrangements crucial to moving along their charges—"Detourists" or "dudes," as they were called—and to ensuring that they were fed and housed to Harvey's high standards. What is more, the Couriers were expected to remain cool in emergencies, working with the drivers to ensure that rocky roads or quirky weather would not spell disaster. One oft-published photo shows a Courier pitching in to wrest a marooned Harveycar from the mud.[28]

The Detours drew on the successful Koshare Tours begun in 1921 by Ethel Hickey and Erna Fergusson, a venture that was absorbed by the Harvey service soon after it was launched in 1926.[29] Colorful advertising in the best of the Harvey/Santa Fe tradition—including a lavish sixty-two-page inaugural brochure that sold both the sights and the comforts awaiting travelers—saturated the nation via Santa Fe and Harvey outlets. The tours proved to be such a success that Clarkson continued to expand and diversify them as the roads improved, adding longer and more luxurious journeys as well as specially tailored excursions. In 1931, with the onslaught of the Depression, Harvey sold the operation to Clarkson, who continued to operate it, still under the Indian Detours name but without the Fred Harvey insignia (the Harvey-

cars became Couriercars, for instance), for many years. The service, transferred to
Clarkson's brother Jim after World War II, lasted until 1968.

As chief of the Santa Fe Transportation Company, a unit managed by the
Harvey Company to provide travel services, and son-in-law of a Santa Fe Railway
vice president, Clarkson was immersed in the La Fonda expansion project. The
newly acquired forty-six-room hotel was too small to meet the growing demand for
rooms and other facilities created by the Indian Detours, not to mention by tourism
to Santa Fe in general. The decision to expand, Harvey and the railway believed,
was a sound one. The numbers continued to support that choice; during 1927, as
the project was under way, Indian Detour patronage jumped 169 percent over the
prior year.[30]

The Santa Fe Land Improvement Company, a subsidiary of the railway, hired
architect John Gaw Meem to design the addition. Meem was an advocate of the new
Santa Fe style who went on to become New Mexico's most celebrated architect. He
attained that status almost by happenstance, however. Schooled as a civil engineer, he
had come to Santa Fe to recover from tuberculosis and was living at the Sunmount
Sanatorium when its director, Frank E. Mera, inspired in him an appreciation of the
region's history and architecture. Meem decided to pursue architecture professionally
and went to Colorado for training, returning to Santa Fe in 1924 to open an office.
One of his first projects, volunteer work for the Committee (later the Society) for the
Restoration and Preservation of New Mexico Mission Churches, was the reconstruction of the Mission of San Esteban (1629–44) at the pueblo village of Acoma west of
Albuquerque. The project stretched from 1924 to 1930, gaining him invaluable experience with the style and structure of adobe buildings. Among the features he added
to La Fonda, his first big nonresidential project, was a six-story tower based on his
reconstructed version of the mission church's towers. The hotel tower, tapering like
those of the church and topped with an open gallery, anchored the building's southwest corner.[31]

The La Fonda project was both an expansion that tripled the hotel's guest rooms and a remodeling of the existing building's layout. The new wing ran prominently along the western side and southern back of the hotel, rising higher but assuming a simpler form and profile than the original Pueblo-Spanish structure. Mary Colter was involved from the beginning of the project, attending its first planning meeting in June 1926 with Meem, Clarkson, and his wife, Louise.[32] Colter's position in the decision-making arrangement was somewhat unusual. Whereas typically the architect and the interior designer were hired by the client (the Santa Fe and the Harvey Company), sometimes as part of the same firm, in this case the designer was part of the client's own staff. This placed Colter in a more powerful position relative to Meem than would ordinarily have been the case. Whether this advantage resulted only from her privileged situation as a Harvey employee, or also from her

The expanded La Fonda was depicted in this 1927 rendering for the Meem firm by T. St. Clair, showing the hotel's west and southern sides, including the new corner bell tower.

greater experience with design in general and hotels in particular (Colter was fifty-seven years old in 1926 and Meem thirty-one) and the force of her personality, is an intriguing question. Knowing Colter's talents and energy, one could safely surmise that all three reasons were in play.

It is apparent from the project correspondence that Colter was concerned with more than the building's interior and that she influenced decisions beyond accoutering its spaces. After one meeting in 1926 with Colter and the others, Meem reported that "Miss Colter was very interested in the elevations" and stated "that she preferred the [proposed] additions to the present hotel. That in her opinion the present structure is much too nervous and indented." She preferred "our using the simplest possible lines to express the plan rather than the wavy lines used on the present structure." Colter let her wide-ranging, and often detailed, approvals and objections be known from the start. The notes to that same meeting reported, for example, that Colter "objected strongly to a stairway," that she "approved of the room arrangement in general," and that she "objected strongly" to the lecture lounge being developed along the lines of a chapel. "In her experience," Meem wrote, "people did not like to lounge in a churchly atmosphere."[33]

Throughout design and construction, Meem reacted favorably to most of Colter's requests and criticisms, often making changes based on them. Although he did not concur with all of her advice, and they had their points of contention, the record is replete with his agreeable responses. When Colter called the existing lobby "dark, dreary and gruesome," for instance, Meem stated: "Everything possible should be done to remove this atmosphere."[34] Colter's suggestion that he not treat two of the bays in the north elevation alike "appeals to me very much, and we are, therefore, going to [make that change]."[35] To accommodate Colter's guest-room furniture layout, Meem assured her that "we will relocate our doors and windows to suit your convenience."[36] Colter's keen support for Meem's simpler design of the addition likely helped ratify that approach; in 1927 he stated that the new part would match the old but "the emphasis will be more on mass than ornament."[37] He was even "inclined to agree with her" when she felt "it would be impossible to stick closely to the straight Santa Fe style," preferring that the interior be "Colonial Spanish, this enabling the hotel to take on a more hospitable and comfortable atmosphere."[38]

The intricate decision-making structure in which Colter worked—taking in her Harvey bosses (J. F. Huckel and company presidents Ford Harvey then Byron Harvey, who became president after Ford's death in 1928), Clarkson, other Harvey staff like Herman Schweizer, plus Santa Fe officials—helped stretch the project out to three years. Always the thorough-going designer, Colter remained closely involved throughout. She tackled issues varying in kind from the width of the halls around the patio and the colors for the floors to the cultural flavor of the dining-room annex (Spanish-Mexican versus Pueblo) and ranging in scale from facades and furniture plans down to towel racks and toggle bolts. She showed practical know-how with structure and other technical matters and a keen grasp of materials—especially metals, a lasting holdover from her early years as a student and teacher of metal-crafting. For example, she took special pains with the design and fabrication of elaborate tin light fixtures for the dining room annex and other rooms, basing them on Mexican prototypes. In a letter to Clarkson, Colter went into great detail about the embossed-tin canopies she wanted for fixtures in the dining annex—their design, materials, and construction (for the brackets, she recommended a metal known as "'long Terne' . . . leaded iron used for automobile bodies").[39]

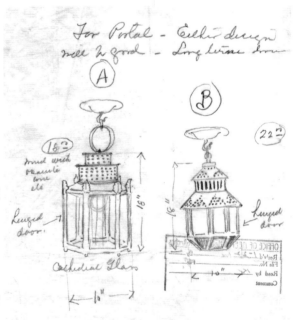

A sketch that Colter made for ceiling light fixtures

The redesigned patio, right, was faced on all sides with windowed partitions that could be removed in the summer.

In the lofty and darkly elegant Lecture Lounge, below, Indian Detourists could take in slide talks on the marvels of the region.

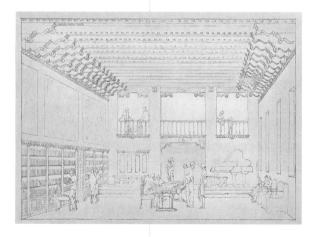

Colter's comprehensive capability should have been no surprise—after all, she *was* an architect. She signed her letters, especially to outside contractors and suppliers, as "Harvey architect and decorator." Throughout her career Colter identified herself as such, even though newspaper and magazine articles persisted in labeling her "the Harvey decorator." Understandably, even her colleagues betrayed the women-do-the-furniture bias of the day. "I trust you and Mrs. Clarkson are now in the midst of a peaceable discussion of furnishings, etc.," Clarkson wrote to Colter.[40]

Three months before the hotel reopened, Colter was involved in an auto accident in Kansas City. The taxi taking her from her apartment at Rockhill Manor to her office at Union Station crashed into a streetcar, sending her to St. Luke's Hospital with facial cuts and hip injuries.[41] She remained there for weeks, but the "smash-up," as she called it, did not stop her from reviewing progress at La Fonda throughout her recuperation, aided in correspondence by her long-term secretary, Sadie Rubins. Within days messages were fired off from the hospital like: "Miss Colter does not want these bancos painted."[42] Meem sent her letters of condolence and, knowing she wanted to keep up on the project, detailed reports.

When La Fonda finally reopened on June 15, 1929, it was a much more commodious and stylish place. The lobby that so offended Colter was enlarged and outfitted with Mexican-style furniture painted on-site by Kansas City artist Earl Altaire, who finished some 800 pieces throughout the hotel, including the guest rooms, according to Colter's design and color specifications.[43] The adjacent patio was pushed back, made square, and bordered by lobby and lounge spaces called *portales* or portals that were outfitted with removable glass window-walls. In its center stood a circular fountain surrounded by a low masonry bench clad in Spanish-Moorish tiles, one of many features that Colter steered vigilantly from sketch through construction. The south portal, further drenched with natural light from glass ceiling panels hand-painted by local artist Olive Rush, was wide enough to serve as a lounge where tea

Adjacent to the patio, the new south portal functioned as both a corridor and a lounge for relaxing around the fireplace.

was served. Arrayed along the hotel's west side was an expanded set of shops, including one of Herman Schweizer's Indian stores, a "curio room" put together by Colter (with ample advice from her friend Herman) to be just as alluring as his other Harvey shops and displays.

Since the Indian Detours helped drive the need for the expansion, La Fonda now included the Courier Lounge, where Detourists and others could obtain information on the tours while being regaled with books, maps, and photographs of the Southwest's alluring sites. A large pictorial map of these attractions, created by artist Gerald Cassidy, hung on the wall. Across the hall was the Lecture Lounge, where in the evening they took in talks on the culture and scenery of the region that were illustrated by hand-tinted lantern-slides. A room that Colter especially liked, this was the hotel's most elegant and imposing space—and its most Spanish. Set down several steps from the lobby, the room rose twenty feet from an oak floor to a heavily beamed ceiling. It was castle-grand instead of inn-cozy, a mead hall for the touring set complete with three balconies opening from an upper level, large windows that admitted light from the south portal, and an imposing hooded fireplace. For the fireplace surround, the hall's two entranceways, and a large wall panel, Denver sculptor Arnold Ronnebeck fabricated warm terra-cotta reliefs that depicted Native American ceremonies and symbols; another such relief was installed above the fireplace in the south portal. Colter also outfitted the hall with imported Spanish lantern chandeliers, imported rugs, and cushy furniture.

"We have tried to give the hotel a true New Mexican and Spanish atmosphere," Colter told a reporter after the hotel opened, "and at the same time embody all of the comforts which tourists from the east demand."[44] As with all of her projects, Colter perceived La Fonda as an integrated work of art that, to delight the eye, required the proper finish. She possessed the clout and talent (and apparently the time) to see her work through to such satisfying conclusion—designing and searching for furnishings and fixtures and engaging artists like Rush, who painted murals for the New Mexico Room (the dining annex, used for banquets and dances) that depicted with whimsy everyday life in old New Mexico. "I got a great kick out of" the preliminary drawing for the murals, Colter wrote from her hospital room two weeks after her accident. "I was especially intrigued with the goat eating a washing. . . . Miss Rush has just the sense of humor that we wish to have."[45] Colter designed a banco, or banquettes, on the perimeter of the room for dancers to rest upon. Rush also garnished with wall paintings some of the guest rooms, yet another part of Colter's domain, each of the 156 of them said to be unique in plan and decoration. Colter labored over their every detail, from hook rugs on the floors to the drapes, hung on wrought-iron poles. The pride of the new hotel were its fifth-floor suites, which she equipped with fireplaces, beds with massive painted headboards, other antiques from Spain, and thick showy rugs. Rustic log beams crisscrossed by wood planks formed the ceilings. Colter called these spaces her "Grandee rooms."

Colter explained the origin of the beds:

THEY WERE PURCHASED IN SPAIN FROM THEIR OLD HOMES BY A DECORATOR TO BE USED IN AN IMPORTANT PRIVATE RESIDENCE IN FLORIDA. WHILE THEY WERE ON THE OCEAN, THE DEVASTATING STORM OCCURRED THAT SWEPT AWAY SO MANY FLORIDA ESTATES [INCLUDING THIS ONE]. ON ARRIVAL, THE BEDS WERE SOLD AT AUCTION FOR A SONG. THE BUYER KNEW I WAS MUCH INTERESTED IN THESE THINGS AND WROTE ME ABOUT THEM. AFTER SEEING THEM, I FELT THAT THEY BELONGED AT LA FONDA AND, WHILE IT IS NOT CUSTOMARY TO USE SUCH FURNITURE IN HOTELS, THE TEMPTATION WAS TOO GREAT. . . . THE BED IN ROOM 520 IS A CATALAN BED OF THE EIGHTEENTH CENTURY. LIKE ALL OF THE CATALAN FURNITURE OF THE SEVENTEENTH AND EIGHTEENTH CENTURIES, IT SHOWS THE FRENCH INFLUENCE VERY PLAINLY; THIS ONE BEING A GOOD EXAMPLE OF DIRECTOIRE OR NEO-CLASSIC. AS A MATTER OF FACT, THE OTHER GENUINE ANTIQUE BEDS AT LA FONDA ARE OF A MUCH EARLIER PERIOD; THE ONE IN SUITE 510 BEING A VERY UNUSUAL AND BEAUTIFUL EXAMPLE OF THE SEVENTEENTH CENTURY. IT IS IMPOSSIBLE TO GIVE YOU AN EXACT DATE OF ANY OF THESE BEDS.[46]

The guest rooms, above, were furnished with all manner of Spanish or Spanish-style fittings, including painted headboards and elaborate fabrics.

For the suites, right, Colter used antique beds from Spain that were originally intended for a private residence.

In each suite the fireplace once again proved a Colter essential. She pushed them throughout the hotel from the start. "The lobby does need humanizing, and nothing will humanize it so much as a fireplace in view," she wrote to Clarkson in 1926. "Nothing will make the place appear so homelike as the introduction of as many fireplaces as are possible in our longing [*sic*] spaces. A fire in [the south portal] on the central axis of the building will be the first thing of note a guest would see onturning from registering at the clerk's desk. It will be distant enough to be intriguing. . . . You may not be able to get all these fireplaces in, but Mr. Frederick Harvey and I are crazy about fireplaces and want to have as many as we can!"[47]

Thanks to preservation of the Meem papers, the record of the La Fonda expansion is likely the most complete of any of Colter's assignments. Showing occasionally through the formalities of official business correspondence are signs of the undertaking's human side. In late 1928, Colter wrote to Meem: "I got your letter saying that the hotel would be ready the first of February. I wonder where you expect to go to when you die? Even the contractor and the railroad superintendent hold out no such hopes. . . . P.S. My secretary suggests that you may be going where all good architects go. On such occasions I do not claim to be an architect."[48] The month after Colter's accident, Sadie Rubins wrote to Meem: "Miss Colter said to tell you that she still expects to get to Santa Fe before the grand opening and 'hopes to regain her strength sparring with you.'"[49]

The new La Fonda proved more than an atmospheric retreat for well-heeled travelers captive to the Harvey/Santa Fe sightseeing agenda, for it was quickly adopted by the city itself as the center for socializing. Local artists, writers, politicians, and the merely wealthy—as well as illustrious out-of-towners—could be found dining, drinking, or otherwise treating the hotel as their second home. In the words of journalist Ernie Pyle, "you never met anybody anywhere except at the La Fonda."[50] In an observation that must have raised eyebrows among the purists of the Santa Fe Style, French writer Simone de Beauvoir, visiting Santa Fe in 1947 as part of a year-long tour of the country, thought the hotel "resembles an African village with its earthen walls and crenellations." She also called it "the most beautiful hotel in America, perhaps the most beautiful I've ever seen in my life."[51] La Fonda is considered one of John Gaw Meem's most masterful works. Given Mary Colter's extensive and influential role in the project, clearly she should share in that praise. ⌖

During the months when the enlarged La Fonda was taking form, the Santa Fe Railway and the Fred Harvey Company were hatching plans for yet another hotel. This facility, in Winslow in the high desert of northeastern Arizona, was to be wholly Colter-designed, as the El Navajo hotel and station had been, and, as it turned out, the largest and most elaborate undertaking of Mary Colter's career.

Winslow was a small town of some 4,000 people on the main Santa Fe line to Los Angeles. Serving as a division headquarters for the railway, it was pretty much a company town. Winslow was also the missing link in the long chain of Harvey towns, since the company offered no first-class hotel between Gallup to the east and the Williams/Grand Canyon area to the west. A Harvey House and depot had stood in Winslow since 1897, but it was a simple affair of brick with sandstone trim that stood on the south side of the tracks. To the Santa Fe and Harvey officials, ever on the prowl to establish resort-like centers for sightseeing, Winslow offered a prime spot upon which to build the capital of a new province of tourism. Ford Harvey, the president of the company, said as much in a 1927 letter to his brother, company vice president Byron Harvey, in which he promoted "the advisability of facilities in Winslow" and pointed to the presence of the Petrified Forest, the Painted Desert, Hopi villages, the White Mountains, and Meteor Crater as attractions that could easily be reached from there by Harvey's Indian-Detour motor-tour operation. "I am convinced there is quite a future there!"[52]

Less than two years later, in January 1929, the Santa Fe Railway announced that it would build the hotel, complete with a new passenger station, and construction began that April.[53] Colter must have worked on plans and drawings for the building in 1928 during the height of the La Fonda project and, given the Harveys' earlier interest in Winslow, she may have been contemplating and sketching out ideas even before that. The company's formula for luring patrons remained the same: southwestern atmosphere served up with Harvey comfort. As she had done so often before, Colter translated that order into specifics by conjuring up a historical tale as her springboard to design. She pictured the building as the seat of a wealthy Spanish colonial family, a sprawling ranch house of the type that might have been found in the Southwest when it was part of Mexico, built in the late eighteenth century and enlarged over the years by consecutive generations. Colter coyly chose 1869 as the point of reference, which not coincidentally was the year of her birth, and the company ultimately named the hotel La Posada, Spanish for "inn" or "resting place."[54]

Instructions given to the Indian-Detour Couriers just before the hotel opened described it as "built in the low, rambling style introduced into Old Mexico and our own far Southwest by the early Spanish emigrants . . . who turned their leisurely attention to the cultivation of the broad vegas and the raising of cattle."[55] Colter articulated her vision of a mature "rancho" through a full-dress package of architecture, interior decoration, and landscaped grounds, which she spread over twenty acres and partly surrounded with walls. She created a compound, an oasis actually, since the desert came right up to the site on the southeastern edge of town—unlike the setting at La Fonda, where the surrounding city separated it from the natural landscape.

Colter further explained her design premise to the *Winslow Daily Mail* when the hotel opened:

The new Harvey House hotel, La Posada in Winslow, Arizona, was in a prime location for tourists to explore the Painted Desert, Petrified Forest, Meteor Crater, White Mountains, and the Hopi lands.

WE WOULD NOT EXPECT THE INTERIORS OF ANY TWO HOMES OR THE ARCHITECTURE OF ANY TWO HOUSES OF THAT DAY TO BE OF THE SAME DESIGN, NOR EXACTLY LIKE THOSE ERECTED IN SPAIN. CERTAIN WOODS ARE ONLY AVAILABLE HERE, AND THE WORKMEN HERE WOULD BE FARM LABORERS AND NOT SKILLED MECHANICS, AND SO THROUGH THE INFLUENCE OF MATERIAL AND LABOR, A TYPE OF HOME ALL HIS OWN WAS BUILT BY EACH OWNER.[56]

Colter fashioned La Posada in the Spanish Colonial Revival style but with a sufficient enrichment of arched openings, arcaded walks, and grillwork and other decorative whimsies to render the building in a mode that might be called Spanish Eclectic. The building is very much of a kind with the Spanish Colonial Revival houses and public buildings that had been built in profusion in the 1920s across the southern tier of the country from Florida to California. Still standing, La Posada is a resolutely asymmetrical but balanced composition constructed of poured reinforced concrete, clad in stucco, and topped with medium-pitched tiled roofs with shallow

165

H-4224   LA POSADA, FRED HARVEY HOTEL, WINSLOW, ARIZONA

overhangs. The 78,000-square-foot structure (including the depot) is long, stretching some 350 feet from west to east, and low, rising only two stories and scraping the sky with but one modest tower. The south facade, facing the tracks, centers on a generous entrance arch in the form of a parabola, a shape that Colter was fond of using in her projects for both interior and exterior arches as well as for fireplaces. At the eastern end stands the one-story Santa Fe Railway passenger depot, fronting the tracks with a multiple-arched portal and linked to the hotel by a long square-columned walkway. On the north side, the hotel's residential arms reach toward Second Street, Winslow's main artery, on either side of a modest entry that opens to a spacious arched hallway. (This was originally the rear door. Much in the way that a southern manor house's principal facade faced the river, La Posada's faced the then-busy tracks.) A heavy timbered balcony is recessed into the western face of the hotel, the wall behind it painted turquoise, said to be Colter's favorite color. One might quibble that the building has too much going on, with its glut of gables and wings and almost ad hoc arrangement of variously sized windows but, after all, La Posada's "history" suggests that it was not built of a piece but had taken form down through the decades. And despite the liveliness of its massing, the building remains crisp-edged and smooth-surfaced—almost modernist in countenance.

　　To enter La Posada, as a passenger alighting from a Santa Fe train or a motorist arriving on the famous Route 66, which ran past the front entrance, was to trade an ever-modernizing America for an older Spanish fantasy world where all was shaded, cool, and unhurried. The wide public halls and cozy guest rooms were furnished bountifully, suggesting the accrued inheritance of a parade of generations, each one passing its distinctive addendum on to the next. Little would have been thrown away. Not since Hermit's Rest, perhaps, had Colter invited the weary traveler into an environment so conducive to the feeling that the owners were still in residence, departing just minutes before. To carry off this effect, she outfitted the hotel

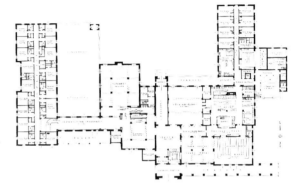

Colter designed La Posada, opposite, as if it had been the sprawling ranch house of a Spanish colonial estate, its asymmetrical collection of wings suggesting a structure that had been enlarged over the years.

The plan of the main floor, above, reveals the generous space devoted to public uses—lobbies, lounges, restaurants, and an enclosed garden.

A large parabolic-arched porch greeted passengers alighting from Sante Fe trains. To the far right stands the railroad terminal.

with a sea of furniture and decorative objects, its mix of the sophisticated and the provincial, even crude, reflecting the owners' travels as well as the exigencies of life on the margin of empire. Colter had hit her stride supplying furnishings and moods for La Fonda; now she reached even farther for variety and evocative power, giving her imagination free reign on a scale as never before.

Benches and chairs, chests and cupboards, tables and stools. If these eye-catching pieces all looked old and rare, then she succeeded in her clever historical deception, for many of them were in fact new. For every antique that Colter shipped in from Spain or Mexico she supplied a copy of another old treasure (and often the original itself), made in the furniture workshop she set up in the depot. There E. V. Birt, a carpenter she had used for La Fonda, and a crew of local workers replicated or created from Colter's own designs a host of pieces—all sawn, carved, assembled, possibly upholstered, and then stained or otherwise "antiqued" to fit into the La Posada scheme. This was a new building with new surfaces and many new trappings, but Colter was determined to project an illusion of antiquity.

Each room had its extraordinary objects. The pride of La Posada was the lounge, a huge chamber located a few dramatic steps up from the lobby that served the mythical ranch family as its great hall. Two layers of pegged-oak planks formed the floor, and the ceiling was painted turquoise with gold and silver accents. Guests

could relax on high-backed tapestry-covered divans set before the hooded fireplace and admire two palm-shaped altar decorations that formerly hung in a Mexican church, hand-made from beads and artificial flowers of tinsel. On other walls was a series of antique engravings of explorer Cortez that depicted the Spanish discovery of America. Standing out amid the jumble of comfortable seating were black-painted confessional stools and walnut horseshoe chairs, both the Spanish original and copies, that sported silk-velour seats and gold-galloon trim. Wrought-iron standing ashtrays thought to be of Colter's own design—abstract jackrabbits, chipmunks, and other fauna (including a man)—supplied comic relief here and elsewhere in the hotel.[57]

Separated by parabolic arches, the long central foyer, the lobby, and the passageway leading to the guest rooms—an orangerie-like corridor later known as the Cinder Block Court for its exposed walls—were lined with conversation pieces. Colter cast her net widely, bringing in (or fabricating) riches that ranged from a 200-year-old chest moved from a ranch house near Winslow and carved benches fitted over radiators to a Mexican pottery-vase table lamp with a goatskin shade and all manner of wall and ceiling light fixtures made of iron, tin, and glass. One especially clever piece that Colter copied was a monk's chair whose circular back folded down to form a table. Most of the hotel's iron work—for example, the sweeping

169

opposite: A recessed wooden
gallery dominates the western wall
of the hotel.

A gated arch west of the hotel
broke the wall between a yard that
represented the crude origins of
the "ranch" and the landscaped
park to the east.

171

172

Colter adorned public areas like the lobby with a melange of furniture and other objects, some of antique vintage and some just built.

The lounge, the mythical ranching family's great hall, cosseted guests in comfort with its fine furniture and welcoming fireplace. Mary Colter sitting at the left in this circa 1930 view.

The Cinder Block Court, which opened on the left to the Sunken Garden, offered its own array of unique furnishings.

baluster on the stairs at the western end of the cinder block court—was crafted on site. Urns, jars, jugs, and pots of various shapes and materials anchored corners and niches. Unifying this veritable gallery were flagstone floors and stucco walls that rose either to rounded arches or to ceilings supported with concrete beams painted with geometric patterns in gold, emerald, and burgundy. All was not Spanish, however. Even in this southwestern wonderland, Colter's love for Asian art surfaced here and there. Blue-and-white Chinese-Chippendale jars and two Chinese candlesticks could be found in the lobby, and the Japanese chrysanthemum motif was carved into certain chairs and tables.

La Posada offered travelers seventy rooms and five suites. Walking up staircases with wrought-iron railings and down halls covered in a tiled linoleum called Linomosaic—designed to quiet their steps— guests entered rooms for which, according to the *Daily Mail*, "nothing has been left undone to give a simple, farmlike impression."[58] That simplicity centered mainly on the oak-plank doors and floors, though, since the chambers were decked out with antique (or antique-style) furniture, ceiling lights crafted from painted tin and mirrors, and brightly colored bedspreads, valenced draperies, and Navajo or Spanish rugs. Much of the furniture was manufactured elsewhere under Colter's supervision. Hammered tin, painted in colors to harmonize with the room scheme, was also used for mirror and picture frames and bedside lamps. Hand-painted shades were installed in the windows. Hanging in each room was a picture of San Ysidro, the patron saint of farming and gardening—a hand-colored linoleum-block print created by Harvey artist Fred Geary that depicted the saint standing behind a plow with oxen and attended by guardian angels, conveying the essence of La Posada's make-the-desert-bloom aura. E. V. Birt made the picture frames in the depot workshop.[59]

One of the suites boasted a corner fireplace, again parabolic, above which was an animated Mexican floral design painted directly on the plaster by Earl Altaire, another artist from the La Fonda job. (Charles Lindbergh stayed in this suite often during the 1930s when he served as advisor for the expansion of the Winslow airport, a major stop for the Transcontinental Air Transport (TAT) passenger route, a joint venture with the Santa Fe and the forerunner of TWA. Many of the passengers on TAT stayed at La Posada, and the hotel kitchen supplied in-flight meals.) Altaire painted flowers in other bedrooms and in public spaces, most winningly a vase bursting with blooms that cheered guests descending the central staircase.[60] He even adorned some window panes with painted flowers and other patterns, tempering the light that entered the main dining room and the end of long hallways. Over the Cinder Block Court's end arches, Altaire painted pastoral scenes with deer.

In case patrons missed fancy Mexican and Spanish tile, they could find it aplenty in the lunchroom, where Colter tiled the horseshoe counters, tables, and the sides and tops of work surfaces with geometric patterns and flowers. The tiles were copies made by a Los Angeles company of various Spanish originals. The dining room next door was surveyed from a tiled niche by San Pasqual, the patron saint of cooking, shown busy at work in his kitchen. In this most Mexican of rooms—one can almost hear the noisy "clunk" of its

A floral mural painted by E.V. Birt in the stair hall to the second level

The "plants" in the foyer were in reality iron light fixtures.

175

provincial wooden chairs against the quarry-tile floor—non-structural log beams finished the ceiling and arched windows inset with doors looked out over a dining patio. Huge wooden hutches in the dining and lunchrooms showed off the hotel's blue-chain-patterned Harvey china. Colter later considered the classic Harvey Girl uniforms too severe for this colorful setting, so she softened the look by adding multicolored aprons with quilted designs that depicted cacti, donkeys, and farm workers dozing under big hats. Between this room and the lunchroom was a dining annex that could be closed off with huge pivoting doors, plank panels painted with multihued abstract motifs. At the hotel's opening, the local press bragged less about the decor in these restaurants than about their "most modern of [kitchen] equipment," touting all that those fancy and often automated machines could do to help the Harvey workers cook and clean. "Envy of every housewife who will see them, are the electric dish and silverware washers."[61]

For La Posada, Colter drew her only complete landscape plan. She introduced guests to this beguiling landscape gradually, starting with the nearest and most inviting space, a sunken garden nestled between the Cinder Block Court and two bedroom wings and enclosed on the north by a stuccoed wall. This was an outdoor room complete with a flagstone terrace, a lawn, flowers and trees, vines on the walls, and yet more of the decorative pieces that Colter had amassed—huge ceramic urns, for instance. One of its two fountains, a lion's head, spouted into a massive petrified-wood stump. In the days before the removal of that material from the Petrified Forest National Monument was outlawed, Colter was evidently able to obtain the specimens she wanted, including some logs she directed to the hotel's south grounds.[62] On that side, facing the tracks, a low and deep tiled-roof porch opened out onto broad lawns landscaped with trees and other plants. There guests could watch some of the dozen or more daily passenger trains arrive and depart or fix their eyes in the foreground on a crown-shaped wrought-iron wellhead that topped a wishing well or

Harvey Girls and guests in the tile-bedecked lunchroom, which faced the railroad

San Pasqual, the patron saint of cooking, surveyed diners in the dining room, above, and appeared on menu covers, right.

gaze up at falcons floating motionless on an updraft. Just before the grassy expanse ended at the brick railroad platform stood a low wall, its narrow stone courses variously stuccoed-over or exposed, that also incorporated sections of open terra-cotta block and dark red wavy fencing that Colter patterned after the Hopi Indian river-of-life symbol.

The western third of the great hacienda was given over to a huge expanse of park and gardens. At its far end stood an enclosure surrounded by a five-feet-tall, exposed-stone wall, an apparent replication of fortifications at Brigham City, an 1870s Mormon colony just north of Winslow.[63] Within the sturdy barricade was another of Colter's ingenious history lessons, a tableau that suggested the mythical origins of La Posada, before the great house was built, as a rough-edged outpost in the desert of northern Mexico. This would have been at first a period of defense, against both the natives and the weather. The scene was marked, as the Indian-Detour Couriers' instructions described it, by "the 'dry water hole' with the broken water cart abandoned beside it, and the old plains Caretta with its huge solid wooden wheels and the bleached yoke of the oxen that dragged it over the roadless desert."[64] Here she intended also to plant a desert garden of cacti and shrubs, but this and other evocative features nearby—a cottage garden, a maze, and a parterre—were never built, possibly due to the Depression.

A tall arch fitted with wooden gates opened between this yard and the more landscaped grounds to the east. Colter inserted more of her thought-provoking contrivances here: a wooden shed that played the role of an old stable (actually used by the hotel gardeners) and in the southwest corner a semicircular faux battlement—complete with loopholes for guns—that guarded the "settlement." Nearby she

In the Sunken Garden, Colter installed a fountain that dripped into a basin of petrified wood.

arranged for a group of Hopi Indians to demonstrate dry-corn farming, overseen by carved wooden statues of San Ysidro, his oxen, and angels. These effigies and other features of the hardscrabble historical portrait, including a hogan to be built and inhabited by Navajo Indians, were planned but apparently never installed.

A variety of trees—American and Chinese elms, cottonwoods, poplars, junipers, and fruit trees—were planted around the hotel. Some of the specimens, like pomegranates and quinces, represented plants that the imaginary founding family had brought with them from Spain. Over the years, as the foliage matured under the care of Santa Fe Railway gardeners, La Posada's environs grew into a lush landscape that softened the architecture and filtered out the intensity of the sun. As she had done with the design of the building, Colter succeeded in mediating between the harsh and windy desert and the travelers' tranquil cocoon of leisure. To brighten and vary the view, early each year the gardeners grew seedlings in the greenhouse located in the northwest corner of the grounds, transplanting them to outdoor beds where they bloomed at intervals over the months. Colter praised the head gardener, Romolo Chacon, as the best of all those who worked for the Harvey system. With such a diverse mantle of vegetation—in the best Colter tradition, both decorous and edifying—San Ysidro would have watched over a bountiful realm.

"Men who had come to this section of America from Spain might come from any one of the provinces and bring very different traditions," Colter explained.[65] To design La Posada, she drew on years of research into such Spanish and Mexican building traditions. A perpetual student of history, architectural history, interior design, and archaeology, she amassed a large library in those subjects, most of the books abundantly illustrated with photographs and drawings. Among the volumes that she possibly consulted for this assignment were *Architectural Details: Spain and the Mediterranean* (subtitled "for use in developing a logical and appropriate style of architecture for California and the Pacific Southwest"); *An Architectural Pilgrimage in*

Old Mexico; and *Spanish Interiors and Furniture*, all of them published in the mid-1920s. A plate in the latter shows a hallway much like those at La Posada. Next to another drawing, depicting the fireplace end of a room, Colter wrote: "Note uneven lines [where the walls meet]." Such irregularities were, of course, her stock in trade. She signed her name below a number of the illustrations in *Spanish Farm Houses and Minor Public Buildings*, a practice she indulged in often, perhaps to highlight designs that she found especially appealing. Her books are littered with notes and markings, and many bear the grooves of paperclips.[66]

The La Posada project brought Mary Colter to Winslow for extended periods. Interaction with local residents and the project team left behind anecdotes of her as an insistent, sometimes difficult, person. One of these stories occurred in 1928, on an early trip to the town. When the bellboy who carried her bags to her room in the old Harvey House could not produce the correct key, an enraged Colter read him the riot act and threatened to have his job. The next day, she came looking for him, apologized, and gave him a big tip.[67] She later stayed at a boarding house run by Clara Schmitz, whose husband, Leon, ran a paint store and decorating business in the back. He would produce any paint color Colter wanted, and together they would test them in relation to materials and objects to be used in the hotel. They also worked on fabric selections. Often during these sessions, Colter insisted on listening to one of her favorite radio programs, an orchestra from Del Rio, Texas. Her presence grated on Clara, who succeeded in getting Colter to move out.[68]

Years later Daggett Harvey, a grandson of Fred Harvey, wrote, "I did know Miss Colter pretty well and have a distinct recollection of the dynamic and authoritative way in which she functioned. She was afraid of no one—from the President of the Railway Company on down."[69] Doubtless Colter was demanding, but in order to accomplish what she did, she often had to be. Ample evidence also exists of her diplomatic and thoughtful side in business dealings and of her kindness to

182

colleagues and friends, not to mention her sense of humor. "I don't think she was irascible. She simply didn't suffer fools lightly. She couldn't stand stupidity," recalled Patricia Smyth, a friend of Colter's in the architect's later years. It is apparent also that Colter was not a self-promoter. "She was secure in herself. She knew what she knew—and what other people didn't know."[70] Colter's "negative" traits tend to stand in sharper profile because of the collective impact of three facts: that she was a woman, a professional, and practiced long before women architects became commonplace. Had none of these conditions pertained, it is unlikely that the difficult side of her personality would have been, and still be, so exposed to comment.

Opening day ceremonies on May 15, 1930, brought top brass from the Santa Fe and the Harvey Company to Winslow to participate in the official formalities. In a widely remembered story, two cowboys (or men dressed as such) decided to celebrate in their own way, riding right into the hotel on horseback, their mounts slipping on the slick flagstone floors. They picked up the diminutive Mary Colter, set her on the lobby counter, fired their guns a few times, and rode off, presumably not into the sunset.[71] In June, Harvey Company photographers arrived in town to take stills and motion pictures of the new hotel. The former were destined for newspapers and the latter for movie theaters, most of these in the East, which was still the nation's population center and thus the mother lode of the Santa Fe/Harvey customer base.

Shortly after La Posada opened, a *Winslow Daily Mail* special supplement touted the new establishment. "This transplantation of the Spanish 'rancho' brings to our community a tourist hotel second to none in the Southwest [and will] make Winslow the home-like headquarters for all detours to Arizona's wonderland of vistas." Indeed, less press was given to the hotel than the area's tourist attractions, from the Grand Canyon to the White Mountains, which one could view with comfort and ease on Harveycar "motor cruises" that fanned out from La Posada. The company showcased visits to Hopi and Navajo Indian villages, although the jaunts were no longer called Indian Detours, as done in New Mexico, but simply Detours. These native peoples were still pictured as exotic and slightly untamed—who could resist the bizarre Hopi Snake Dance or the "brilliant barbaric rugs" woven by the Navajos—but, as one headline in the supplement reassuringly put it, "The Navajo Is Becoming Civilized." Not too civilized, it was probably hoped, to make them unfit for tourism.[72]

How many tourists would come to La Posada was open to question in any event, since, unfortunately, Winslow's lavish new hotel debuted seven months after the stock market crashed. As the nation sank into the Depression, the travel industry suffered along with other sectors of the economy. This was surely on the mind of the Santa Fe official who sent a telegram to the Harvey Company: "Congratulations on the new building, La Posada. Hope income exceeds estimates as much as the building costs did."[73] As it turned out, La Posada was the last of the great railroad hotels that the Santa Fe Railway would build for the Fred Harvey Company, but despite the economic bottomland into which it was born, the hotel endured for nearly three decades and even enjoyed a measure of prosperity.

For all of its regional and national value to the two companies that built it, Mary Colter's creation also proved enormously important to Winslow itself, serving the local population for many years as a much-loved center of social and civic life. All of the Harvey hotels functioned as unofficial civic centers for their communities, large and small. La Posada was the finest place in the region at which to dine and to celebrate family rites. Weddings, for instance, were held in the lounge, and the receptions that followed could take advantage of the fine array of outdoor settings that the "rancho" offered. Clubs and business groups from Winslow and elsewhere in northern Arizona held meetings there. And in much the same way as the Alvarado had done for Albuquerque, La Posada served as Winslow's connection with the "real" world. In the evenings, before television claimed their attention, families would stroll

The full staff of La Posada, including a bevy of Harvey Girls, posed in 1930 on the south lawn.

down to the hotel to see the sleek Santa Fe super-trains come in, hoping to glimpse famous faces getting off—Lindbergh, Errol Flynn, Howard Hughes, Carole Lombard, Clark Gable, and other celebrities and heroes of the day. Colter had brought more than a building into being.

Return to Grand Canyon

LA POSADA SHOWED OFF SUPERBLY how Mary Colter was able to reach into regional history to produce themes that directed the designs of her buildings. The impetus for her projects was always practical, of course, but she was able to mask that practicality well—clothing it not only in style and architectonic effect but also in narrative. Each Colter building told a story. Each had its own "reality," constructed in Colter's mind as the product of fastidious research and planning, then later planted in the imagination of the traveler.

With her next building commission, the Watchtower at Desert View, Colter once again drew on southwest history to conceive a structure that told tales. Rising from the rim at the eastern end of Grand Canyon National Park, the tower was a fine match for La Posada in terms of conception, size and expense, and atmospheric results. With the Winslow building, Colter's monolith stands at the summit of her architectural career.

The Watchtower project brought Colter back to the Grand Canyon for what would be a series of buildings conceived in response to the rise of tourist traffic. The number of annual visitors to the national park had grown from approximately

For her Watchtower at Desert View, Colter drew on the characteristics of a number of Indian ruins.

187

The Round Tower at Cliff Palace in Mesa Verde National Park, shown here in a photo taken by Colter circa 1931, inspired the form and proportions of her tower.

44,000 in 1919 to more than 200,000 in 1929. The Depression crimped those figures, but by the mid-1930s they were again on the rise, reaching 300,000 in 1937. The Santa Fe's relative role in bringing in those sightseers had been declining for some time; by 1926 the majority were arriving by automobile.[1] In fact, overall passenger traffic on the Santa Fe Railway had been decreasing nearly every year since it peaked in 1920.[2] But the fact that vacationers were taking more and more to their cars mattered less at the canyon than elsewhere, since the two companies had sewn up most of the market there for entertaining and lodging tourists, no matter their mode of travel. The railroad and the Harvey Company pressed ahead with expansion plans, most of which were gestating before the stock market crash.

Harvey had been interested in beefing up its presence at the eastern end of the park, which lay some twenty-five miles out along the south rim from the main huddle of attractions in Grand Canyon Village. In 1931 a new road, the East Rim Drive, was finished from the village to the area, known as Desert View for its stunning vistas of the far-off Painted Desert. The company's tour buses drove that route, but tourist facilities were limited to a 1930 building used as a rest stop and canyon-viewing point.[3] What developed from Colter's imaginative interpretation of the company's needs, however, was far more than another rest stop with a gorgeous view. Returning to her fascination with Native American architecture and art, first essayed so ingeniously at the pioneering Hopi House and later at El Navajo, and to her love of conjuring up effects from the spirit of a site, so well realized at Lookout Studio and Hermit's Rest, she envisioned a new fusion of purpose and form.

"First and most important," Colter wrote in a handbook for tour guides about how she came to conceive the observation tower, "was to design a building that would become a part of its surroundings;—one that would create no discordant note against the time eroded walls of this promontory." She also wanted a structure that would enhance the view, not only of the Painted Desert and of a generous amount of

188

canyon and river below but of "*the entire circle of the distant horizon.*" Obviously, the structure would have to be a prominent one, but to avoid making it stick up like a sore thumb she rejected modern design and materials. Ultimately, she "hit upon" the idea of an Indian watchtower, which would provide the necessary height but could assume the guise of a "prehistoric building" whose "time-worn masonry walls would blend with the eroded stone cliffs of the Canyon walls themselves."[4]

Like La Posada, the Watchtower exemplified Colter's work as an exhaustive researcher. Even before she came up with her watchtower notion, she had become familiar with the architectural remains of ancient Indian villages scattered about the Four Corners region (at the junction of Arizona, New Mexico, Colorado, and Utah) and elsewhere in Arizona. She had probably visited most of those locations already. In 1927, in the middle of the La Fonda project, she prevailed upon John Gaw Meem to obtain copies of photos of various of these ruins from a museum in Santa Fe.[5] Colter was especially fascinated by the stone towers that stood among these remains: scores of monoliths in round, square, oval, and other shapes. The most well-known were found among the cliff dwellings at Mesa Verde National Park in southwestern Colorado—Square Tower House, for example, and the Round Tower at Cliff Palace— but others stood at Canyon de Chelly, Wupatki, and Montezuma's Castle, all in Arizona. Most numerous were the towers at Hovenweep National Monument in southeastern Utah, which led Colter to speculate that the tower form had originated there. She wrote of the Hovenweep structures: "They play 'hide and seek' among boulders in the arroyos; chase each other up the rugged sides of cliffs; hang to the very brink of the canyon walls; and scramble to the slanting crowns of monolithic rock pinnacles. We cannot but question what it is all about!"[6] Indeed, the impetus for building the towers remained a mystery. Some seemed to be watchtowers used for defense, others habitations or storehouses for grain. One intriguing theory held that they were centers for astronomical observation.

Colter also photographed Square Tower House at Mesa Verde, among many other Indian sites.

189

Colter peers into the kiva at Cedar Tree Tower at Mesa Verde.

The only way for Colter to study the towers' construction techniques and materials more closely was to visit them again, so she took off six months to do just that. By then in her early sixties, she apparently thought nothing of chartering a plane to pinpoint tower locations from the air—including new discoveries—, bouncing over rough roads in a Harveycar to her targets (she could command this relative luxury), then scampering to, into, and over the rocky ruins to sketch and photograph them.[7] The photographic record of these trips, most likely made in 1931, which she later had bound into four elegant albums, includes in addition to the structures a treasury of images of ancient petroglyphs and pictographs, prototypes for many of the decorations built into or applied onto the Watchtower. Colter's expeditions also yielded some of the best of the few photographs ever taken of the architect herself. They captured her in safari-like garb poking through the ruins, at times in the company of the Harvey driver and her colleague and project collaborator Herman Schweizer, at other times alone, standing in the solitary opening of some long and deftly fabricated rock wall.

Colter chose Mesa Verde's Round Tower as the direct inspiration for the form and proportions of her Watchtower. However, that tower's stones had been hewn to shape, coursed regularly, and pecked into a uniform dimpled texture, whereas the rock she had to build with at the canyon could not be hewn or tooled, she claimed, "without losing the *weathered surfaces* so essential to blend it with the Canyon walls."[8] Also, the builders at Mesa Verde had used stucco to smooth their walls, which were protected from the elements by the overhanging cliffs above. Stucco would not work

Colter perches below the Twin Towers ruin at Hovenweep National Monument, whose towers provided the inspiration for the Watchtower's masonry.

on the more exposed Watchtower. As it turned out, the stone at Hovenweep was closer to that available at the canyon and had not been much modified for the towers, which were, like hers would be, fully exposed to the weather. Thus for the masonry she opted for the example set by Hovenweep, supplying her workmen with enlarged photographs of wall details from those towers to use as guides. Back in her studio, Colter crafted a clay model of the proposed structure and its setting, photographing it from different angles to weigh its design and its effect on the site, a promontory previously known as Navajo Point that overlooks the canyon and the Colorado River as it bends to the west. She first arranged to have the park's naturalist, Edwin D. McKee, build a base model of the topography around the site.[9] To further measure the watchtower's impact and precisely gauge the views it would offer, she had a seventy-foot tall wooden platform built on location, the same height as the finished building.

"[T]his building should NOT be called a 'copy'; a 'replica'; a 'reproduction' or a 'restoration.' It is absolutely none of these," Colter insisted, preferring to call it a "re-creation" since "various ruins contributed characteristic features." The "primitive architect never intentionally copied anything," she pointed out, each of his buildings differing as to site, materials, and purpose.[10] Colter's structure is taller and larger than any of the originals (even as first built), tapering in diameter from thirty feet at the base to twenty-four feet at the roof. Attached at its base is a one-story also-circular structure, forty feet in diameter, that "re-creates" a kiva, a chamber used primarily by the Pueblo Indians for religious rites and other gatherings. Many of the ancient towers, including a number of those at Mesa Verde, were built in conjunction with kivas.

As with most of the Fred Harvey projects, construction of the Watchtower was supervised by the Santa Fe Railway, but it was undertaken in this case by the S. C. Hichborn Company of Los Angeles, which had built many bridges for the railway.[11]

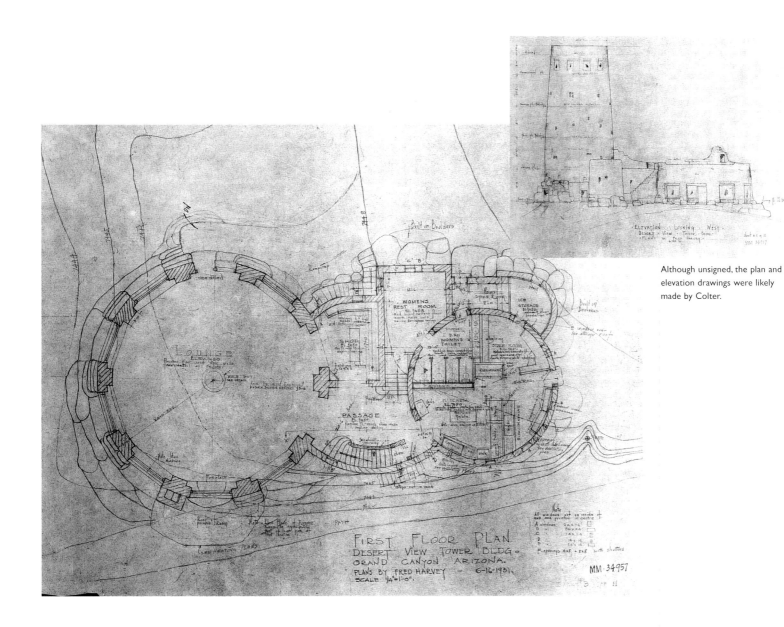

Although unsigned, the plan and elevation drawings were likely made by Colter.

The detailing of the walls of the tower and kiva show Colter at her most imaginative and exacting. Underpinning the "ancient" structure is a modern steel frame, right.

The tower is built over a steel-frame structure erected on a concrete base. Just as she had done at her other rim-side projects, however, Colter took great pains to tie the building visually to the terrain, making the Watchtower look like it sprouted from the site. Thus she masked the foundation with boulders "so huge that they seem to preclude the possibility of being placed by man," looking as if they were part of the natural rock strata, especially when viewed from below the rim. The massiveness of these lower walls also reduced the apparent size of the kiva and helped raise its view windows above any distracting foreground.[12]

An outside stairway, now closed, led to the roof of the kiva.

From this hefty geological base soars Colter's commanding anthropological cylinder. It is a resolute vertical composed of clever horizontals—some of the most imaginative patterning of stone to be found anywhere. Colter had been working on rustic walls for most of her career, and this was her finest. Local stone was used pretty much as it was found in the small canyons nearby, much of it plucked from already-built Indian habitations dating back centuries. She did not want to create "conspicuous scars" by altering it, so each piece had to be selected carefully. "Time, the lost principle in much modern construction, was taken to select each rock for the outer walls."[13] The generously textured surface may seem ad hoc at first sight, but she plotted it with precision, fitting stones of myriad sizes and shapes together into bands of different widths and colors.

Colter sundered the pattern here and there with larger, oddly shaped, or protruding pieces, and even purposely introduced a large crack in the masonry. She found it necessary to break up the facade in this way—creating shadows and invigorating the walls—since it had greater height and surface area than the ancient towers in the field. Some of these ornaments were suggested by motifs on the proto- types that Colter had selected. A series of triangular stones, for example, extends only part way around the tower beneath the unevenly finished parapet. "The suggestion for this treatment came from a wall at Wupatki where it played the same erratic trick," Colter noted.[14] Likewise, three conjoined diamonds near the main entrance were copied from a detail at Pueblo Bonito in Chaco Canyon. She even incorporated T-shaped door recesses filled in with rubble that appear "as if done in haste in the fear of the attack of an enemy."[15] This was not just Colter the designer; this was Colter the teacher, taking us back through the centuries to eavesdrop on ancient builders. The Watchtower is Colter at her most hypnotic.

Native Americans were fond of stones that resembled animals, Colter claimed, so she attached one onto the tower wall, a long jagged protrusion that resembled Balolookong, the great plumed serpent of the Pueblo Indians. At various places on the tower and the kiva, Colter also inserted petroglyphs—human, animal, or other figures pecked or otherwise carved into stones—that were taken from the vicinity of Ash Fork, Arizona.[16] This use of authentic artifacts would in later years be frowned upon by Indians and others, and finally prohibited by federal and state laws.[17]

The relentless rockiness of Colter's bastion is relieved by the cool smooth glass of deep-set windows. The windows are mostly small squares and rectangles that look as if they were thrown randomly at the wall. Only at the top are they large and regularly spaced around the tower; they taper upward, aping the lines of the building itself. Intended for the same purpose—viewing—huge picture windows break through the kiva's wall where it overlooks the canyon.

Like most of her works, the Watchtower is a stage set and Colter a master of special effects. To show how the ancient tower builders would often appropriate the site and materials of prior structures, Colter planted a "ruin" directly next to the tower, an unfinished roofless set of stone walls that looks as if it had been plundered to build the Watchtower. She also designed the structure to illustrate the condition in which ruins could often be found in the region, remains that she had visited for

Mary Colter chats with Don Hichborn of the S. C. Hichborn Company, which built the tower.

Among the unique stones that Colter used to break up the pattern of the wall is a diamond-shaped series. The source for this, at Pueblo Bonito in Chaco Canyon, is shown below.

Another source for the Watchtower were the incised stones, above, copied from a ruin at Marsh's Pass Arizona, and used above the outside stairway.

The T-shaped doorway at Pueblo Bonito, right, inspired those used on the Watchtower.

this project. "It was impractical to design the Watchtower in as ruinous a condition as usually prevails and the adjacent broken down walls to the west add to the desired atmosphere."[18]

Visitors enter the Watchtower through the kiva, which, unlike the historical model, was built above ground. Modern use necessitated other deviations: windows, a fireplace on the outer wall (directly beneath a window) instead of a fire pot in the middle, and absence of the traditional hole-in-the-ceiling entry. Colter did honor the original, however, with a floor-to-ceiling ladder and small circular fireplace in the center of the chamber. The timbers for the ceiling were salvaged from the log-framed Grandview Hotel (mid-1890s), the canyon's oldest inn, which stood some twelve miles west and was being razed. Colter called this reuse "one of the most pleasing features of this whole building." Patterned after the ceiling of the large kiva at Aztec, New Mexico, this low dome was ingeniously assembled of crisscrossing logs laid inward and upward in ever-smaller circles toward the center, topped with horizontally placed timbers.[19] As so often was the case with Colter's projects, virtually none of the decoration in the kiva could have been ordered from an architectural catalog. The reflectors over the wall lights were either shields decorated with designs taken from an initiation ceremony or headdresses worn in important dances. A bench was cut from a tree trunk and placed before the fireplace, and an owl stool was fashioned from a grotesque tree root found by park ranger and Harvey guide Edwin Cummings and given copper deposits for eyes. Cummings also made rawhide-covered chairs for the room. Two of the ceiling lights descended from decorations in Zuni kivas.[20] It was a simple and barely adorned room that, before it evolved into a crowded gift shop, must have impressed the visitor as almost sanctuary-like.

Nothing, however, could have prepared that visitor, climbing from the kiva into the Watchtower, for the vision at the top of the stairs—a balcony-ringed, cave-like column of space that rises three stories and surrounds one with an

200

enthralling display of colors and folk images. A phantasmagoria of abstract architecture and art, it is a romantic, even mystical creation whose imagery suggests a fusion of modern paintings—Klee and Chagall come most immediately to mind—freed from their frames and spread onto the crudely modeled walls and ceilings. Yet all of these hundreds of images are derived from southwestern native America, and it all can be elucidated. The first of the three gallery floors is a paean to the Hopis, the people most closely associated with the Grand Canyon. The nearest native neighbors to the canyon, the Hopis believe that their ancestors arrived on Earth from its depths. Decoration of this chamber brought Colter together with Fred Kabotie, a Hopi painter in his thirties from the Second Mesa village of Shungopavi who would become one of the most celebrated Native American artists of the Southwest. Working with Colter on the designs for the room, Kabotie shaped the artwork to communicate the physical and spiritual origins of Hopi life.

He depicted many symbols and scenes around the room: a wedding, a women's dance, a winged figure under a rainbow and clouds who represents the forces of the heavens, and gods of germination, war, and echo. But two works dominate. In the center, protected under glass, is an altar derived from one in the Snake Kiva in Oraibi, Arizona, and used for the famous snake (rain) dance. The work consists of a sand painting and such artifacts as religious crooks, carved *katsina* figures, and a tray of sacred corn meal. Kabotie created the painting, a square bordered by colored lines with the figure of a puma in the center, by slowly dribbling

Fred Kabotie finishes his mural of the Hopi snake legend on the wall across from the altar.

The kiva, opposite, is a modern, above-ground interpretation of the Indian prototype, complete with picture windows for viewing the canyon.

201

Kabotie's murals as they appear
today

fine colored sand held between a thumb and two fingers. This was Colter's second use of the medium, after the sand paintings with which she adorned El Navajo in 1923, but her first use of the genuine article. Unlike traditional sand paintings, which are swept away after use, this one is permanent, although it is said to have been slightly changed to satisfy Hopi leaders. On the wall Kabotie created the building's most famous artwork, a large circular mural that portrays the Hopi snake legend—the story of the first man to navigate the Colorado River. The painting is divided into quadrants that illustrate the adventures of a young man sent out in search of the snake clan, who possessed the much-sought-after power to make rain. As this and other paintings in the room reveal, the search for rain is at the heart of Hopi life and legend.

The interior of the tower, above right, is a multi-level chamber embellished with a profusion of southwestern Indian images.

The ceiling of the third level, top left, groups images from the Abo caves in New Mexico.

Colter praised Kabotie's representations of traditional Hopi art. "In it every line he draws is as sure as truth itself, whether…with brush and pigment on the wall or with colored sand in the mosaic of the altar."[21] Years later, Kabotie remembered:

MISS COLTER WAS A VERY TALENTED DECORATOR WITH STRONG OPINIONS, AND QUITE ELDERLY. I ADMIRED HER WORK, AND WE GOT ALONG WELL…MOST OF THE TIME. BUT ONCE IN A WHILE SHE COULD BE DIFFICULT, ESPECIALLY WHEN IT CAME TO MATCHING COLORS. I REMEMBER ONE DAY SHE KEPT SENDING ME UP IN THE TOWER WITH LITTLE DABS OF OIL COLORS, TOO SMALL TO MATCH. I DON'T KNOW WHETHER YOU'D CALL HER THRIFTY OR STINGY, BUT I FINALLY LOST MY PATIENCE. "LET ME HAVE THAT TUBE," I SAID, AND SLASHED IT OPEN. I SQUEEZED EVERYTHING OUT, AND STIRRED IN THE COLOR I FELT WAS RIGHT.

"WE'RE THROUGH—YOU'VE RUINED EVERYTHING," SHE GASPED. "AND YOU'VE USED UP ALL THE PAINT!"

"BUT MISS COLTER, WE HAVEN'T TRIED IT YET," I SAID.

I TOOK A LITTLE DAB AND RAN BACK UP IN THE TOWER. FORTUNATELY IT MATCHED, THE VERY COLOR WE'D BEEN SEEKING. SO THAT SAVED MY LIFE—AND HERS. SHE WAS QUITE A WOMAN. WE DIDN'T ALWAYS AGREE, BUT I THINK WE APPRECIATED EACH OTHER.[22]

Included in the archives is a sketch Colter drew indicating the colors to be used for the Kabotie wall painting of Muyingua, the god of germination.[23]

The feast of imagery continues up through two more levels, each accessed via a stairway fitted into the curve of the outer wall and open to the floor or floors below. Variously sized windows admit shafts of light. The similarity to Frank Lloyd Wright's Guggenheim Museum, in both design and use, is striking.[24] Harvey artist Fred Geary painted the walls and ceilings of these galleries, copying pictographs (images painted on rock) and petroglyphs from originals at sites in the Southwest that Colter had visited or studied. Here one encounters gods and monsters, humans, birds and animals (real and mythical), flowers, rainbows and other heavenly phenomena, geometric contrivances, and even handprints. The ceiling decoration over the upper

Colter specified the colors for the tower's art, as shown opposite top, in her sketch of Kabotie's mural of Muyingwa, the god of germination.

Fred Kabotie works on the sand painting of the snake altar on the first floor of the tower in 1932.

level is an adaptation of rock paintings at the Abo caves in central New Mexico. Colter based the design on drawings that Herman Schweizer had made in 1908 on a trip to the caves (actually cliff alcoves). Among them is a thunderbird he sketched that was adopted as a trademark by the Harvey Company and used on stationary and in company publications.[25] On the stairwell to the third level are paintings copied from pottery found at ruins of the Mimbres Indians in southwestern New Mexico, whimsical figures like a pelican eating fish and a rabbit riding the moon. Colter would again use Mimbres drawings for china she designed later in the decade for the dining car of the Santa Fe's Super Chief. But she was already taken by them: "The spirit of caricature is rivaled only by the perfection of draftsmanship."[26]

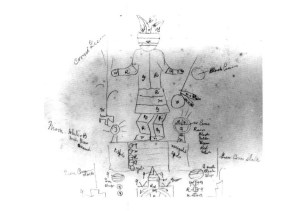

One more floor awaits the visitor. From this top-most room, which Colter dubbed the "Eagle's Nest," one gazes through the tower's large top windows out over the panorama of northern Arizona. The walls and ceiling, painted indigo, are devoid of images that might compete with the vast natural tableaus. An observer of the newly built Watchtower commented: "When lifted up by it, glories become visible to the traveler which no man has ever seen before."[27]

If Colter had missed out on breaking into the dominant masculine milieu of the typical architectural practice, her career path not having taken her to an independent commercial firm, she encountered the male-only environment in full force on the job site. There she worked with a range of men, from project managers and engineers to masons and carpenters. The Watchtower was especially challenging to build, given the intricacies of its stonework, and therefore for her to supervise. But supervise she did and with great presence. During construction she was ubiquitous, ensuring the tower would turn out just the way she designed it. Any element that did not measure up was simply torn down and rebuilt, vexing her workmen and reinforcing her reputation as an exacting taskmaster. Colter was immovably self-confident. She knew precisely what she wanted and headed straight toward that goal,

The lavish opening-day ceremonies for the Watchtower were crowded with both spectators and Indian ritual performers. The booklet for the festivities, above, explained the ceremonies.

whether it be an architectural detail or a personal response. Michael Harrison, a Park Service ranger at the Grand Canyon during the 1920s and '30s, recalled Colter—factually and sarcastically—as "a woman among men." She had a powerful personality and "knew what she was about. . . . Evidently she knew her job or else she wouldn't have had it as long as she did."[28]

The date for completion of the tower, although specified to occur December 31, 1931, was extended several times finally to November 30, 1932, although the tower did not open officially until May 13, 1933. (According to Frank Waters, "two days before it was opened the Hopis held a dedication ceremony. [Colter] was the only White invited."[29]) As they had done almost exactly ten years earlier at El Navajo, the Harvey Company and the Santa Fe Railway pulled out all the stops, staging a grand ceremonial for hundreds of guests that stretched from early afternoon until past sunset. The day was given over completely to Indian ritual and culture, beginning most substantially with "De-ki-veh," an elaborate Hopi blessing of the kiva and tower. Four scenes of ritualistic drama enacted inside and outside of the building concluded with the Kiva Chief solemnly naming and sanctifying Colter's building. Other dances and rites, performed by Hopi and Navajo men, women, and youths in lavish costume, ensued along with a Hopi feast (barbecue for the less adventurous). Wrote one reporter: "It is the Indians' day."[30]

To explain the Watchtower to the Harvey tour guides who had pestered her about the meaning of the stark and enigmatic fortress and its ocean of imagery, Colter wrote a handbook, the *Manual for Drivers and Guides Descriptive of the Indian Watchtower at Desert View and Its Relation, Architecturally, to the Prehistoric Ruins of the Southwest*.[31] The typewritten manual is remarkably lively and accessible, thanks to her liberal use of capitalization, underscoring, and quotation marks, not to mention the author's curiously appealing turns of phrase. The handbook confirms Colter's own pedagogical nature. She had taught high school years before, and the manual—like

206

the Watchtower itself—shows her still a teacher at heart. And in the facts she amassed, the theories she propounded, and the questions she raised, it portrays her also as the perpetually curious student. In the cover letter for the manual, addressed "Dear Boys," Colter chides the guides for having brought the book upon themselves "by asking questions about this and that and the other thing. . . . So it's your own fault if you are scared by the bulkiness of this manual." She assures them they "aren't expected to learn it by heart," that they should familiarize themselves with what they would say to their charges. "You'll get lots of practice!—and it won't be long before you begin to rattle it off 'parrot fashion'—and when it comes to that point, I won't love you any more!" She signed the letter: "Your very sincere friend and happy passenger, M. E. J. C."[32]

The Watchtower at Desert View is the most abstract and least domestic of Mary Colter's works. This was not a hotel or a cozy corner for relaxation but more of a pure architectural experience. Despite Colter's desire to ensure that the structure would intrude but modestly on the land, it commands one's attention, competing with the Grand Canyon itself. At the same time, the tower is Colter's most powerful cultural statement. It went the farthest of her buildings to introduce the depth of Native American culture to the traveler, while taking them the farthest from their own realities as white Americans. For the best of reasons, the Watchtower intrudes immodestly on the memory. ⌗

The need for additional lodging at the Grand Canyon, more modestly priced than at El Tovar, had been on the National Park Service's agenda for years. Little had been done to meet that need on the south rim, however, even during the prosperous 1920s, other than to build automobile-camp log cottages[33] and to squeeze travelers into the Bright Angel Hotel and its retinue of cabins and tents, together known as Bright Angel Camp. Elsewhere in the park, Phantom Ranch opened in 1922 at the

207

bottom of the canyon, offering limited room, and the Union Pacific Railroad completed the Grand Canyon Lodge in 1928 on the remote north rim. As far back as 1917, as part of implementation of the Grand Canyon Working Plan, the Harvey Company was planning to replace the Bright Angel (1896) with a more modern facility, one enticing enough to join the company of Harvey's acclaimed chain of southwestern inns. The 1917 Working Plan, whose map for the village showed a proposed cottage community at the rim, pointed out:

THAT EVEN THE CHEAPER RATES AT THE BRIGHT ANGEL HOTEL DO NOT MEET THE REQUIREMENT FOR WHAT IS CONSIDERED TO BE THE MOST DESIRABLE CLASS OF TOURISTS AND VISITORS. EDUCATORS, SCIENTISTS AND ARTISTS AS A RULE CANNOT AFFORD TO STOP AT EL TOVAR, AND PRIDE MAKES BRIGHT ANGEL ACCOMMO-DATIONS NOT QUITE SATISFACTORY. IT IS FOR THOSE THAT THEY NOW PROPOSE...THE CONSTRUCTION OF A GROUP OF ARTISTIC AND PLAIN, BUT CLEAN AND LIGHT HOUSEKEEPING COTTAGES.[34]

At that time Mary Colter had drawn up preliminary schemes for such a community of cottages, but the company diverted her to other projects, mostly outside the canyon, and ultimately the Depression intervened. Tourism sagged to a low of 89,000 visitors to the south rim by 1933. Recovery from the sharp drop-off was on its way, however, and visitation began to rebound the next year, and in 1935 reached 175,000. The lack of an adequate water supply had also hampered development in the village. Water had for years been hauled in railroad tank cars from 125 miles distant. A new system completed in 1932 tapped a more generous supply from Garden Creek at Indian Garden, located halfway down the canyon. To transport materials and workers down to the Garden, a cable tramway was built. A pumping plant was constructed that sent water up to the rim through two-and-a-half miles of pipe.[35] Before the tram was dismantled at the end of the project, Colter rode it down to Indian Garden, suspended high above the canyon in a wooden box. A well-known photograph shows her staring soberly out from the crude gondola surrounded by bemused construction workers and park officials.

The recovery of tourism and the augmentation of the water supply spurred the Harvey Company and the Santa Fe to thaw out their expansion plans. According to one account, "they were, in fact, pushed by National Park management, concerned about inadequate facilities, faster than the profit picture encouraged them to go."[36] Construction of accommodations resumed, led by the new Bright Angel Lodge.

The goal was to sweep away the old hotel, two other major buildings adjacent to it, and the military-base-like grid of cabins and tent sites that crowded behind them, in favor of much more felicitously designed and sited hostelry. The Harvey/Santa Fe planners knew that their addition had to hew to the Park Service's policy that improvements should harmonize with the landscape. They also retained the basic notion of the new facility as a village, in this case centered on a main lodge. Colter submitted proposals for the lodge, which she first interpreted as an imposing stone building. One of her alternatives called for a two-story structure perched directly on the rim whose roundness, rugged walls, and tapered windows echoed the recently completed Watchtower. But the Park Service objected to building right on the rim, since it would interrupt the promenade of tourists.

Colter came back with a new building not only pulled back from the rim but radically redesigned as a low ranch-like lodge built of logs and stone. To its west she arrayed a bevy of cabins and other guest buildings set informally but carefully onto the rocky rise above the promenade. The Park Service approved this scheme. Prior to construction, Colter built a scale model of the entire complex, which covered a table

Mary Colter prepares to descend into Grand Canyon on the tramway used to help build a water line from Indian Garden.

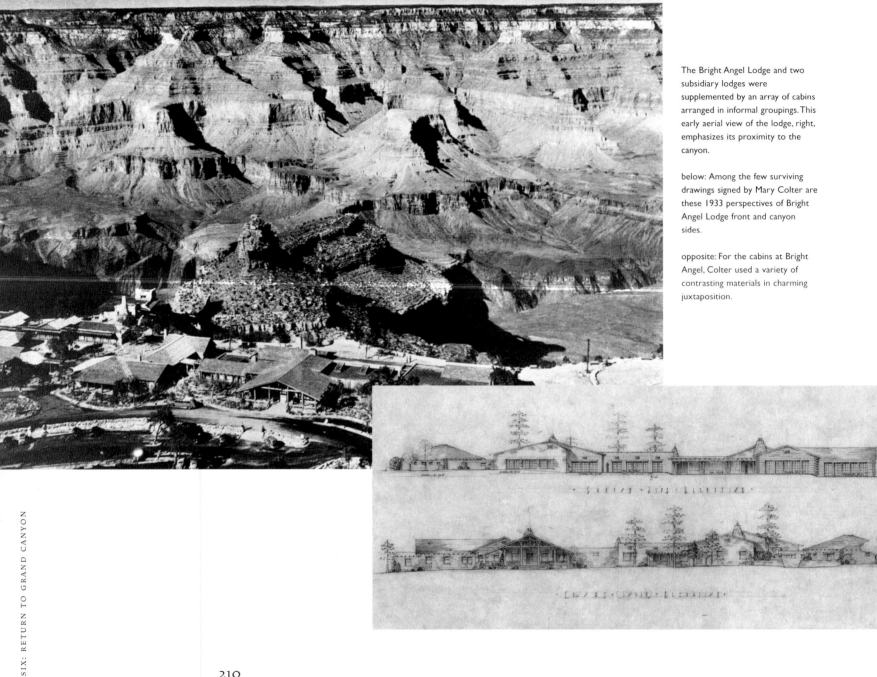

The Bright Angel Lodge and two subsidiary lodges were supplemented by an array of cabins arranged in informal groupings. This early aerial view of the lodge, right, emphasizes its proximity to the canyon.

below: Among the few surviving drawings signed by Mary Colter are these 1933 perspectives of Bright Angel Lodge front and canyon sides.

opposite: For the cabins at Bright Angel, Colter used a variety of contrasting materials in charming juxtaposition.

more than six feet long. Every building was represented—fashioned in its particular architectural style and colored to show the various stone, log, or stucco finishes—and every tree was inserted into the maquette, using sprigs from actual trees.[37]

"In the development of the new Bright Angel lodge, park visitors will see a pleasant and practical innovation in national park construction," reported an account of the September 1934 meeting (attended by Colter and her boss, J. F. Huckel, Santa Fe Railway officials, and the park's superintendent, Miner R. Tillotson) at which the project was announced. "In their rambling, one story design, the buildings suggest an interesting little village which has gradually grown up on the rim of the canyon."[38] Colter did not seek to present a specific "history" to her hamlet, as she had done with some of her other projects, but the amiable assembly suggested such. With the informality of its plan and the simplicity and diversity of its architecture, the grouping gave the air of having accumulated slowly over the years. She located some of the guest rooms in two small lodges linked to the main lodge by covered walkways and scattered the rest in cabins reached by pathways and curving automobile lanes.[39] Junipers and piñons softened and unified the compound.

Fourteen Bright Angel cabins, single-story buildings of one to four units, were completed by June 1936, one year after the main lodge opened.[40] They are among Colter's most inventive works. Here her talent for styling and juxtaposing materials proved especially successful. Picking from a menu of log slabs, rough stone, straight or wavy-edged clapboard, board-and-batten siding, irregular wood shingles, and stucco (studded with vigas), Colter created composite facades whose abrupt changes of material, texture, and color expressed the individual units within each structure. The results, rather than awkward, were whimsical and endearing. The encounters between different rooflines—gabled, flat, and shed—were also arresting; several cabins reveal their four units within through a pinwheel of shed roofs. In the Bright Angel assemblage no single style fits all, although it is tempting to coin a new inclusive mode: Woodsy Meets Rocky Meets Santa Fe. Colter occasionally used the same "accidental" meeting of dissimilar elements to diminish the uniformity and massing of the two lodge buildings.

The guest quarters, done up in a rustic but comfortable manner, were cozy and home-away-from-home-like—"all of them low, picturesque, welcoming, restful."[41] Contemporary photos show bed and sitting rooms furnished with rocking chairs, brightly patterned rugs and drapes, bedspreads enlivened with cowboy or other designs, oil-lantern-style ceiling and wall lighting, and Colter's oft-used wrought-iron standing ashtrays. True to its original charge, Bright Angel offered three levels of comfort. Economy cabins were finished with inexpensive wallboard and wood trim. Moderately priced rooms featured vertical wood paneling, and deluxe cottages on the rim provided the greatest luxury and Grand Canyon views, not to mention rugged stone fireplaces and more extensive use of natural wood. It is interesting to observe that the higher the price of an accommodation, the more romantically rustic its interior.

In developing Bright Angel Lodge and Cabins, some forty of the old cabins were moved to the Fred Harvey Auto Camp to the southwest.[42] Not all of the old buildings were removed, however; Colter insisted on retaining the Buckey O'Neill Cabin, a gable-roofed log structure that had been incorporated into the Bright Angel Hotel, and the Cameron Hotel (or Red Horse Station), another log cabin, which had been moved to its present site and enlarged with a second story. It served from 1910 to 1935 as the U.S. Post Office. Both buildings were woven into the Bright Angel Lodge complex—the Buckey O'Neill (circa 1896), the oldest surviving building on the rim and likely the first built there, as part of the seventeen-room lodge just west of the main lodge and the Cameron (circa 1890), reduced to its original single story and outfitted as a free-standing two-unit guest cabin in the western corner of the property. Not all of the cabins originally planned were completed.

Entry to the main lodge was through a wide porch roofed by an extension of

Travelers arrive at a Bright Angel Cabin in this period photo, opposite. Interiors, below opposite, were furnished cozily with cowboy bedspreads, oil-lantern lights, sturdy furniture, and other western touches.

the ranch-house-like building's low-pitched gable. Supported by stripped log columns that forked at the top to receive roof beams and retained their branch stubs, a device Colter used throughout the Bright Angel complex, the portico might have stepped out of a Hollywood western that opened with the arrival of a stage coach rather than a Harveycar. The lobby inside was encased in logs and planks, except for a flagstone floor and a fireplace at the rear that was fashioned with immense slabs of Kaibab limestone. Above it hung a painted and feathered wooden thunderbird, an Indian symbol of the "powers of the air" that Colter had also used in the Watchtower, based on a 1908 drawing by Herman Schweizer and adopted as a Harvey Company trademark. By installing a wooden bench on each side of the fireplace, Colter contrived a small inglenook.

For the lounge just off the lobby Colter designed the most amazing fireplace of her career. This is the so-called "geological" fireplace, an intricate stack of stonework that imitates the strata of the Grand Canyon just outside the room's square and heavily framed picture windows. Here stands the geologic marvel in miniature—layered up from the worn hearthstones removed from the Colorado River bed to the Kaibab limestone at the top of the pile, taken from the canyon rim. Sandwiched between, in stones varying from slender slices to thick slabs, are bands of Vishnu schist, Muav limestone, redwall limestone, Hermit shale, Coconino sandstone, and other geologic evidence of the river's six-million-odd years of wearing down and washing away. In a span of ten feet from floor to ceiling, Colter mimicked the mile-deep canyon, working with park naturalist Edwin D. McKee to make sure the composition turned out accurate. "This was planned and designed largely on the basis of a similar rock

Another sketch by Mary Colter of the entrance side of Bright Angel Lodge

214

The lobby of Bright Angel Lodge, left, includes a fireplace crafted from huge slabs of Kaibab limestone and topped by a painted thunderbird. The "geological" fireplace in the former lounge, far left, is layered up with stones representing the strata of Grand Canyon from river to rim.

The lounge was intended to be a quiet refuge in which to gather by the fire or gaze out at the immensity of the canyon (whose drama was heightened in this mid-1930s photo by the insertion of a canyon photo into the window space).

column that I had previously built on the porch of Yavapai Station [the observation building designed by Herbert Maier east of the village]," recalled McKee years later. "At Mary Colter's request, I helped her work out the scale, locate appropriate rock specimens and check for accuracy in rock thicknesses and positions....Whenever possible specimens containing fossils were selected and at one stage we planned to have additional fossils in an corresponding column adjoining."[43] When he suddenly left the job temporarily, she wrote to him:

> YOU DESERTED ME LAST WINTER WITHOUT EVEN A GOOD-BYE! WHEN I FOUND YOU WERE GONE I POST-PONED THE BUILDING OF THE FIREPLACE TILL YOUR RETURN....WON'T YOU PLEASE, IN THE MEANTIME, CHECK THE ROCK [PARK RANGER] ED CUMMINGS HAS COLLECTED AND SEE IF THERE ARE ANY IMPORTANT OMIS-SIONS....I KNOW THE *DESIGN* I WANT BUT I DEPEND ENTIRELY ON YOU FOR THE GEOLOGY. YOU KNOW I AM NOT TRYING TO SHOW *EVERY* STRATA AND VARIATION IN *EVERY PART* OF THE WHOLE CANYON, ONLY THOSE THAT OCCUR EITHER ON THE BRIGHT ANGEL OR THE SOUTH RIM PART OF THE KAIBAB TRAILS. I WANT IT TO BE AS AUTHENTIC AND THEREFORE AS INTERESTING AS POSSIBLE OF COURSE.[44]

The tall, tapering showpiece, designed and pieced together with lapidary precision, was contrived with Colter's usual originality and persistence. An emblem of her long career, it again showed her fixation on scrupulously researching a project and doggedly stalking its materials as well as her need to closely manage the construction process. And once more it manifested Colter as a teacher, laboring to ensure that a work result not only in beauty and charm but also in instruction—of the most unexpected and pleasurable kind.

To reinforce the Bright Angel's pioneer-day aura, Colter hunted down unique and appropriately picturesque pieces to use or copy for her interiors. For the lobby and elsewhere, she converted hanging oil lamps to electricity.[45] For the cigar shop, she procured a life-sized carved wooden statue of Jenny Lind, "the Swedish Nightingale," that held cigars, said to be one of only two such figures to have survived.[46] Another prop was a Northwest Coast Indian thunderbird that she equipped with an electric light inside its head.[47] The sturdy wooden furniture she had made for the coffee shop in the main lodge—commodious curved-back chairs and dark-stained table tops supported by X-shaped legs—were the very embodiment of the term "chow down" rather than "dine." Whimsical softening was never far away, however; echoing La Posada, she painted the room's window-transom panes with colorful designs and adorned the lower halves of the stout log columns with mosaics of applied color. Colter's yen for the picturesque extended to the curio shop, another in the long line of Harvey Indian Department stores; Colter equipped it with a corner fireplace and styled its bounty of Native American and Mexican goods, working with Herman Schweizer. The thrill of the chase came through in a news story in which Colter confessed her frustration in searching for one type of item: "The lodge will be furnished with comfortable, sturdy pioneer furniture. Miss Coulter [sic] says, 'There wasn't a single covered wagon crossing the prairies but carried one of those old grandmother rocking chairs. Where are they?'"[48] She must have found some, since two mammoth rockers appeared in the lounge.

Two thousand people gathered on June 22, 1935, to celebrate the opening of Bright Angel Lodge and Cabins with a barbecue. Cowboys entertained with songs and Hopis performed ceremonial dances. In attendance also were members of the Navajo and Supai nations as well as state and federal officials and bigwigs from Fred Harvey and the Santa Fe Railway. "Because the Hopi Indians have for years been master of the art of masonry," commented one observer, "the dedicatory ceremonies for the new lodge featured members of a near-by Hopi tribe. Qu-Ja-Ho-Now (white bear), a 5-year-old Hopi, wielded a trowel in expert manner as the corner-stone for the hostelry was laid."[49] For the fete Colter added yet another layer of Old West atmosphere by decorating the lodge's lobby with westerners' hats, including a sombrero allegedly worn by Mexican revolutionary Pancho Villa.[50] That year at Christmas she added seasonal trimmings, recalled Ruth Stephens Baker, who grew up at the canyon:

> THEY HAD THE MOST BEAUTIFUL CHRISTMAS TREE IN THE LOBBY. MARY [COLTER] WAS THERE, AND SHE WANTED TO HAVE IT LOOK LIKE AN OLD-FASHIONED CHRISTMAS. WE SPENT THE AFTERNOON WITH THE SNOW GENTLY FALLING OUTDOORS, STRINGING POPCORN AND CRANBERRIES. THE BIG FIREPLACE WAS GOING, AND WE WERE SINGING CHRISTMAS CAROLS, AND GUESTS WOULD COME IN AND SING WITH US. IT WAS ONE OF THE MOST BEAUTIFUL THINGS YOU CAN IMAGINE.[51]

In its "primitive" architecture and interior design and its vernacular site plan, the Bright Angel complex can be seen as a descendant of Phantom Ranch carried out at a larger scale and with more elaborate appointments and facilities. Beginning with Hermit's Rest and Lookout Studio more than two decades prior, continuing through her Indian Garden sketches and Phantom Ranch, and culminating with Bright Angel, Colter helped pioneer and reinforce the approach to design that later came to be called "National Park Service rustic." This idiom—which emphasized simplicity, ruggedness, and the use of native materials—dominated architecture in the national parks nationwide from the 1920s into the early 1940s, producing a diverse body of highly original buildings and other improvements that attempted, above all, to fit in to the natural environment. Historian Linda Flint McClelland praises Bright Angel as one of the best such developments in the national parks for "provid[ing] model solutions for maintaining a harmony between the accommodations and the natural setting."[52] Like her earlier rustic essays, Colter's Bright Angel was also recognized in its time; *Park and Recreation Structures*, the National Park Service's grand 1938 album of exemplary structures and landscape architecture, devoted several pages of text, photos, and plan in praise of this "imaginative" and "enormously successful" project:

NOWHERE ARE THE POTENTIALITIES FOR INTEREST BASED ON A VARIETY OF
MATERIALS AND FORMS MORE COMPLETELY REALIZED THAN IN THE BRIGHT ANGEL LODGE AND ITS CONNECTED
DEPENDENCIES ON THE SOUTH RIM OF THE GRAND CANYON. THE RESULTING INFORMALITY OF THE ENSEMBLE
IS APPEALING IN THE EXTREME, DESERVING OF CLOSE STUDY, AND SHOULD INSPIRE THOSE CHARGED WITH THE
DESIGN OF LARGE-SCALE OVERNIGHT HOUSING IN PARKS WITH A DEEP DESIRE TO CREATE INFORMAL INDIVID-
UALITY OF REGIONAL FLAVOR IN AN EQUIVALENT DEGREE.[53]

By the mid-1930s, with completion of the Bright Angel group, Grand Canyon
Village development between the railroad and the canyon rim had coalesced into a
modernized Fred Harvey precinct that extended from Hopi House and El Tovar on
the east to the Bright Angel Cabins and Lookout Studio on the west. The company
had finally caught up, if briefly, with rising demands for lodging and other visitor
services. Little would be added to this Harvey hamlet until more hotel construction
was begun between the Bright Angel Lodge and El Tovar in the late 1960s. Until
then, most of the rim-side buildings in which tourists stayed or through which they
ambled were the product of Mary Colter.

Bright Angel proved to be the last major architectural commission of Colter's
career. Her final buildings—and her only non-public ones—were two employee
dormitories built nearby and soon thereafter. Although the Harvey Company had
long intended to house its workers better, the go-ahead did not come for the first of
the pair until 1936. Completed in July 1937, the Fred Harvey Men's Dormitory was
sited near the company's auto camp southwest of the attractions on the rim.[54] The
two-story, fifty-room hall was built of variously sized concrete blocks left exposed on
the exterior—"pressed cinder blocks," as they were known, similar to those Colter
had employed in the Cinder Block Court at La Posada. The use of clapboard siding
for gable ends and rough stone for a chimney and lower portions of walls softened

SIX: RETURN TO GRAND CANYON

220

Mary Colter shows plans in 1935
to, from left, Miner Tillotson,
superintendent of Grand Canyon
National Park, and Mrs. Harold
Ickes, wife of the Secretary of the
Interior.

the building's somewhat utilitarian countenance, and its shallow V shape and low hip roof pared down its apparent size. A small one-story clapboard-and-stone wing, housing a lounge, jutted out beside the entrance. The only decorative touch were panels executed in a concentric diamond pattern between lower and upper window groups. Still standing, the dormitory is a modest, background building that might not seem especially Colter-like—until one notices adornments like the panels or the wavy edge to the clapboards in the gables or the fact that the strict geometrically patterned walls of cinder blocks rise from courses of rough, irregular, and sometimes quite large, stones—a transition so typical of the architect.

Colter specified the cinder block for the Fred Harvey Women's Dormitory, which was finished in December 1937 on a sloping site just behind El Tovar. That material was dropped in favor of roughly coursed natural stone, however, possibly so the building would better match the prominent stone foundation of the hotel. The

The Fred Harvey Men's Dormitory at Grand Canyon National Park, shown in 1939

The Fred Harvey Women's Dormitory, shown in an early view

seventy-five-room structure was of similar size and shape to the men's dormitory and like it bent slightly in the middle. The use of stone chimneys and wavy-edged clapboards in the gable ends also show kinship to the earlier hall. To fit the building appropriately onto the site, Colter stepped the structure down with the slope. As was the case with the men's building, the primary interior space was a common room centered on a large fireplace; heavy wood beams lined the ceiling. Construction of the women's dormitory required the removal of four buildings, including a laundry and the

Backward - turn backward
Oh, Time in your flight
Make me a girl again --
Just for tonight.

Long enough to wish Curly
a Very Merry Christmas
with all the correct cos-
tumes and action !

" *Mary Jane* "

December 25, 1933

Colter sent this handmade Christmas card in 1933 to her Harvey Company driver, Curly Ennis.

original photography studio; the Lookout that Colter designed on the rim became known subsequently as Lookout Studio. Elimination of these buildings finally achieved the Park Service's goal, dating to its takeover of the park in 1919, to remove unsuitable architecture from the area.[55] Both of the Harvey dormitories were later renamed, the men's to Victor Hall in honor of Victor Patrosso, long-term manager of El Tovar, and the women's to Colter Hall in honor of the architect.

Interspersed among her major architectural and interior design projects, Colter worked on a number of remodeling jobs for the Harvey Company at the Grand Canyon and elsewhere. As the firm's chief architect, she was on call throughout her career to update public spaces as well as guest rooms in hotels and other attractions. The jobs might entail solely decorating or also encompass architectural changes. In the early 1930s, for example, she designed and supervised the installation of bathrooms in twenty-five of El Tovar's bedrooms.[56] Later, before starting on the Bright Angel project, she added some decorative zest to El Tovar's new cocktail lounge. Prohibition had ended in 1933, and Harvey and the Santa Fe were eager to cash in on the trade that that termination promised by inserting bars into their hotels. In 1934 she consulted with John Gaw Meem on the creation of a "tap room" at La Fonda in Santa Fe, part of a scheme to reconfigure a portion of the hotel's first floor.[57] At El Tovar, the original bar, which served also as a soda fountain during the Prohibition era, was reborn as the cocktail lounge, to which Colter added her usual unusual items. She had found a flock of ceramic roosters in a shop in Malibu, California, and displayed the colorful, variously sized birds on a wooden ledge on either side of the bar. Over the entrance she installed a highly polished copper rooster to signify the cocktail lounge, which she furnished with red leather-upholstered chairs and banquettes. Apparently Colter was wont to count the birds periodically and one day found two of them missing. The next day all of the remaining roosters were wired down.[58] A series of seven humorous drawings by western artist Dean Fausett that depicted the stages of an encounter among partying cowboys further augmented the decor. The titles tell the story: amicose, bellicose, comatose, jocose, lachrymose, verbose, and vamose.

Gale Burak, who worked many years at the Grand Canyon starting in the early 1940s, for the Harvey Company and later for the Park Service, remembers Colter working on El Tovar, probably during World War II. "I knew Byron Harvey, Fred's grandson, who then headed the company," she recalled. "He'd come once or twice a year in his private railroad car, ostensibly to check up on operations. One time I recall that he showed up when Mary Jane was doing a renovation in El Tovar. Repainting walls in the hotel rooms and long hallways meant also that the large Indian motifs and other symbolic designs, which took the place of framed pictures, had to be repainted, too. She had the crew in a tizzy, which seemed to amuse Byron and didn't help the situation."[59] Burak also knew Rose Callum, a research botanist who worked summers in the rim forests. "If Mary Jane, as we all called her behind her back, came to the canyon when Rose was there they'd have lunches together where I worked [in 1942 at the Harvey auto camp]. They'd spend an hour or so over their meal, heads together and animatedly conversing. Rose introduced me to Colter, telling her of my intensive inner canyon hiking and my 'Boston background,' which didn't seem to impress her very much."[60] Those who knew Colter well enough to address her by her first name (even behind her back) tended to use "Mary Jane" rather than just "Mary." In business and other formal situations that necessitated the use of her last name, Colter and colleagues put both middle initials on display, as in "Mary E. J. Colter" or "M. E. J. Colter."

Serving the Traveler

DESPITE THE OPTIMISM FOR THE FUTURE signified by the opening of the Bright Angel complex, the national economy remained lethargic as the Depression wore on. The Santa Fe Railway, like most companies, suffered heavy losses. By 1934 passenger revenues had plummeted to one-third of their 1929 level, and the railway was forced to cut fares and eliminate many of its short-line trains in favor of through trains from Chicago to California.[1] Revenues did not rise significantly throughout the decade.

The Harvey Company also had to retrench, closing many of the small lunch and dining rooms and hotels that had once been the backbone of the enterprise—restaurants in Emporia, Kansas, and Kingman, Arizona, for instance, and hotels in Trinidad, Colorado, and Vaughn, New Mexico. In 1938 El Ortiz—the hotel in Lamy, New Mexico, which Colter had decorated in 1910—was shuttered. The growth of faster trains with dining cars and the reduction of branch-line routes, not to mention the rivalry of other modes of travel, helped spell the death knell of these Harvey Houses. Additionally, local competition had eaten into their once exclusive domain. The loss was felt keenly. "Everyone in these small towns in the 1930s was acutely

The Santa Fe Railway's 1937 Super Chief, for whose dining car Colter designed the china, was one of the new generation of streamline trains.

aware that the railroad was their lifeline to the outside world. The aura of importance and excitement brought in with the daily trains would never be replaced," wrote Lesley Poling-Kempes in her study of the Harvey Girls. "The Great Depression was more than an economic condition in those small communities."[2]

Other, more sudden changes were coming to the Fred Harvey Company. In March 1936, Mary Colter's long-term boss, John F. Huckel, died after nearly four decades with the firm. A company vice-president and general manager, Huckel had been the driving force behind designing and supervising the construction of Harvey's hotels, restaurants, and shops. He was devoted to the history of the Southwest and successfully promoted the incorporation of its Spanish and Native American architecture and art into the new buildings of the Harvey chain as it expanded in the region after the turn of the century. "He knew that historic and aesthetic values could be joined with business development to the benefit of the latter and of general social wealth," stated an article shortly after his death.[3] With the support of his wife, Minnie Harvey Huckel, he had established the company's Indian Department in 1901 and nurtured the growth of its collection of Native American and Hispanic art. He worked for years with the department's director, Herman Schweizer, beginning with their shared effort in establishing the Indian Building at the Alvarado Hotel alongside the Santa Fe Railway tracks in Albuquerque. As Colter's superior, Huckel operated closely with the architect on many of her undertakings—molding the concepts for such structures as El Navajo and the Watchtower and then implementing their construction. With Huckel's passing, Colter lost her closest professional collaborator.

The next month saw another big loss when the company's chief vice-president, Frederick H. Harvey, and his wife, Elizabeth, were killed in a plane crash. Harvey, a grandson of the first Fred Harvey, had been the heir apparent to the Harvey empire. His death at forty and the loss of Huckel shifted power and responsibility from the company's Kansas City headquarters to its Chicago offices, where Frederick's uncle Byron worked as president. The decision to move the Harvey Company head offices to Chicago was neither surprising nor long in coming; the transfer was completed by 1938.[4]

The Bright Angel and dormitory buildings were Colter's final architectural projects. Whether she suspected this at the time is not clear, but surely she realized that economic conditions and mounting competition from the automobile and airplane were depressing the demand for Harvey/Santa Fe construction outside of the Grand Canyon. Yet she remained a versatile, and thus valuable, designer for the Harvey Company. The Arts and Crafts sensibility that had permeated Colter's education shaped her outlook on the visual arts and informed her professional performance. She was the complete designer, able to assemble adroitly architecture with its allied arts into big-picture projects. She could focus on the components of a job—its interior or landscape, for example, or even such particulars as a mural or a chandelier—with as much enthusiasm and authority as on the building itself. This aptitude carried over into her decorating and other non-architectural projects, many of which were renovations, even of her own work. Adaptability helped her to serve long after she had designed her last building. Colter turned sixty-eight in 1937 but was about to sail into a series of new design projects.

Among its financial woes, the Santa Fe was facing increasing competition from other railroads like the Chicago, Burlington and Quincy, and the Union Pacific, which had launched passenger fleets of new streamlined trains powered by diesel locomotives. A new era was beginning of faster, more efficient, but also more stylish trains. The Santa Fe responded in kind with the sleek and speedy Super Chief, a first-class-only weekly train between Chicago and Los Angeles that was pulled by a diesel locomotive engineered by the Electro-Motive Corporation. It superseded the Chief, which had been the top-flight train since 1926. The Super Chief's eight cars, air-

conditioned and uncommonly luxurious, were planned by celebrated architect Paul Philippe Cret in collaboration with Chicago designer S. B. McDonald and the Santa Fe's advertising chief, Roger W. Birdseye. They lavished southwestern colors and Native American motifs throughout the nine-car, all-Pullman train. Cars were given evocative Indian pueblo names—Laguna, Isleta, Taos, and Oraibi for the sleepers—and outfitted sumptuously with an array of materials. Enjoying special prominence were wood veneers crafted from such exotics as satinwood, sycamore, ebony, and teak. Passengers in the beige, brown, blue, and orange Acoma lounge car could rest their cocktails on a bar of zingana wood. Custom woven carpets in Indian motifs and Art Deco lighting fixtures stood out among the other deluxe trappings. In perhaps the ultimate statement of opulence, the Navajo sleeper-observation car was decked out in a turquoise-painted ceiling, reproductions of sand paintings, goatskin lamp-shades, and upholstery based on Navajo motifs.[5]

The Cochiti dining car was named for a pueblo surrounding the Mission San Buenaventura de Cochiti, which was located on the Rio Grande north of Albuquerque and dated back at least seven centuries. The designers paneled the car, operated by the Harvey Company, in Bubinga wood and colored it in warm brown, brick red, ebony, and burnt orange. They asked Mary Colter to design its table china in a Native American vein. Colter adorned the china with motifs from pottery made in the thirteenth century or earlier by the Mimbreño Indians, inhabitants of the Mimbres Valley in present-day southwestern New Mexico. She was already quite knowledgeable about their whimsically stylized, animated representations of animals and birds, fish and insects, and humans, having used some of these figures to decorate the walls of the Watchtower. She continued her Mimbres research for the Super Chief project, as southwestern writer Erna Fergusson, a friend of Colter's, depicted:

The Cochiti dining car was, like the other Super Chief cars, sumptuously designed in a southwestern motif.

Ancient pottery made by the
Mimbreño Indians supplied the
motifs Colter used for her Super
Chief china. A set of original
Mimbreño dishes, opposite,
photographed in 1937.

WHEN MISS COLTER OF THE HARVEY SYSTEM DECIDED TO USE THOSE AMUSING FIGURES, SHE WENT TO THE MUSEUM OF NATIONAL HISTORY IN NEW YORK. THEY HAD, SHE FOUND, NO END OF THE MIMBRES POTTERY IN A WAREHOUSE OVER IN BROOKLYN. A DAY'S TAXI-FARE, A LONG SEARCH FOR THE MAN WITH THE KEY, HOURS OF COPYING IN A HUGE LOFT UNDISTURBED FOR YEARS, AND THESE VIVID AND HUMOROUS RUNNING QUAIL, INQUISITIVE RABBITS, AND TENDER FAWNS WERE BROUGHT OUT FOR THE JOY OF MODERN TRAVELERS.[6]

The Mimbres' art was one of the great discoveries of the heady early twentieth-century era of southwestern research. The Mimbres and their pottery were first publicized by anthropologist Jesse Walter Fewkes in a series of essays begun in 1914. Renowned archaeologist Alfred V. Kidder reported on Mimbres culture and art as part of his well-known study of southwestern archaeology in the 1920s,[7] and more information came to light from a site excavated by Harriet ("Hattie") Cosgrove for Harvard University, starting in 1924. In about 1935, Colter bought a book about that venue, *The Swarts Ruin: A Typical Mimbres Site in Southwest New Mexico*, that included drawings of pottery sporting the designs that she decided to use on the Harvey china.[8] Colter reproduced the figures, changing them very little, and also used the ancient pieces' cleverly varied geometric borders, which Kidder had praised as "extraordinarily well executed, with a delicacy of line and an accuracy of spacing unequaled in Southwestern ceramic art."[9]

The Santa Fe commissioned the Onondaga Pottery Company of Syracuse, New York (the predecessor of the Syracuse China Company) to manufacture the service. The company had for years made china for the railway. Colter worked with Onondaga's talented chief of product design, R. Guy Cowan, who arrived at the company in 1932 after an illustrious career in Cleveland as the head of the Cowan Pottery.[10] Not surprisingly, given her typical insistence that instructions be carried out to the letter, Colter turned down Cowan's first samples. As Max Palmer, who worked at that time for the china firm's Chicago distributor, E. A. Hinrichs &

Company, described it, "[t]he black used was a solid ceramic black, a color the Mimbres could not or did not produce. Furthermore the lines were too perfect. They did not look like they had been painted by a twig that had been chewed. This was the method the Indians employed in their pottery painting. Soon Syracuse caught the spirit."[11] As she had done so many times before, Colter favored authenticity over regularity. "Miss Colter knew what she wanted and she generally got it," Palmer observed. "All respected her authority in this area and bent to her dictates completely. While she may have been critical of someone's interpretation or attempts to develop her wants, she was always kind in her criticism of their efforts, and allowed them a second chance."[12]

Using a brick red accented by a blackish brown, Cowan applied the thirty-seven different Mimbreño decorations that Colter interpreted to an ivory body color, creating a service of thirty-nine different pieces. Over time, fifty-four pieces were made. The results were fetching—as striking as and in happy harmony with the Cochiti's modern interior. Stamped on the reverse of each piece was a circular logo enclosing one of the Indian figures and reading "Ancient Mimbreño Indian Designs Made Expressly for Santa Fe Dining Car Service." Used on both the Super Chief and an upgraded Chief, the service turned into a hit with the public. On its maiden run the Cochiti offered diners an array of dishes artfully served on Colter's china—among them poached tranche of salmon (70 cents), old-fashioned boneless chicken pie (85 cents), and sirloin steak for two ($2.75). *The Hotel Monthly* showcased the chinaware in a 1938 article that stated that "Miss Mary Colter . . . created a truly American design" and went on to illustrate it with various foods from the trains' soup-to-nuts dinner menu.[13] Onondaga produced the Mimbres china from 1937 until 1970 for the Santa Fe, which used the ware until it ended its passenger service in 1971.[14]

In creating the Mimbres ware, Colter was adapting to the smooth simplicity of the Art Moderne style that had come to pervade much of architecture and interior

design in the 1930s, most eloquently in transportation design. Through the use of horizontal banding, flowing lines, and curving concave and convex surfaces, the style expressed speed and efficiency in trains, cars, airplanes, ocean liners, and even road-side buildings. Materials like stainless steel, glass, enameled metal, and linoleum were popular. Art Moderne suggested effortless, unimpeded movement; it also connoted progress, a notion particularly appealing during the Depression. The visual effect was known as "streamlining," and the style itself came to be known as the Streamline Moderne. "Streamliner" was the label for the shiny new generation of trains like the Super Chief that were replacing the boxy trains that had long traveled the country. The first Super Chief departed Dearborn Station in Chicago on May 18, 1937, in a blizzard of publicity, its christening attended by actress Eleanor Powell and other celebrities. The train reached Los Angeles in just under thirty-seven hours, setting a new record and even beating its own schedule. The Santa Fe had turned out a new and sophisticated star, and Hollywood's own screen idols soon made the train the fashionable mode of transcontinental travel, bringing instant glamour to the cities and towns in which it stopped.[15]

The Westport's cocktail lounge was a bright, curvilinear room outfitted in the fashionable colors and materials of the day.

Art Moderne was very much the inspiration behind Colter's next project, the Westport Room, a new Fred Harvey restaurant and cocktail lounge in the Kansas City Union Station. It replaced the dining room that she had decorated when the building opened more than two decades before but that, grand as it was, had been losing money. With its lowered ceiling and smaller size the new facility was more subdued and much simpler than the old. Colter finished the room with smooth, undecorated surfaces—walls of uniform bleached aspen wood, plain round ceiling lights set into a soft-gray acoustical ceiling, and shiny round bronze-finished columns. She installed cove lighting and blocked out the old windows that brought in daylight, which were positioned too high for the new room, in favor of stylized and indirectly lit openings

237

equipped with glass Venetian blinds and framed by copper "drapes." Hard edges were softened with a dark blue-black carpet and dark red mohair-covered chairs and banquettes (or "bancos" as they then were known) along the walls. Colter designed the furniture specifically for this installation, finishing the chair legs in Swedish birch of the same color but darker than the walls and topping the plywood tables with bleached aspen veneer. Serving tables were given the same treatment. "Even the side table is modern," boasted Restaurant Management magazine, encapsulating the modish intent of the project and showing how magical and specific the tag "modern" still was at that time.[16] When the Westport Room was fitted out for dinner with tablecloths, it became a worldly, almost nightclub-like space—a fitting cousin to the streamlined trains pulling into the tracks below. Soon after the restaurant opened in June 1937, a local society weekly pronounced it "a delightful new setting for Fred Harvey's famous cuisine."[17]

At either end of the restaurant room, three large murals were installed, two depicting pioneer life along the Missouri River landing in Westport, the 1840s settlement that grew into Kansas City, and a third showing the Santa Fe Trail. One of the former portrayed the arrival of a steamboat, and the latter showed the departure of a covered wagon; the foregrounds of all three were filled with animated men, women, and children. The muscular and high-minded murals were painted by Hildreth Meiere, a prominent New York City artist whom Colter hired. Meiere's murals and mosaics adorned many American public buildings, New York's Temple Emanu-El and St. Bartholomew's Church among them, and she also crafted tile and marble mosaics for the extraordinary Nebraska State Capitol that Bertram Goodhue designed.[18]

For the adjacent cocktail lounge, Meiere painted a less sober set of settlers from the early days, cartoonish figures shown singing, dancing, playing instruments, and otherwise enjoying themselves. Color lithographs of some of these murals were used for the wine-list covers. This bright little room was even more modern—and

The sleek Westport Room, shown opposite left on a Fred Harvey menu cover, marked a departure for Colter.

The Westport Room wine list, opposite right, used figures from the room's Meirere murals.

The Westport Room

**IN THE UNION STATION
KANSAS CITY, MISSOURI**

Fred Harvey "3000 MILES OF HOSPITALITY" Series
See back of menu for description and further details about this series.

Wine List

FROM MURALS BY HILDRETH MEIERE
IN COCKTAIL LOUNGE

The Westport Room

Fred Harvey
Union Station
Kansas City, Mo.

239

with its curvilinearity, moderne—than the dining room. Shaped like a pear and adorned with a semicircular bar, curved banquettes, and round tables, it seemed all curves. Colter even turned an unavoidable and conspicuous structural column from a defect into a standout: a fat round pillar wrapped in ivory linoleum that handsomely anchored the bar. The color scheme was light—chairs and banquettes upholstered in golden-yellow imitation leather, wooden chair frames and table bases stained silver gray, tables and the bar topped with a composition material in another gray, and the bar front finished with yellow linoleum. A dark gray carpet helped ground the composition, and mirrors added depth. The foyer between the bar and restaurant mediated between the two through use of the same carpet as in the bar, for example, and by sporting a dark blue wall that picked up the hue of the dining room carpet. A bit of the old Colter whimsy shone through here with her inclusion of wrought-iron standing ashtrays, the witty abstract animals that she had used in so many prior projects.

Colter carried off the Westport Room and bar with aplomb. Photos show them as well-tailored, intimate spaces, their suave modernity burnished by Meiere's narrative murals. It is intriguing to compare Art Moderne's emphasis on the new, the progressive, and the international, however, to Colter's lifelong passion for age, history, and regional reference. The romantic look of instant age that she applied to materials, the irregularities of construction and finish that she insisted upon, and the notion that a room could be a museum of charming or even obscure objects were not to be found here. The murals supplied the only element of regional and historical character, aside from ornate dinner-menu covers retained from the prior restaurant and the full skirts and cameo pins worn by the waitresses. It is not known whether Colter chose the rooms' modern theme or if her company wanted it that way. The death of John F. Huckel, which had removed an enduring presence from Colter's professional life, also dissolved the aesthetic compact that the two had built up over the years. Colter had to please a new boss with tastes new to her. In the Kansas City area, moreover, the railway, Fred Harvey, and probably Colter herself would not have been as drawn to the use of motifs based on native Americana as they were in the Southwest, and Hispanic cultural reference in the vicinity was nonexistent. Furthermore, the landscape of the region was far from the captivating spectacle that it was in the Southwest. Colter restricted regional derivation to the region itself. 🖭

For her next job, designing the restaurant for the new Los Angeles Union Passenger Terminal, Colter was offered the chance to blend contemporary architecture and art with historical reference in a way she had not done since the El Navajo hotel and depot in the early 1920s. The terminal, the last of the nation's great metropolitan railroad stations, did not open until 1939. This tardiness was ironic, since Los Angeles and southern California had long been both the geographical objective of the Santa Fe line—the end point implied by the timeless slogan, "Santa Fe All the Way"—and the golden goal that had sent so many thousands of passengers westward in the first place. The fresh young city by the blue Pacific, the soft climate, and the region's agricultural wealth—a mind's eye confection of orange groves stretching to the horizon—exerted a tremendous pull on the imagination of easterners. True, the advertising imagery that the railway and its Harvey partners employed so

A "streamlined pueblo," the Los Angeles Union Passenger Terminal, was the last of the big-city stations. The pavilion to the right housed the restaurants that Mary Colter designed.

241

successfully for so long centered on the Southwest. But without California as the direct or implied goal for the rail journey, fewer people might have been bold enough to travel through or tarry in New Mexico and Arizona. The journey "all the way" was hardly new: One of the first of the railway's trains to head toward Los Angeles, and its first luxury train, was called the California Limited; it debuted in 1892, five years after the first Santa Fe train arrived in that city on its own tracks.

Yet, to the city's embarrassment, the rite of that arrival paled beside the style and drama of departure via the noble stations of Chicago and Kansas City or even the fanciful mission depot of Albuquerque. Since 1896 the Santa Fe in Los Angeles had occupied La Grande Station, a peculiar jumble of Victorian motifs crowned with a Moorish dome. The other transcontinental lines, the Southern Pacific and the Los Angeles and Salt Lake (later absorbed by the Union Pacific), operated from a series of modest terminals. The dearth of a union station was not for lack of trying, however. Since the 1910s the three railroads had been urged to consolidate into a single station near the historic plaza where Los Angeles was founded, but they fought the idea, fearing increased competition. Even after the state railroad commission ordered construction of the station in 1921, nothing ensued other than continued resistance to the project. In 1926 a public referendum backed by the city and the *Los Angeles Times* approved the plaza terminal. Once again the issue foundered. The combatants fought all the way to the U.S. Supreme Court, which in 1931 threw out the railroads' opposition. Construction finally started in 1934.[19]

"There may be larger terminals in many of the metropolitan cities of the east and midwest but none more modern or better planned and none so beautiful and glamorous," declared California's *Architect and Engineer* magazine.[20] The new building's style was a latter-day interpretation of the Mission Revival that had long been the choice for stations and hotels built throughout the Southwest by the Santa Fe and other railroads. The revival flowered most fully in southern California, where

243

it was born in the late nineteenth century and used for city halls and other civic buildings, churches and schools, and houses. This station was no Alvarado, however—no florid, parapet-walled, tower-happy fantasy of Spanish California but a stripped-down, clean-cut, and modern-day rendition. (The fond parlance of the day was "ultra-modern.") The building has also earned the label Spanish Colonial Revival, among others.[21] The lead architects were John and Donald B. Parkinson, father and son, who designed many iconic Los Angeles landmarks, including city hall, Memorial Coliseum, and the Bullocks Wilshire flagship department store.[22] They fashioned the station as a long asymmetrical cluster of variously sized pavilions and wings interlaced with arcades and patios. In its style, massing, and rather "rancho" appearance, it seems a cousin to Colter's La Posada. Hewing to the Spanish theme, the roofs are of red tile and the walls of stucco. Three huge arched windows and a matching entryway sculpt the facade next to a tall but polite clock tower. Ornament, discreetly applied on the exterior, breaks out in greater profusion within, much of it as tiled floor and wainscot mosaics that, along with geometric lighting fixtures and pencil-gothic signage, exude an Art Deco air. Superbly trussed and coffered wooden ceilings, however, dispel any doubt that this was meant to be a Spanish building. The Santa Fe summed up the effect crisply: "streamlining a pueblo."[23]

Through an open-air arcade to the right of the main entrance stands Colter's project, the interior of the Fred Harvey restaurant pavilion, which enclosed lunch and dining spaces and an adjacent cocktail lounge. The main dining room and lunch counter occupied the primary space, a large and lofty hall framed by three massive Moorish-style arches. Colter fashioned the floor of red, black, and buff cement tile whose colors and pattern—a staccato of black-and-buff bars at the sides framing lightning-like zigzags that gather together in a crescendo at the center—suggest a modern Navajo weaving. The pattern is also Art Deco in its nervous geometry. Just as ingenious are the two sculptural forms that Colter designed to mask air vents on

For the cocktail lounge at L.A. Union Station, Colter devised a heady blend of the historical and modern.

The outside entrance to the cocktail lounge, below, framed Spanish doors with striking Art Deco boxes.

either side of the glass-paneled entry arch. Looking like huge brooches, perhaps, or upside-down Deco-fantasy facades, they step upward from the bottom and outward into the room, framing metal grills elaborated with spirals. Fixed with stair-step brackets at the base, they distantly echo the architectural trappings of El Navajo. At the same time, six circular chandeliers with shiny metal banding speak a more Moderne language. Colter carried the Spanish aura of the rest of the station through with wall panels finished in diamond-patterned colored tile mosaics, within which perch images of parrots. The diamonds are mimicked in paint in the ceiling coffers.

The traditional lunch counter was still a Harvey House feature, although Colter shrank it here to a single horseshoe near the kitchen that seated twenty-seven; tables in the center, set with nail-head-trimmed leather chairs, and raised booths next to each of the long walls accommodated 200 more. The niches were sectioned off with low leather-covered partitions that were tooled in the corners with a floral pattern. Perched above, behind an ornate metal balustrade on a balcony that rests on heavy brackets, is the mezzanine dining room, a recessed space that Colter styled Spanish provincial with random-width white-pine paneling and a vaulted ceiling finished in patterned acoustical tile. She carried some of the historical aura into the cocktail lounge with a floor of herringbone-patterned paving bricks, leather-seated barstools with spindle legs, and rivet-studded leather-clad entrance doors, but surrounded the entry with a bright up-to-date statement: projecting box panels of back-lit bubble glass adorned with "cocktails" spelled out in an Art Deco face. A copper-sheeted bar, mirrors, curving walls and soffit reminiscent of the Westport Room lounge, and strips of red indirect lighting further "ultra-modernized" the room.[24] Beyond the bar Colter built in two facing rows of curved booths separated by copper-backed, bubble-glass mirrors and undulating walls whose juncture with the ceiling was accentuated by continuous strips of recessed red lighting. The effect must have been intoxicating, even without the aid of alcohol.

As in so many other train stations, the restaurants were patronized both by travelers and city residents, and the owners made a point of encouraging this. The Fred Harvey Company took out its own newspaper advertisement, bidding Angelenos to "come down during Opening Week and see your beautiful new Union Station, and pay a visit to the City's newest fine Restaurant."[25] Reigning Hollywood gossip columnist Hedda Hopper soon gave the place her kiss of celebrity approval: "Newest rendezvous in town is cocktail room at our Union Station. So pleasant there it's a joy to miss your train. No one wants to catch one."[26] Her last sentence was unwittingly prophetic, an augur of lean days to come for both the passenger railroads and the station.

Not a hint of that dolor was in the air in May 1939, a month after Colter turned seventy, when a proud Los Angeles opened the $11-million edifice to the world. Some 500,000 people showed up for the first event of a three-day fete: a parade of military equipment, floats, and marching bands down Alameda Street—including the Santa Fe's famous All-Indian Band from Winslow, home of its La Posada hotel. Dubbed "Railroads Build the Nation," the cavalcade climaxed with a procession of historic rolling stock from the three railroads that built the terminal. Tours, receptions, and a formal dedication followed, and the crowd was treated daily to a historical pageant entitled "Romance of the Rails," staged with help from the railroads, Hollywood studios (DeMille, Twentieth Century-Fox, Paramount), the Federal Theatre Project, and even the Boy Scouts of America. A men's chorus of railroad workers supplied the music.[27] The debut of Union Station was a gigantic party that portrayed the story of the railroads as a lustrous yesterday fated to be followed by a radiant tomorrow. ⌗

In 1940, with the station project out of the way and the Fred Harvey Company main offices recently relocated from Kansas City to Chicago, Colter decided to move from her apartment in Kansas City and into the Altadena, California, house that she had bought years before for her late sister, Harriet.[28] Colter had been spending much of her time there anyway during the station job and likely figured that she would continue working for Harvey in the Southwest, so she would still be conveniently situated. She packed up her considerable Kansas City possessions, which included oriental furniture, a large collection of Indian jewelry, pottery, and baskets, and an extensive library of books on architecture, design, and history. Some she transferred to storage in Kansas City and the rest to Altadena.

Soon Colter was at work on another remodeling, the design of a new cocktail lounge at the Alvarado in Albuquerque, the hotel where she had begun her Harvey career nearly forty years before. Here she was back in her old element of steeping an environment in atmosphere and age to suggest a story or long-ago place. Colter contrived the lounge, La Cocina Cantina (literally "the kitchen barroom"), to represent an old Mexican ranch kitchen agreeably recast as a bar. The room featured a large whitewashed-brick fireplace of the type one could cook in. Plans were made, in fact, to cook and serve Mexican food in the hearth during the winter. All around she placed her finds: old tiles with letters on them that she arranged to spell out Spanish sayings like "a vuestra salud" (to your health) and "no con quien naces, sino con quien paces" (not with whom you were born, but with whom you pasture); old European bottles, including one that was an 1852 miniature of opera star Jenny Lind; and drop lights fashioned from Mexican parrot cages. According to one account, "there was some talk of having a live parrot in one of them trained to say: 'Another old-fashioned, please.'"[29] The floors were brick, and the front of the bar was built of brick, tile, and brass. Once again Colter brought in Harvey artist Fred Geary, this time to paint designs in turquoise, magenta, deep purple, orange, and green between the layers of double-glazed windows. The panes washed the lounge in the afternoon with tinted sunlight.

For the newly created outdoor patio next to the lounge, Colter hung lamps on tall iron standards. She had found the lamps at a racetrack in Mexico, where they had survived a fire, their colored glass fusing into iridescent shades. Adorned with wrought-iron railings, a flagstone floor, trees, vines, and flowering plants and separated from the street by a high wall punched with small grilled windows, the patio was "the perfect place to spend a leisure hour."[30] Commented one review of the Cantina's opening in July 1940:

> ONE'S FIRST IMPRESSION IS OF GAIETY AND COLOR. ONLY LATER DO YOU REALIZE THE LACK OF BRAND-NEWNESS [SIC] THAT USUALLY ACCOMPANIES OPENING DAYS. EVEN BEFORE IT WAS QUITE FINISHED, PREVIEWERS REMARKED AN AGED-IN-THE-WOOD QUALITY THAT IS THE ESSENCE OF CHARMING INTERIORS AS WELL AS GOOD BEVERAGES. YOU CAN CHALK UP THAT MIRACLE TO THE UNFALTERING TASTE OF MISS MARY COLTER, WHO HAS BEEN DECORATING HARVEY HOUSES FOR A GREAT MANY YEARS. THOSE WHO WORK WITH HER SAY MISS COLTER NEVER SPARES HERSELF EITHER RESEARCH OR TROUBLE TO ACHIEVE AUTHENTICITY AND HARMONY.[31]

Colter also designed a fittingly decorous uniform for the lounge's waitresses, a Spanish-style dress with a long flowing skirt that she topped with a boldly patterned scarf worn like an apron. Harvey Girl Violet Bosetti, who was assigned to the Cantina when it first opened, described her encounter with Colter:

> MARY JANE COLTER SAW ME AND PULLED ME ASIDE AND SAID SHE WANTED TO MAKE A SPECIAL COSTUME FOR ME TO WEAR IN THE CANTINA. I WAS NOT BEAUTIFUL, BUT DIFFERENT-LOOKING—ITALIAN, A LATIN TYPE. A SEAMSTRESS CAME IN AND MADE ME THIS BEAUTIFUL DRESS LATER WORN BY ALL THE HARVEY GIRLS IN THE CANTINA. THEY WERE ALL LOVELY WOMEN AND IT MADE THE CANTINA VERY ELEGANT.[32]

"Within and without these new-old rooms and gardens, you are invited to seek your pleasure," stated a Harvey Company brochure,[33] and it was not long before La Cocina Cantina became popular for both travelers and Albuquerqueans. Among the more famous regulars was journalist and war correspondent Ernie Pyle, who lived in the city in the early 1940s. He wrote that "we like it here because you can do almost anything you want to, within reason. In four months, I haven't been out of overalls more than a half dozen times," he wrote. "And I go to the Alvarado Hotel's swell Cocina Cantina always in my overalls, and nobody raises an eyebrow."[34] ⊡

After the United States entered World War II in December 1941, the national economy shifted gears. Non-essential travel was frowned upon, and difficult and lavish vacations a near impossibility. Patronage for the Harvey Company's hotels, tours, and other attractions all but evaporated. Yet the war proved a shot-in-the-arm for both Harvey and the Santa Fe. Although the tourism industry may have been unnecessary for the war effort, with the railway's facilities the two organizations amassed invaluable know-how. Soon the Santa Fe found itself in the business of shipping troops and Harvey in the industry of feeding and lodging them. "Every month more than a million meals are prepared in diners, in hotels and restaurants operated by Fred Harvey," the Santa Fe reported, "and most of these meals are for Uncle Sam's fighting citizens."[35] Sagging patronage recovered at Harvey Houses along the line, and some of the closed houses were even reopened.

Harvey's traditionally gracious service and lavish environments had to give way—most painfully at the larger, more luxurious hotels like Colter's La Posada. Since it was a major meal stop for hundreds of troops at one time, the Winslow hotel's serving space was stretched far beyond its normal capacity. The dining and lunchrooms were supplemented by porches, the lounge, the lobby, and hallways, and the round dining tables were replaced by banquet seating. Throughout the system,

Harvey had to placate local residents who found themselves shunted aside. In response, the company took out ads in national magazines portraying a fictional Private Pringle who symbolized the many actual soldiers who ate, slept, and traveled by train to Harvey facilities. "We're grateful for your good-humored acceptance of this temporary situation," read one of the ads. "When Private Pringle's big job is done we promise you again the Fred Harvey hospitality you have learned to expect.[36]

Because of the war, the Harvey Company's active planning for new or remodeled hotels and restaurants ground to a halt, and much of the time Mary Colter found herself without a busy work agenda. She may have been involved in making some of the physical arrangements at hotels and restaurants to accommodate the troop traffic. Meanwhile, in November 1943 her colleague and friend Herman Schweizer died at the age of seventy-two. The enduring genius of the Indian Department, which he had helped found in 1901 under the patronage of John F. Huckel and his wife, Minnie Harvey Huckel, Schweizer had for decades been recognized for his understanding and promotion of Native American art. He was unusually well rounded, serving as an accomplished trader, retailer, and advisor to museums and individual collectors. Among the latter was newspaper czar William Randolph Hearst, who amassed a large collection of Navajo textiles that he purchased through Schweizer over some thirty-five years. Directly and indirectly, Schweizer encouraged public appreciation of Indian art and artists. He hired potter Maria Martinez and her husband, Julian, for example, to work for Harvey making pottery at the 1915 Panama-California Exposition in San Diego; this was years before they

became nationally famous.[37] Schweizer also ran the company's curio shops at stations and hotels and worked with Harvey's public relations force on many of its promotional publications.

Schweizer had helped Colter in one way or another on most of her projects— from the very first, her decoration of the Indian Building at the Alvarado, through the great hotels, tourist attractions, and interiors that she designed in the 1920s and '30s. He accompanied her on trips to study ancient Indian towers in the Four Corners area in preparation for her Watchtower project. In 1990 writer Frank Waters recalled their relationship: "Miss Colter worked closely with Herman Schweizer, was very fond of him, and told me much about him."[38] Like Colter, Schweizer never wed but enjoyed a remarkable professional marriage. By the end of the 1930s, however, his role in the Harvey firm was diminishing. Tourists' tastes and buying habits had changed, a trend to which he was not blind. "People just simply are not looking for anything except modern products and mostly cheaper things," he complained in 1939.[39] Moreover, travelers were no longer captives of the Santa Fe and Harvey and could find their own way, usually by car, to the Southwest's scenic and ethnic attractions. Pressured by Huckel, the Harvey Company had earlier sold parts of the Indian Department's collection to museums in Kansas City and elsewhere. The company's president, Byron Harvey, was well aware of the changing market and tried to further shrink the department's holdings. "With the new fast train schedules eliminating or cutting down the stop at Albuquerque," he wrote to Schweizer in 1939, "you have practically no opportunity now to handle these things as you used to be able to handle them and this situation probably will get worse rather than better."[40] Harvey's entreaties to Schweizer to sell off more inventory apparently failed, however. Schweizer's intent all along had been to have the art reside in a museum, possibly at the Grand Canyon; ultimately, some eighty percent of the remaining collection was loaned to the Heard Museum in Phoenix.[41] 🔲

opposite above: Herman Schweizer at Mesa Verde's Cliff Palace on one of Colter's 1931 research trips

opposite below: Schweizer probably took this photo of Colter perched high up at Cliff Palace.

After the war ended, Colter stayed on with the Harvey Company, although she had passed her seventy-sixth birthday and had been working for the firm, in either full- or part-time mode, for forty-four years.[42] The days of her conjuring up and fastidiously planning hotels and other choice tourist destinations had come to an end. The demand for such attractions continued to decline, in large part due to the decrease in tourist travel on the railroads, the popularity of which had been set back by the combined impact of the Depression, World War II, and the continuing ascendancy of the private automobile. Indeed, the wartime revival of some of the smaller Harvey Houses was quickly snuffed out with the arrival of peace, and even some of the larger ones closed, like the Castañeda in Las Vegas, New Mexico, which shut its doors in 1948. El Ortiz failed to make it even that far. Closed in 1938, the little inn in Lamy, New Mexico, was razed in 1943. This was the first of the buildings on which Colter had worked to be demolished. A commentator on El Ortiz' demise wrote about the clientele it had once attracted: "the great and near-great; salesmen and statesmen; financiers and shoe clerks; artists, writers and musicians; Santa Fe 'high society' . . . all of whom would mourn the passing of the 'littlest hotel in the littlest town.'"[43] That same year, but before El Ortiz fell, Minnie Harvey Huckel, who had conceived the idea of the hotel with her husband, died.

Harvey had foreseen the ebb in railroad travel and was beginning to test the waters at off-track locations—scenic and urban sites and, in later years, highways and airports. In the meantime, Harvey's sizable and still successful presence in Grand Canyon National Park, which was much less dependent on railroad traffic, helped buoy its financial situation. At the canyon and elsewhere, the company knew it could rely on Colter's interior design talents, even as she neared retirement. She was intimately familiar with its entire system of hotels, restaurants, and shops and was an obvious choice when it came to remodeling or enlarging her own buildings and interiors. She had been attending to them for years. Thus Colter found herself back in the Grand Canyon in 1946, altering Phantom Ranch. She designed a laundry-room addition to the main lodge, a new luxury for the ranch, which had always sent its laundry up to the rim for washing.[44] Whether she rode down on muleback to inspect the site is not known, but such a feat would have been quite in character for Colter, even in her late seventies.

One of the postwar projects took Colter and the company to a location off the railroad that was fresh to both of them—the Painted Desert Inn. Situated in the northern portion of what is now the Petrified Forest National Park, near Holbrook, Arizona, the diminutive building overlooked the remote and windy Painted Desert. It was the product of a long and somewhat unsettled history. Holbrook businessman Herbert D. Lore had built the structure in 1924 as his private retreat and a tourist stop, dubbing it Stone Tree House, since he had incorporated blocks of petrified wood into its walls. To attract travelers, Lore constructed a dirt road from Route 66, the transcontinental highway that lay but a few miles to the south, and equipped the inn with a lunch counter, six sleeping rooms, and an Indian trading post that sold local Navajo and Hopi crafts.[45]

Lore's lodge was somewhat Prairie Style in appearance, with a low horizontal profile, a hip roof, and exposed stone walls. After the National Park Service acquired the building and surrounding territory in 1936, the agency laid plans to radically remodel the structure.[46] Using labor from the Civilian Conservation Corps and designs by Park Service architect Lyle Bennett, the renovation was begun in 1937. Unfortunately, the original lodge had been built on unstable clay soil, causing structural problems that slowed the reconstruction and that plague the building to this day. After nearly three difficult years a stucco-clad Pueblo Revival building brushed with Spanish Colonial flourishes emerged—a slant-walled, viga-adorned adobe composed of multiple cubic volumes that would be right at home among its brethren in Santa Fe. Inside, the inn was outfitted with heavy carved furniture, tin light fixtures of Mexican inspiration, and glass ceiling panels painted with Hopi pottery motifs.[47]

The Painted Desert Inn opened in 1940, with the addition of six guest rooms, Park Service exhibits, and expanded dining facilities. The war shut its doors in 1942, and service resumed only in 1946. Patronage did not begin to recover, however, until June 1947, when the Fred Harvey Company added the inn's concession to its familiar and highly regarded chain of lodges, restaurants, and shops. By the end of 1948 business had doubled over the previous year. In the meantime Mary Colter was brought in to redecorate the interior to Harvey standards. Arriving on site in December 1947, she promptly launched a repainting project.[48] Upon its completion, over the winter, she made or designed other improvements, most notably the replacement of windows in the curio shop and dining room with four large picture windows that enhanced the view out over the multihued landscape. These substantial plate-glass openings were reminiscent of windows she had designed for the same reason fifteen years before for the kiva/observation lounge of the Watchtower at Grand Canyon National Park and, a few years later, for the lounge of that park's Bright Angel Lodge.

As is the case with practically all of her work, Colter's scheme for the Painted Desert Inn shows her fascination not only with the natural landscape but the human as well. To the latter end, in May 1948 she brought in her old associate and friend, Fred Kabotie, to create a series of murals and other decorative art in the lunch- and dining rooms.[49] In 1933 Colter had hired Kabotie to paint the murals and craft the sand painting for the Hopi Room of her Watchtower; for the inn he once again drew from Hopi life and legend. The largest of the murals depicts the salt legend, the ceremonial journey of young men who, as an initiation into manhood, are sent to gather that essential mineral from a salt lake far from their home. "Salt is very, very important" to the Hopis, Kabotie explained. "To get this salt of theirs, the Hopi really make a big ceremony out of it. Those who are volunteered to go for [it] get the salt for their aunts. . . . When they go from home they take food that their aunts have prepared for them to take along."[50] Another mural shows a rainbow that encloses a number of

4548— THE PAINTED DESERT INN, PETRIFIED FOREST NATIONAL MONUMENT, ARIZONA   8B-H72

Painted Desert Inn shown after the building was enlarged by the National Park Service

human and bird symbols, and the third illustrates the Hopi Buffalo Dance, held in January both to venerate the animal and to ward off the cold weather. Kabotie (circa 1900–1986), who by that time had become a world-famous artist, finished the murals by July. In 1958, he had one last contact with a Colter building, although not with the designer, when he painted murals in the cocktail lounge of Bright Angel Lodge that depict native and tourist life. The dining room at the Painted Desert Inn was dedicated the Kabotie Room in 1976.

The Harvey Company promoted the inn as the destination of a quick but memorable trip off the main highway: "Here the rim juts peninsula-like into the frozen sea of brilliantly tinted waves, ridges, mounds and buttes. . . . The inn commands the finest view of the dazzling sea of colors."[51] In one respect, the park that includes the inn was not entirely new to Colter. In 1930 the Petrified Forest National Monument had supplied petrified wood to Colter for her use in decorating La Posada, the Harvey hotel in Winslow, Arizona. She employed one log section as the base of the lion fountain in the sunken garden and others to adorn the railroad side of the building.[52]

With the Painted Desert Inn project completed, Colter decided to retire from the Fred Harvey Company after forty-six years in its service. The year before, in April 1947, she had sold her house in Altadena, California, and was planning to settle back in the Southwest, most likely Santa Fe.[53] By this time in her life, she was making plans also to dispose of her collections of Native American artifacts. Mesa Verde National Park was one of the repositories that she had considered, as she described in a letter that month to Don Watson, a naturalist there whom she had known for years:

Here I am in California. I had expected to be back in Arizona and New Mexico a long time ago. I have just sold "Ifcroft"—my Altadena house of many years and have commenced to pack up my many belongings. The question arises as to what to do with my Indian things. Not the Jewelry but particularly the bulkier things like Baskets and Pots. My pottery is mainly Pueblo and I feel belongs in the Pueblo Country. As you know I favor the Mesa Verde Museum and that seems pretty close to home.

My pots have more than the usual significance in as much as I know the year in which every piece was *accquired and while some of it was bran [sic] new—just out of the oven—on the day I got it other pieces were very old even then and some of it prehistoric. The <u>first</u> piece *accquired in the collection was sent to me by friends who went to Acoma in the year 1897. Just fifty years ago! I have pieces of Hopi that I saw Nanpaio [Nampeyo] make and decorate in the years 1904 & 1905. I have owned all of it for over 40 years myself and have the date and place of buying of every piece. There are between two and three dozen pieces representing nearly every well known make....(haven't seen some of it for quite some time, myself).

IF YOU HAVE A PLACE FOR IT I WILL SEND IT TO YOU. *TOGETHER*—IT HAS CONSIDERABLE VALUE—SEPARATED—IT WOULD JUST BE POTS—SOME OF THEM VERY EXCEPTIONAL BUT SOME JUST ORDINARY....NOW IF YOU WANT IT YOU WILL HAVE TO LET ME KNOW *RIGHT AWAY*....OF COURSE, I CAN SELL IT ALL OR GIVE IT TO THE SOUTHWEST MUSEUM OUT HERE BUT IT DOES NOT SEEM TO BELONG OUT HERE. IT WILL GO EITHER TO YOU OR JESSE'S LABORATORY [THE NEW MEXICO LABORATORY OF ANTHROPOLOGY IN SANTA FE, DIRECTED BY ARCHAEOLOGIST JESSE NUSBAUM]—I THINK—OR PERHAPS THE ALBUQUERQUE UNIVERSITY.

I HAVE BEEN HAVING A REGULAR SIEGE WITH NEURITIS IN MY RIGHT ARM AND HAND. WRITING IS VERY HARD WORK—AS IS ALSO PACKING AND WORK GENERALLY. WHAT DID YOU THINK OF MY JANE [AN ASSISTANT WHO MARRIED FRANK WATERS IN 1947]? WELL—SHE GOT A FINE MAN IN FRANK WATERS! I REALLY BELIEVE HIS "MAN WHO KILLED THE DEER" COMES CLOSER TO HITTING THE BULL'S EYE THAN ANY OTHER BOOK ON AN INDIAN SUBJECT I HAVE READ.

I EXPECT TO GET BACK TO THE COUNTRY AROUND ALBUQUERQUE SOME TIME AROUND THE LAST OF MAY. WHERE WILL YOU BE? HOPE TO SEE YOU.

Among the myriad remarkable pieces of Native American art that Colter collected over the decades was this 1904 bowl made by the famous artist Nampeyo.

THE VERY BEST EVER TO YOU—
MARY E. J. COLTER

ADDRESS FOR TWO WEEKS—
526 E. LAS FLORES DR., ALTADENA, CALIF.

* IT TAKES 2 C'S TO SPELL THE WORD IN MY ESTIMATION AND I INSIST ON 'EM![54]

Colter subsequently sent the pottery and baskets to him. As for her Indian jewelry, Colter had already signaled her intent to bequeath that large collection to Mesa Verde. She knew the national park and its world-famous ruins of early Native American habitations quite well and had visited them often, most notably in the early 1930s as part of a study trip to prepare her design for the Watchtower. Located there was the National Park Service's first and largest museum. Colter had visited the park in the summer of 1944, bringing half of the jewelry with her to show Kenneth Ross, acting naturalist during Watson's war service in Europe, and acting superintendent Jesse Nusbaum, whom she had known since at least 1914, when they collaborated on the Painted Desert Exhibit for the 1915 San Diego exposition. Colter informed them that she was considering Mesa Verde among a number of museums for her bequest. In 1945 she made her decision, writing to Ross: "I have been making over my will lately and have decided to leave my Indian Jewelry to the Mesa Verde National Monument [sic] Museum. I have . . . left a certain amount of money for building such cases as would be necessary for its special housing."[55] Ross and Nusbaum were delighted. The latter man, close enough to Colter to address her as "Mary Jane" and kid her, added: "P.S. Wonder what new treasure you have recently acquired that you will tantalize me with for three years before I am privileged to see it for the first time?"[56]

To Colter, the Southwest was home. Its countryside and Native American and Hispanic cultures were what had drawn her to the region nearly a half century before. There stood the buildings she had imagined and then designed, and there lived many of the people she had come to know, either through work or socially. Ironically, Santa Fe, where she chose to retire, would be Colter's first official southwestern address. She was moving to the region that she had long studied, worked in, and loved, but home during her working years had meant mainly Kansas City, Altadena, and the

Harvey hotels and Santa Fe trains out on the line. The New Mexico capital offered a particular draw; it was a historic and cultured city and one with which she had been familiar since at least the late 1920s, when she was working with John Gaw Meem on the expansion of La Fonda.

Colter retired to a residence at 2 Cerro Gordo, a street situated east of the center of town.[57] Soon, however, her former employer came calling once again, interrupting her days of leisure with a project that would take her back to La Fonda: the expansion of La Cantina cocktail lounge. Given her familiarity with the hotel, proximity, and long record of accomplishment, the Harvey Company made a wise choice in Colter. She designed the new bar and dining space, called La Cantinita, with a rustic Spanish ambiance that recalled her 1940 treatment of La Cocina Cantina at the Alvarado. The new space was in fact vintage Colter, echoing a career's worth of evocative design, from its fireplace-dominated south wall to its hodge-podge of antique or pseudo-antique props. Colter built the homey fireplace and its simulated ovens around two structural columns, using century-old handmade bricks from the old New Mexico capitol laid up in a purposely messy manner. The wainscoting was also brick. "She made the man who did the brick dado tear that out twice because he was too meticulous and she wanted it sloppy looking," recalled Patricia Smyth, who knew Colter for many years.[58] On and above the mantel, Colter placed antique copper kettles retrieved from old Harvey Houses. The ceiling lights were progeny of Mexican chandeliers, essentially metal racks outfitted with bedroom candlesticks that were lowered at bedtime, allowing each guest to take a lit candle off to bed. Finely crafted tin wall lights recalled the folk-style fixtures that she had used in the hotel years before. The tabletops were crafted from solid walnut cured for gun stocks during World War I, and the buffet was styled like an old Mexican chest. "The warm, nostalgic charm of an old Mexican Kitchen which pervades 'La Cantinita,'" commented Harvey's company magazine, *Hospitality*, "is another tribute to the

Colter's last professional commission was La Cantinita, a new bar and dining room at La Fonda. Here she used her familiar battery of techniques to create a room from old Mexico.

imagination and ability of Mary E. J. Colter, 'retired' Fred Harvey designer and decorator.... [T]he results bespeak 'Mary Jane Colter' to anyone at all familiar with her artistry in decorating many, many Fred Harvey rooms."[59]

La Cantinita opened in July 1949. Since its construction filled in an outdoor space at the front of La Fonda, one of the hotel's many expansions over the years, it was necessary to build a new entrance down the street to the west. Colter designed

The expansion of La Fonda necessitated a new entry corridor, for which Colter brought in artist Dorothy Stauffer to paint a mural of the original *fonda*.

the entry, hiring Santa Fe artist Dorothy Stauffer to decorate one wall with a painting depicting the *fonda*, or inn, that had stood on the site of the present La Fonda three centuries before. Indians and traders, *caballeros* and *señoritas* peopled the long mural.

La Cantinita was Colter's last professional commission. Nearly a half century after she had first come to the territory of New Mexico to work for the Fred Harvey Company and its Santa Fe Railway partner, Mary Colter retired completely. In 1952 she moved to a house in a compound called Plaza Chamisal, located south of the Santa Fe River that bisects the city. The loosely organized group of Pueblo Revival houses around a looping lane had been built in the early 1930s by another woman architect, Katherine Stinson Otero (1896–1977). Otero was a pioneer in American aviation who had founded an aircraft company with her mother and enjoyed an illustrious career as a pilot, chalking up a series of feats— the first woman to fly over London, to fly at night, to fly in the Orient, and to skywrite. After developing tuberculosis, she moved to New Mexico in 1920, later marrying prominent politician Miguel A. Otero, Jr. Although she was not professionally trained as an architect, her interest in southwestern architecture led her to acclaim

Colter's last residence, left, was a house beyond the gate shown here at Plaza Chamisal in Santa Fe.

Mary Colter devoted life and career to the study of Native American art and culture, often visiting Indian villages and ruins. In 1939 she traveled to Awatovi in Arizona, below left, an abandoned pueblo that was being excavated by the Peabody Museum. The photo was probably taken by celebrated archaeologist Harriet Cosgrove, a friend of Colter's.

Colter offers a puff to a symbol on a Harveycar, below.

for remodeling or designing several houses in Santa Fe, including one she designed for herself and husband in Chamisal, situated across a private drive from Colter's. Katherine Otero was a close professional associate and personal friend of John Gaw Meem, who had been a fellow patient at Sunmount Sanitorium in the early 1920s.

The Chamisal buildings share a vocabulary of stuccoed walls, flat parapeted roofs, porches supported by carved wooden posts and corbels, and protruding vigas and canales. Their walls have rounded corners and are set with wood-plank doors and multi-paned wooden casement windows. Some of the window and door openings in the compound are framed in wood crowned with low pediments, typical of the Territorial Style common in New Mexico. Creating a hushed and private atmosphere, walls link houses to outbuildings to form private gardens like the one that Colter enjoyed next to her one-story dwelling. Her house also featured an extra-height studio in one corner with a fireplace. Otero designed her own two-story house in a sleeker Meem-type form. The other units are more rustic, exuding an added-on-to look that Otero heightened by using recycled windows, doors, fences, gates, and in one case, an old building—a very Colter-like way of imparting an air of age. It is no wonder that Colter was attracted to Plaza Chamisal.[60]

Colter's old colleague and friend, Miner Tillotson and his wife, Winifred, also lived at the Plaza. She had known Miner, who had served as superintendent of Grand Canyon National Park from 1927 to 1938, since at least the early 1920s. His final post, in Santa Fe, was director of the Park Service's regional headquarters. The Tillotsons or other friends accompanied Colter to cultural events in the city and region, including such Indian celebrations as the Inter-Tribal Ceremonials in Gallup. Retirement offered Colter new freedom to pursue the interests that had long appealed to her, and to none was she was more devoted than Indian art and life. The ceremonials had offered dances, games, art exhibitions, and other attractions annually since 1922, the year before El Navajo opened in that city, and Colter had been in attendance every year since 1924.

Colter's interest in Native American art was first kindled in childhood, when a relative, John Graham, gave her a collection of drawings made by Sioux Indian prisoners interned at Fort Keogh after the 1876 Battle of the Little Bighorn. Graham, who was stationed as paymaster at Fort Keogh, became intrigued by paintings that the prisoners made on buffalo skins. He asked them to draw their symbolic signatures—a lizard or black bear, for example—on notebook paper he provided. They gave him not only those but also sketches representing exploits of both the white man and the Indians, one of which showed an Indian buying firewater from a soldier for two and a half dollars.[61]

Colter's years of collecting were launched in earnest after she went to work for the Harvey Company in 1902, which brought her to a region rich in native art and exposed her to the milieu of its history and creation. To her advantage, employment with the company offered Colter insider purchasing privileges. "She bought so many of the pieces at cost from the Fred Harvey Company that [Herman] Schweizer finally moved to stop her," wrote Byron Harvey III.[62] But that didn't discourage Colter; she kept collecting—buying jewelry and other items at the Inter-Tribal Ceremonials and other Indian festivals, trading posts, and curio shops as well as from individuals. This, after all, was a woman with an exceptional drive and talent for tracking down just the right furnishings for her buildings.

By the time Colter retired, she had acquired more than five hundred pieces of jewelry—including such familiar forms as squash-blossom necklaces, belts, pendants, and rings, but also specialties like hat bands, fetishes, boxes, carved shells, and sculptural pieces, as well as buttons, clips, and pins. The items ranged in age from the prehistoric to the twentieth century. Colter seemed especially interested in the spectrum of creativity that they represented. She was drawn to pieces that displayed a whimsical touch—a tiny silver airplane is one example—and many of them represent animals: cowheads, mountain sheep, insects, and reptiles. Indian

Colter's jewerly, a small portion of which is shown here, included such unusual pieces as the silver biplane at the left and the large carved bone with a beaded buffalo head, below.

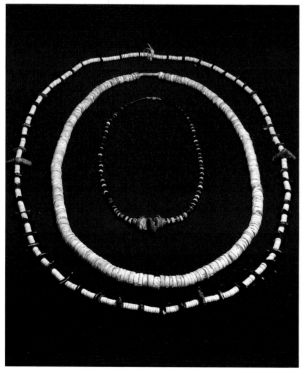

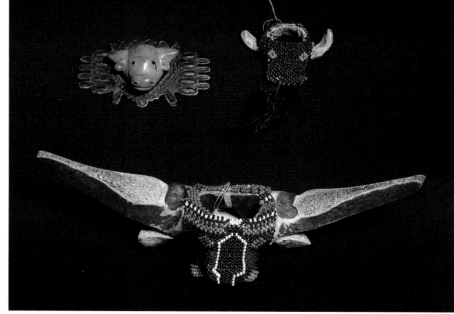

jewelry blends representational art with abstraction—the reduction of physical features or flora and fauna to lines, crosses, dots, or geometrical figures. This attribute must have particularly appealed to her design instincts; it was one she employed in architectural and interiors projects. She also admired the ingenious use of off-beat or low-cost materials—old phonograph records or hairbrush handles, for example. But metals—primarily silver but also copper, steel, and others—frequently set with stones like turquoise were the most prominent materials. Their treatment must have fascinated her as a metalworker of long standing.

Colter enjoyed the stories behind the making and acquisition of her jewelry and had made notes at purchase that proved useful when she later had to describe the pieces for donation. Under "silver necklaces," for example, she listed "necklace of coral bead and silver crosses. Crosses represent water bugs; double cross represents dragonfly with egg sack. Made at Isleta. Purchased at McMillan Shop, Santa Fe, 1945." A silver belt was described as "very old silver conchas on leather belt. Purchased from Indian in 1905." Among modern adaptations was a "necklace made from handles of brushes and combs, purchased probably from 5 and 10-cent store. A few waste turquoise— all set in DuPont cement. Black is probably battery compound." Among the odder items were ancient pieces of wampum: "Found in ant hills near Gallup, New Mexico, where ants had carried them up from graves. . . . The beads were sieved out of the ant hills."[63]

In April 1952 Colter put her jewelry on public exhibition at the Laboratory of Anthropology, a 1930 Spanish-Pueblo Revival building in Santa Fe designed by John Gaw Meem. The display illustrated the myriad forms and materials, and beguiling origins, of Native American craftsmanship. For the preview party, hosted by the Indian Arts Fund, she adorned herself fittingly. "As she moved among the guests," reported the local newspaper, "the jewelry she was wearing was as spectacular as the pieces she had chosen to be put in the cases. Everyone who remembers Miss Colter

Colter shows off a set of necklaces at the preview party for the Laboratory of Anthropology exhibition of her jewelry.

remembers her rings."[64] Indeed, almost every finger was bedecked with one, including a "path of truth" ring, set with two large sky-blue turquoise stones representing footprints that flank an oval turquoise. The symbolic use of footprints and handprints was common in Hopi and Navajo jewelry. Hands also appeared often, one on a ring that Colter was wearing that evening on an index finger; it was a coral hand, the index finger of which sported its own tiny turquoise ring. Colter had asked an Indian artist to make the ring from the hand, which was left over from a necklace she had commissioned. She was also wearing necklaces—a double one of high-quality turquoise given to her by the famous Arizona trader Lorenzo Hubbell and a long strand of wampum shells and turquoise beads; its coral inserts were spines from spiked oysters found by Indians in the Gulf of California and used for trading.

Colter often, but not always, wore jewelry. Fred Harvey's great-grandson Stewart Harvey recalled her sartorial habits: "Sometimes she wore very simple clothes, always with a jacket, but no jewelry or anything, and at other times she loaded on the jewelry like you wouldn't believe. Rings on every finger, including her thumb. Sometimes multiple rings on a finger, and the few times that I stared at her, she would bring me over and she would comment on each ring. Each ring was a treasure. And either you would be interested or you would be dismissed, so you better be interested."[65]

Age was taking its toll on Colter, curtailing her activities and sapping her energy. The Harvey Company, which from time to time reported on her activities in *Hospitality*, noted the occasion in early 1955 when she broke her hip after falling at home. Two operations were required at St. Vincent Hospital, and she spent months recuperating in bed. But the injury never healed completely, and she was mostly confined to a wheelchair from that point on. Colter was fortunate at this time to have the friendship and aid of Alvina Zimmerman, who served as her secretary and handled many of her business affairs, including the time-consuming work of cataloging her jewelry to ready it for shipment to and exhibit at Mesa Verde National Park. Colter had known Zimmerman, many years the architect's junior, since at least the time she had arrived in Santa Fe. A secretary at the National Park Service's regional office in Santa Fe, Zimmerman was helpful in many essential ways, including the writing of letters when eye or arm trouble prevented Colter from doing so.[66]

Colter had begun to organize her jewelry before the hip accident, arranging visits from Don Watson of Mesa Verde National Park to help sort out and interpret the material and from C. G. Wallace of Zuni, New Mexico, to appraise it. After Wallace's work, not performed until March 1956, Watson took the jewelry back with him to Mesa Verde. Colter also provided $2,000 in her will for display cases, expressing to Watson her "perfect confidence in whatever you do in the arrangement for the exhibit."[67] (In earlier years, she probably would have relished the task of designing the displays herself.) One thing, however, was anathema to her. In 1945 she had written to Mesa Verde's acting naturalist, Kenneth Ross: "I have specifically directed that it should not be called a *'collection!'*"[68] She did not want the jewelry or the pottery and other arts that she donated to be linked with the story of her amassing them. Instead, she wanted them arranged to narrate the history of Indian artistic endeavor—"displayed to emphasize the culture, (as shown in their artifacts used for personal adornment), of the Indians of the Southwest, from prehistoric times to the most modern developments."[69] This was Colter's final act as a teacher.

Although she was never able to visit the Mesa Verde Museum, park archae-ologist Carroll Burroughs showed her color slides of the exhibit there that Watson had prepared in the spring of 1957, a seven-panel display installed in the Colter-funded cases.[70] The exhibit was chronological, and the cultural significance of the pieces—their spiritual meaning and the way they were worn—was emphasized along with their artistry. Colter's jewelry, pottery, and baskets are now on display as part of a revised exhibit at the Far View Visitor Center, which opened in 1968, one of the many modernist structures that were built in the parks as part of the Mission 66 program.[71] Colter also donated much of her library to Mesa Verde—books on history, architecture, interior design, and archaeology that encompass many cultures, including Native American. Among the lot are such early acquisitions as *Handbook of Ornament* by Franz Meyer, signed "Mary E. J. Colter 1893." Here and there, through an inscription to her in a gift book or her own notes and markings, the finer grain of Colter's life is revealed. Pasted into many of the volumes is the bookplate that she had designed in 1899 and used all her life—a quintessential Arts and Crafts composition incorporating the initials "MEJC," a simple line drawing of a Viking ship, and a quotation: "on the other side the world we're overdue," taken from a refrain in an 1897 poem by Rudyard Kipling, "The Feet of the Young Men." Colter also bequeathed many books to the Grand Canyon National Park's community library, which was destroyed in 1994 by a fire that consumed most of her books with it.

Colter donated her Sioux drawings to the Custer Battlefield National Monument in Montana (since renamed the Little Bighorn Battlefield National Monument), returning them to the land where they had been made some eighty years before. She still maintained contact with friends she had known for decades, including the Minneapolis family of Arthur Larkin, a Mechanic Arts High School student in St. Paul whom she had befriended half a century before (see page 86). "Aunt Mary" corresponded with her namesake, Arthur's now-married daughter Mary Colter Larkin Smith, and sent her gifts, many of them treasures she had picked up over the years. One was a monk carved and painted many years before in Mexico by a "quite famous" artist whose name Colter had forgotten. "The reason I sent him to you," Colter wrote Smith, "was because I thought he would fit in quite well with your modern surroundings and that he would be happy there. I never thought he was happy with me!"[72] She had recently sent Mary a brass koumiss jug for her fireplace, of the type "used by all the Tartar Tribes of Central Asia," she explained. "This one was evidently made by one of the Tribes that kept to their old religions as witness the six armed god with which it is decorated and the Chinese letters also. No telling how old it is."[73] Arthur Larkin's sudden death in the fall of 1954 came as a shock to Colter.[74] That winter Colter's neighbor and colleague, Miner Tillotson, also died.

The world that Mary Colter knew was dimming. The great touristic collaboration of the Fred Harvey Company and the Santa Fe Railway, once Colter's passage to a singular and flourishing career, was fading away as many of its hotels and restaurants closed or fell to the wreckers. In late November 1956, the companies shuttered the dining and lunchrooms and newsstand at La Posada. That finale, while no surprise (the hotel had been operating in the red), was distressing to residents of Winslow and northeast Arizona, who found themselves suddenly deprived of the beautiful dining and gathering place they had enjoyed for many years. In what has become the architect's most famous statement, a doleful Colter remarked: "There's such a thing as living too long."[75] The hotel itself ceased operating in January 1959, after efforts to find new management or sell the property failed, and Fred Harvey concluded its twenty-nine-year lease. The elaborate furnishings that had made La Posada seem timeless, if not permanent, were photographed, hauled away, appraised, then auctioned off. Meanwhile, in July 1957 the hotel portion of El Navajo, Colter's adventurous essay in modernism, was torn down to make room for the widening of Route 66.

Mary Elizabeth Jane Colter died on January 8, 1958, three months short of her eighty-ninth birthday. Services for Colter were held at Memorial Chapel in Santa Fe, and she was buried in Oakland Cemetery, in her home town of St. Paul beside her parents and sister and next to a granite family gravestone carved "Colter." A number

Colter's points out details of the fireplace wall at La Cantinita to hotel manager David Cole.

of newspapers noted her passing, chiefly in the cities from Cleveland to Los Angeles that had enjoyed a Fred Harvey presence, in small articles headed variously "Grand Canyon tower architect," "decorator," "woman architect," or "national figure." The Harvey Company's *Hospitality* devoted most of a page to Colter, lauding buildings that "stand as memorials to her great ability and devotion to the work. . . . She had a distinguished career and was widely known for her work, particularly in the Southwest. Her contribution to the culture of the Southwest was of inestimable value." Mary Colter the person also shone through: "Many of the older members of our organization will remember her with admiration and affection not only for her great creative imagination, phenomenal energy, [and] youthful spirit, but also her colorful temperament and salty method of expression."[76]

Several years before her death, writer and husband of Alvina Zimmerman, Frank Waters, recalled Colter:

Her collections of old baskets, and Navaho and Zuñi silver, are the best I have ever seen. But it has always been life itself which has interested her most. And to it she has brought both an Irish mysticism and Irish wit, a tender heart and a caustic tongue. Indian medicine-men know her by one, her Anglo business associates by the other. If ever she can be induced to write her memoirs it will be as valuable Americana and as penetrative a study of Indian life as any we have obtained.[77]

Sadly she never did.

Colter designed this Arts and
Crafts-style bookplate with its
quotation from Kipling during her
Mechanic Arts High School days in
St. Paul and used it for the rest of
her life.

273

The Colter Legacy:
"After Me Cometh a Builder"

EIGHT

"TO MAKE WAY FOR THE WIDENING of U.S. Highway No. 66, it has become necessary to demolish our El Navajo Hotel at Gallup, New Mexico. The hotel was closed May 25th."[1] So ran a note in 1957 in *Hospitality*, the Fred Harvey magazine, announcing the passing of one of the finest buildings that the company and its life-long partner, the Santa Fe Railway, had ever contrived. The curtness of the message was understandable. El Navajo had become a minor building in an ever-booming West that paid little heed to the old and presumably obsolete, and its connection with the shrinking fortunes of the passenger railroad all but ensured that it would slip into the night unnoticed.

opposite: In July 1957 the hotel portion of El Navajo was demolished, opposite, sand paintings and all.

But some outside of Gallup did notice. That August, John B. Hungerford began his travel column for the *Los Angeles Times*, entitled "Death of an Inn," with a plaintive image: "When the lights were turned out not long ago at El Navajo, the Harvey House at Gallup, N.M., an era ended in the West—the era of the railroad hotel-restaurant. Without fanfare Gallup's hostelry . . . closed its doors to make way, of all things, for a new State highway." Hungerford had recently paid El Navajo a call:

ON NEXT TO THE LAST NIGHT I STOPPED OVER AND HAD A FINAL SAD LOOK.
OTHERS WHO HAD HEARD OF THE CLOSING HAD COME FROM AS FAR AWAY AS NEW YORK, ALL EAGER TO REVIVE
FOND MEMORIES BEFORE THE CURTAIN WAS DRAWN. THE SAME PRIM WAITRESSES WHO HAD GROWN GRAY IN
SERVICE WERE THERE, THE INDIAN BELLBOYS WERE ON DUTY AS USUAL, THE ENGINEER'S WIDOW WHO ACTED AS
ROOM CLERK WAS UNCHANGED. BUT THE ATMOSPHERE WAS THAT OF A WAKE; WE ALL FELT IT. TRAINS CAME
THROUGH, MOTOR TRAFFIC RUSHED PAST TO THE MOTELS, NOBODY CAME IN.

Hungerford's most disheartening sentence was surely this: "With the razing of El Navajo the Indian sand painting designs which adorned the walls of the main lobby will be destroyed."[2] That loss must have been especially bitter for Mary Colter and those who admired her hotel. Neither of the two articles mentioned her, however, even though she had first visualized El Navajo four decades before and then designed the little building with the grand Indian-Spanish name. With this exuberantly modernist hotel and its daring interior, Colter had taken the Harvey Company's embrace of indigenous America to a new level of confidence and style.

A year and a half later, and 125 miles to the west, the much larger La Posada sank into a forty-year slumber, emptied of its eclectic bounty of furnishings and the chatter of tourists and townspeople. The adjacent Route 66 that had threatened the passenger railroads was itself superseded in 1979 by Interstate 40, which bypassed Winslow to the north, further isolating the idyllic oasis. The great hacienda by the railroad tracks was nevertheless luckier than its Gallup sibling, for the Santa Fe Railway chose to use it for divisional offices. Although that meant ripping out the restaurants and many of the guest rooms and carving the lobby into smaller spaces, the structure, the gardens, and the railroad depot were preserved, holding on until better days came along in the 1990s.

As for Colter's interior designs, most of those along the main railway line vanished—predictably so in a culture that grants commercial interiors an even shorter shelf life than buildings. The restaurants and shops in Chicago Union Station were remodeled out of existence; those in the concourse were lost in any event when that building was razed in 1969. The Westport Room in Kansas City Union Station, itself a replacement for an earlier Colter interior, proved but a brief flower, lasting until tastes after World War II veered away from such '30s modes as the Moderne. In 1958 a steamboat-theme restaurant took its place. The Hildreth Meiere murals survived but were covered with multi-paned windows to give customers the fantasy of gazing out onto a scenic riverside. The walls were covered with gold-on-dark flocked paper, the windows hung with white-satin Austrian curtains, and new furniture installed: black plastic-cushioned benches on one wall, white on another, and curving white-leather banquettes. "An old Chinese gong was placed near the entrance and was struck whenever an order of Chicken Maciel was sold."[3] One can picture what Colter's reaction might have been. The restaurant and other Harvey shops closed in December 1968, the murals acquired by a private party, and the station shut down in 1983.[4] The restaurant at the Los Angeles station fared better. After it was shut in 1967 the furniture was removed but the interior left largely intact, which opened the view of Colter's splendid tiled floor. The station had become a ghost town, victim of the plunge in postwar passenger-railroad traffic. "Dust gathers in its once jammed restaurant and young children scoot wildly about on baggage carts in nearly empty tunnels," the *Los Angeles Times* reported two years later.[5]

The rooms that Colter decorated or designed at the Alvarado—in the Indian Building, her first Harvey project, as well as in the hotel itself—were lost to the Santa Fe Railway's controversial razing of the Albuquerque landmark in February 1970.[6] The spaces had been altered over the years anyway, and the Indian Building had faded out with the shrinking of Harvey's trackside empire, especially after Herman Schweizer's death in 1943.[7] The citizens of Albuquerque fought the demolition of the Alvarado passionately, appealing all the way to the federal government for help. One participant recalled the struggle:

WE TRIED. MY GOD, HOW WE TRIED...WE WERE JOUSTING WITH WIND-
MILLS, AND THE BIG BOYS MUST HAVE LAUGHED AT US. WE RESENTED DEEPLY THAT THE SANTA FE RAILWAY...
[WAS] NOT WILLING TO GIVE US, OR SELL AT A REASONABLE PRICE, THIS JEWEL OF THE RAILROAD ERA, THE
SOCIAL, CULTURAL AND SENTIMENTAL HEART OF EARLY ALBUQUERQUE. WE WERE DEFEATED, BUT IN ONE LAST
GRAND DEFIANT GESTURE, WE STAGED THE INAUGURAL BALL OF THE MUSEUM OF ALBUQUERQUE...IN THE
ALVARADO A FEW MONTHS BEFORE IT WAS RAZED. WE ALL DRESSED UP IN OUR FINEST, INVITED DIGNITARIES,
SERVED CHAMPAGNE AND OYSTERS, HIRED BANDS, WALTZED IN THE MOONLIGHT, AND PROMENADED ALONG THE
BEAUTIFUL ARCHED WALKWAYS...JUST AS THE PEOPLE OF NEW MEXICO HAD DONE FOR MORE THAN SIXTY YEARS.[8]

Expansion of La Fonda in Santa Fe, which first brought Colter to work on the
hotel, has recurred often, each enlargement erasing more of her presence.[9] Some of
her later work, including the space that was La Cantinita cocktail lounge (now a
pastry shop) and the front entrance hall, lives on, as do certain earlier features in the
guest suites and public spaces, lighting fixtures and occasional pieces of furniture
among them. The Lecture Lounge, now called the Santa Fe Room, offers perhaps the
best remaining sense of a true Colter room, with its dark Spanish dignity and charm.
The work of artists brought in for the first addition remains, including the sculp-
tured-tile fireplace and door surrounds of Arnold Ronnebeck and the Indian Detour
map by Gerald Cassidy. In 1969 the Santa Fe Railway sold the hotel to Sam Ballen.

The luckiest thing that can happen to a building is for it to remain in use. This
has helped protect Colter's legacy at Grand Canyon National Park. All of her structures, from Hopi House to the two Harvey dormitories, stand and mostly serve their
original purposes. Like La Fonda, Bright Angel has endured additions and remodeling, but less destructively; new wings on the eastern end have marred its shape and
blurred its bone structure, and interior tinkering has compromised spaces like the
coffee shop/dining room, lounge, and curio shop. Views of and access to the outside
are fewer; for example, the lounge's direct access to the canyon-side porch was sealed

Some of the artists' work for the 1920s addition to La Fonda remains, including the tile reliefs designed by Arnold Ronnebeck, shown right. One of his door surrounds in the Lecture Lounge is shown here.

opposite: Although its furnishings were removed, Colter's restaurant at the Los Angeles terminal remains intact, as shown in this 1990s photo.

279

off. Yet the rustic essence of the lodge and cabins survives along with delightful features like the lobby and the geological fireplace. The other Colter landmarks stand less diminished, although denatured by the creep of commercialism. That now-quaint-sounding function, the curio shop, has been pumped up exponentially over the decades, filling in spaces with goods and storage rooms at the expense of visual and aural serenity. Places conceived for rest and contemplation of natural wonders are now chockablock with *things*. The mutation became especially obvious at Hermit's Rest, Lookout Studio, and the Watchtower kiva. Hopi House was intended from the beginning to devote prominent space to the sale of Native American wares. Over the years it too suffered from overuse and crowding, but a 1995 rehabilitation reopened the long-closed second floor and otherwise improved operations and appearance. The original room vignettes created by Colter were not reinstated, for various reasons. Marketing to tourists was the original intent of all these attractions, of course, and that end endures, but at an often painful scale.

Physical ailments have also crept in—leaking roofs and, for all their seeming toughness, sagging or eroding structural members, wood, and stonework. Repointing with hard Portland cement mortar in the 1930s exacerbated the decline of stone walls at Hopi House. Seepage has been most grievous at the Watchtower, damaging large portions of the Indian murals. The steel superstructure proved inadequate to support great masses of visitors; as it flexed, out of synch with the stone exterior, that facade began to crack. The leakage is exacerbated by the deep mortar joints, fissures, jagged roofline, and other "historical" peculiarities that Colter specified. Her quest for irregularity did have its consequences. How might she react today, though—insist that the building be fixed or prefer that it molder into a real ruin?

Mary Colter's buildings endured, especially at the canyon. They grew familiar to the armies of visitors to the park there, but she herself did not. What small notice she received during her lifetime diminished even more after she died, as the

Harvey/Santa Fe promotional culture, like that of the passenger railroads, faded away and architectural fashion moved on. Modernism prevailed over the romantic-historical and site-derivative approach embodied in Colter's works. By the 1950s, architectural policy for the national parks discarded the rugged rusticity that she had promoted so successfully. Colter's obscurity, even while she lived, can also be explained by the fact that she was a woman in a predominantly male profession, that she served as the Harvey house architect for nearly all of her career, and that her production was modest and generally far from urban centers. Yet even these reasons fail to fully explain the silence surrounding her—why, for example, one could search in vain for her name in virtually every history of American architecture. Mary Colter remained outside the pantheon, a rara avis even on the rosters of also-rans.

Happily, that oblivion has proved impermanent. All along there were local Colter mavens, scholars who tended her flame, and those who looked after her buildings. Their work and changing times have brought Colter's name into a prominence that she never enjoyed herself. Many shadowed corners of history ultimately get their due. Cultures may quickly forget, but they rediscover, also, and this has been true of American architecture. Studying the design of earlier eras closely, we have reinstated once-prominent practitioners and shed needed light on unknowns like Colter. Numerous obscure regionalists have thus been retrieved. The loosening of modernism's grip on architectural culture has buoyed this reassessment. So has the rise of the American historic preservation movement, especially since the 1960s; its empowerment has not only saved buildings but also spread the stories of their creators. An important part of the preservation process, the listing of sites on the National Register of Historic Places or as National Historic Landmarks, has been particularly helpful in confirming Colter's repute.[10]

Ronnebeck's La Fonda reliefs endure also on fireplaces in the South Portal, below, and the Lecture Lounge, right. That hall still exudes some of the elegance and distinction that Colter designed for it.

The demands of merchandising have compromised some of the interior spaces that Colter designed at the Grand Canyon, as evidenced here in the main hall of Hermit's Rest.

A plateau in public awareness was reached in 1980 with publication of Virginia L. Grattan's biography, *Mary Colter: Builder Upon the Red Earth*, the first book to cover the architect's life and works. Yet a 1982 review of it in the *Journal of the Society of Architectural Historians* peevishly dismissed most of Colter's achievements, especially those after El Navajo. Deeming that structure her "most significant building," the writer judged the rest of her output a regression into eclecticism. The verdict for the Grand Canyon buildings was harsh: "Her work [there] scarcely deserves the designation of architecture. It is the work of a decorator dabbling in the natural environment."[11] Curiously, perhaps tellingly, the writer misspelled the architect's name as "Coulter" throughout the critique. An earlier review, in the *AIA Journal*, stating that the Grattan book "rescued Mary Colter from a position . . . completely out of the mainstream," asserted that Colter's "work clearly deserves recognition."[12]

In 1984 Colter was inducted into the Arizona Women's Hall of Fame, a division of the state hall-of-fame museum that honors women who enriched Arizona's development. By the end of that decade, thanks partly to a blossoming of interest in the contributions of women to architecture, her name was appearing more often in books and magazines, a trend that has continued. Public interpretation of Colter buildings, especially at the Grand Canyon, began to refer more frequently to the architect who designed them and who, after all, was an important figure in the park's history. A pamphlet distributed at the Watchtower is revealing; once devoid of reference to Colter, it was revised to credit her as well as cite her strenuous research at Indian ruins.[13] Another watershed occurred in 1996 when the Heard Museum in Phoenix mounted an exhibit on the Harvey Company's role in "inventing" the Southwest. Giving Colter prominent billing, the show helped uncloak her signal contribution to Harvey's marketing machine—credit not freely given in the past.[14] Soon she was the star of two film documentaries, one of them shown nationally on public television.[15]

In the meantime Colter's largest and most lavish work, La Posada, was stirring back to life. In the late 1980s rumors that the Santa Fe was about to transfer staff from the building fed worries that it would be shut down and maintenance would end. The company had not said it would raze the structure, but the long decline of the Santa Fe/Harvey empire—and the destruction of El Ortiz, the Alvarado, and most of El Navajo—was sufficient omen. Determined to prevent the same fate for their beloved landmark, local preservation activists Janice Griffith and Marie LaMar mounted a public rescue campaign. They took the story of the Harvey Houses and Mary Colter to the public in Winslow and beyond. Most people had lost their La Posada memories, but the duo gave talks, held tours, and badgered the media enough so that the notion of restoring the hotel finally began to take hold. They enlisted resident volunteers and the city to maintain the hotel grounds after a water line ruptured, the group dubbing itself the Gardening Angels, and also helped Winslow win a federal transportation-enhancements grant to help restore the property. Alerted earlier to La Posada's endangerment by a report from the National Trust for Historic Preservation, Los Angeles resident Allan Affeldt and his wife, Tina Mion, bought the hotel in 1997 and launched its restoration—opening up long-divided spaces, reinstating decoration, and furnishing rooms in their original style, on occasion with pieces brought back from their diaspora. During the process, in November 1997, they reopened the hotel. La Posada had been closed for four decades, longer than it had been open.

Other Colter structures have come back. In 1995, ninety years after it debuted, Hopi House was rehabilitated by its owner, Amfac, a Honolulu-based real estate development company, which strengthened the structure, installed a new roof, and replaced much of the original Moenkopi red sandstone facing with matching stone from the original quarry, located 125 miles east of Grand Canyon Village.[16] It is hoped that collaboration between the National Park Service and Amfac or any

La Posada today, above

The stair hall to La Posada's second level appears much as it did in 1930, above right.

opposite: The lounge at La Posada, relieved of the encrustation of decades, shines again.

successor concessionaire will bring about the restoration of other Colter buildings, including the Watchtower, Hermit's Rest, Lookout Studio, and Bright Angel Lodge and Cabins.[17] In some cases, retailing and food services should be reduced in size or relocated completely from landmark interiors that need restoration. Bright Angel Lodge, the most compromised of the buildings in terms of functions and floor plan, will require the most renovation.

In Gallup, the surviving railroad station portion of El Navajo came back to life in 1995. Using local, state, and federal funds, the project transformed the neglected landmark into a city-owned multimodal transportation center that offers Amtrak train and bus services as well as a tourist information center, history museum, shops, and offices of a cultural center operated by the Southwest Indian Foundation. Much of the original exterior appearance was regained through restoration of doors, windows, and facade elements; inside, woodwork and other vestiges of the early design were retained, including large wooden doors that once rolled open for baggage. A plaza on the street side, used for public events, has woven into its pavement pattern an echo of the distant heyday of the western passenger railroad: a large abstract of the Santa Fe Railway's memorable circular emblem.[18] ⌑

In *American Visions*, his 1997 exploration of the evolution of art and national character, historian and critic Robert Hughes discusses the "cultural tourism" developed by the Harvey Company, calling the Southwest "the home of mythic American primitivism." After describing Hopi House, he adds: "A gifted architect named Mary Colter, whose name deserves a permanent place among the pioneers of the American theme-park mentality, constructed ancient kivas and 'prehistoric' watchtowers with still 'older' ruins on the south rim of the Canyon, with a close eye for archaeological accuracy." A quotation follows from Colter's *Manual For Drivers and Guides* that explains the "ruins" she designed just west of the Watchtower.[19] With this citation in a nationally popular book, Colter had arrived at last, referred to favorably (perhaps ironically and slightly inaccurately) in a three-centuries-long chronicle of artistic and social change.

The linking of Colter with theme parks comes as a bit of a jolt, especially after the happy discovery of her name in the index. Yet upon reflection, the insight in this portrayal is right on target. If one weighs the role of the Harvey Company in the rise of tourism, a parallel can be seen between present-day impulses and devices and those that emerged a century ago. Harvey and the Santa Fe and their artistic executor, Colter, used time and place—history and location—to attract and delight the traveler fleeing the everyday world. They were as inventive and as successful at this theme-driven tourism then as Disney and its designers are now. Hughes's characterization infers the reliance on one of Colter's favorite practices, the endowing of new structures with quotation-mark age, albeit accurately done. Such "olding up," perhaps less scrupulously carried off, is a popular technique today. Packaging the art, architecture, and performance of Hispanic, Native American, and pioneer cultures for the convenience of the tourist, Harvey indeed "invented" the Southwest. Into, through, and beyond the twentieth century, the seduction of the traveler by carefully, even overly, wrought environments has built upon precedents set in the West by Colter and her employers. Our assessment of Colter need not shy away from this observation.

There are differences between then and now, of course, beyond the obvious one of scale. Most importantly, Colter's environments were strictly in and of the Southwest; she mined the region's history and landscape for themes as well as for myriad particulars. She remained true to the region. That is not the case today, when all the world is a stage. Las Vegas gives us not only the Southwest but also New York City, Paris, Venice, and other global venues. Southwestern imagery has, in fact, been largely discarded, the Sands and its breed replaced by Bellagio and Company. (It is intriguing that, as the last century opened, western tourism design had been purged

Rehabilitation of the remaining portion of El Navajo, top, has retained many of its original features, including the rolling baggage doors, below.

of non-American reference; as it closed, those sources were back in full vogue.) Within the framework of one region, Colter strove for cultural authenticity, whether she imitated models more or less whole (Hopi House) or synthesized a set of precedents (La Posada). For furnishings, also, she brought in or faithfully duplicated originals or designed anew in sympathy with the old. Fits of authenticity occur often enough in modern theme park architecture and interiors, oddly with the more ornate designs, but to a greater degree they are essays in exaggeration and omission. In another contrast, Colter gleaned materials from the region or even the site, an unusual exertion even in her day and more so now, when neither necessity nor sentiment require such practice. Finally, she made the site the wellspring for the building and skillfully synthesized the two, shunning any "discordant notes," as she wrote in her plans for the Watchtower. Today's architecture of entertainment rises at a scale and with a self-importance that render the site moot.

Mary Colter took pride in her work. That is evident in the confidence and thoroughness with which she carried it out. Yet she was not a self-promoter. If she viewed her buildings as monuments to anything, it was to histories and cultures. Did she nonetheless picture herself within the evolution of American architecture? Colter knew that her work was important and that it was successful. As a careful student of history, architectural and otherwise, she surely sensed more acutely than usual that there is precedent and continuation, that she might fit into history's stream. A confirming intimation of this can be found in the research that she conducted in the early 1930s in preparation for designing the Watchtower. After her travels, Colter produced four handsome albums of the photographs she had taken of Indian ruins. In the introduction to volume one (Chaco Canyon and Hovenweep) she bound a poem by one of her favorite poets, Rudyard Kipling, her moving ode to the Native Americans and the towers they left behind, to the inspiration they provided her, and to the builders and towers yet to come:

"THE PALACE"
—Rudyard Kipling, 1902

When I was a King and a Mason—a Master proven and skilled—
I cleared me ground for a Palace such as a King should build.
I decreed and dug down to my levels. Presently, under the silt,
I came on the wreck of a Palace such as a King had built.
There was no worth in the fashion—there was no wit in the plan—
Hither and thither, aimless, the ruined footings ran—
Masonry, brute, mishandled, but carven on every stone:
After me cometh a Builder. Tell him, I too have known.
Swift to my use in my trenches, where my well-planned ground-works grew,
I tumbled his quoins and his ashlars, and cut and reset them anew.
Lime I milled of his marbles; burned it, slacked it, and spread;
Taking and leaving at pleasure the gifts of the humble dead.
Yet I despised not nor gloried; yet, as we wrenched them apart,
I read in the razed foundations the heart of that builder's heart.
As he had risen and pleaded, so did I understand
The form of the dream he had followed in the face of the thing he had planned.

When I was a King and a Mason—in the open noon of my pride,
They sent me a Word from the Darkness. They whispered and called me aside.
They said—"The end is forbidden." They said—"Thy use is fulfilled.
"Thy Palace shall stand as that other's—the spoil of a King who shall build."
I called my men from my trenches, my quarries, my wharves, and my sheers.
All I had wrought I abandoned to the faith of the faithless years.
Only I cut on the timber—only I carved on the stone:
After me cometh a Builder. Tell him, I too have known![20]

ONE

1   Frank Waters, *Masked Gods: Navaho and Pueblo Ceremonialism* (Chicago: The Swallow Press, 1950), 111.

2   Harold D. Mitchell, "Architecture in America: Its History up to the Present Time," *The California Architect and Building News* (February 1882): 29.

3   Linda Flint McClelland, *Building the National Parks: Historic Landscape Design and Construction* (Baltimore: The Johns Hopkins University Press, 1998), 113.

4   Albert H. Good, *Park and Recreation Structures, Part III, Overnight and Organized Camp Facilities* (Washington, D.C.: National Park Service, 1938; reprint, New York: Princeton Architectural Press, 1999), 73.

TWO

1   Virginia L. Grattan, *Mary Colter: Builder Upon the Red Earth* (Grand Canyon, AZ: Grand Canyon Natural History Association, 1992), 2. Mary E. J. Colter, "Mary E. J. Colter," two-page typed autobiography, October 25, 1952, Fred Harvey Collection, Heard Museum.

2   The West in American history has always been a moving target, starting as the region just over the Appalachian Mountains and receding in stages toward the Pacific. "Time was when Ohio was West, Alabama and Tennessee Southwest," wrote Erna Fergusson in *Our Southwest* (New York: Alfred A. Knopf, 1940), 2. One indication among many of the former "westness" of today's Midwest is the title of the professional journal *Western Architect*—published not, as its name implies, in California or the far West but in Chicago. The upper West in the nineteenth century, including Minnesota, was also commonly known as the Northwest.

3   In 1883 the Northern Pacific Railroad, which joined St. Paul to Portland, Oregon, was completed (Grattan, 4). Ultimately that line, as part of the Burlington Northern Railroad, would be merged with the Santa Fe Railway—one of Colter's two career-long employers—into today's Burlington Northern Santa Fe.

4   Alan K. Lathrop, "Architecture in Minnesota at the Turn of the Century," in Michael Conforti, ed., *Art and Life on the Upper Mississippi, 1890–1915* (Newark: University of Delaware Press, 1994), 29.

5   *St. Paul Globe*, May 1, 1887, as quoted in Herbert Y. Weber, "The Story of the St. Paul Globe," *Minnesota History*, Minnesota Historical Society (Winter 1965): 331.

6   The guild apparently was named after the Art Workers' Guild in London, a prominent organization that is said to have given birth to the phrase "arts and crafts." Wendy Kaplan, "The Lamp of British Precedent: An Introduction to the Arts and Crafts Movement," in Wendy Kaplan and others, *"The Art That Is Life": The Arts and Crafts Movement in America, 1875–1920* (Boston: Museum of Fine Arts, 1987), 56.

7   Quoted by Marcia Gail Anderson in "The Handicraft Guild of Minneapolis: A Model of the Arts and Crafts Movement," in Bert Denker, ed., *The Substance of Style: Perspectives on the American Arts and Crafts Movement* (Hanover: University Press of New England: 1996), 217.

8   New Century Club records, Special Collections, Minnesota Historical Society.

9   Grattan, *Mary Colter*, 4.

10   Mary E. J. Colter to John A. Aubuchon, letter of October 26. 1956, referenced in Matilda McQuaid with Karen Bartlett, "Building an Image of the Southwest: Mary Colter, Fred Harvey Company Architect," in Marta Weigle and Barbara W. Babcock, eds., *The Great Southwest of the Fred Harvey Company and the Santa Fe Railway* (Phoenix: The Heard Museum, 1996), 24. Grattan, *Mary Colter*, 2, 110.

11   Nemesis Productions, *Mary Jane Colter: House Made of Dawn*, documentary film, 1998.

12 Birgitta Hjalmarson, *Artful Players: Artistic Life in Early San Francisco* (Los Angeles: Balcony Press, 1999), 28–32. *The San Francisco Art Association, 1871–1906*, exhibition brochure (San Francisco: California Historical Society, 1996). The school, one of the first such art academies in California, was renamed the Mark Hopkins Institute of Art in 1893 when it moved with the association into the Mark Hopkins mansion on Nob Hill. Both were destroyed in the 1906 earthquake.

13 The name of the firm is not known. Colter's brief 1952 autobiographical outline (note 1) states that she "studied architecture in office of San Francisco Architects."

14 Harvey L. Jones, *Mathews: Masterpieces of the California Decorative Style* (Layton, Utah: Gibbs M. Smith, 1985), 12–31.

15 It is also possible that Colter's architectural apprenticeship was with Mathews' father and brothers.

16 Nemesis Productions, *Mary Jane Colter*, 1998.

17 Richard Longstreth, *On the Edge of the World: Four Architects in San Francisco at the Turn of the Century* (Cambridge: MIT Press, 1983).

18 City of St. Paul Board of Education, "Report of Board of Education" (1899): 55. Mechanic Arts High School records, Special Collections, Minnesota Historical Society.

19 Douglas Baldwin, "The Spirit of Mechanics," in a booklet entitled "M" (St. Paul: Mechanic Arts Literary Society, 1916), 29. Mechanic Arts High School records, Special Collections, Minnesota Historical Society.

20 Mary E. J. Colter, "A Song to the Cause," in "M," 40. In another essay for "M" in which she describes the origin of the school yell, "Boom-a-Lac-a," Colter wrote: "[We] had with us the fear of extermination, perhaps, tomorrow; [we] counted daily our ranks lest even one fall out and jeopardize our cause."

21 "Mechanic Arts High School," typed manuscript, February 23, 1932, 1. Mechanic Arts High School records, Special Collections, Minnesota Historical Society. Among famous later graduates from Mechanic Arts were sculptor Paul Manship, civil-rights leader Roy Wilkins, actress Joan Davis, and Supreme Court Justice Harry Blackmun. Manship (1885–1966) would have attended the school when Colter was teaching there and may have had her as a teacher.

22 It has not been determined exactly what products were exhibited. Baldwin, "The Spirit of Mechanics," 29.

23 Unidentified St. Paul newspaper, January 19, 1905. Mechanic Arts High School records, Special Collections, Minnesota Historical Society.

24 Some contemporary newspaper accounts reported that the medal was shared by Mechanic Arts with Minneapolis' manual-training high school, which had an adjoining exhibit at the fair. St. Paul, however, as touted in the unidentified St. Paul newspaper article noted in note 23, "stood alone as an exhibitor of the most ambitious display attempted by any competing high schools." The same article reported Colter as one of "Prof. Weitbrecht's aids [*sic*]" at the display in the high school. "Mechanic Arts School Shows Art Exhibit," unidentified undated newspaper article. Mechanic Arts High School records, Special Collections, Minnesota Historical Society.

25 Grattan, 44, 46.

26 Grattan, 6. Colter, "Mary E. J. Colter."

27 Art Workers' Guild of St. Paul, "Annual Report of Secretary, Year Ending May 1, 1906." Art Workers' Guild of St. Paul records, Special Collections, Minnesota Historical Society.

28 Marcia G. Anderson, "Art for Life's Sake: The Handicraft Guild of Minneapolis," in Conforti, ed., *Art and Life*, 174.

29 Colter, "Mary E. J. Colter."

30 A typed obituary (1958) from the Santa Fe Railway files states that she did "her reading and writing of reviews of books during the wee small hours of the morning."

31 New Century Club files, Special Collections, Minnesota Historical Society, including a booklet by Lily A. Long, "The New Century Club, 1887–1922." The name "New Century Club" was not unique, for it was adopted by similar organizations during that period in New York City, San Francisco, Oakland, and Philadelphia as well as in London.

32 "The Armory Decoration," undated unidentified newspaper article in M.A.H.S. scrapbook, Mechanic Arts High School records, Special Collections, Minnesota Historical Society.

THREE

1 John W. Ripley and Robert W. Richmond, eds., *The Santa Fe in Topeka* (Shawnee, KA: The Shawnee County Historical Society, 1979), 10. The Santa Fe called itself a "railroad" before switching in 1895 to "railway" after a financial reorganization. Marta Weigle and Barbara W. Babcock, eds., *The Great Southwest of the Fred Harvey Company and the Santa Fe Railway*, (Phoenix: Heard Museum, 1996), 1.

2 Lesley Poling-Kempes, *The Harvey Girls: Women Who Opened the West* (New York: Marlowe and Company, 1991), 29–36.

3 Keith L. Bryant, Jr., *History of the Atchison, Topeka and Santa Fe Railway* (New York: Macmillan Publishing, 1974), 2.

4 Poling-Kempes, *The Harvey Girls*, 25.

5 Dee Brown, *Hear That Lonesome Whistle Blow* (New York: Holt, Rinehart and Winston, 1977), 144.

6 Bryant, *History of the Atchison, Topeka and Santa Fe Railway*, 107.

7 James D. Henderson, *Meals by Fred Harvey: A Phenomenon of the American West* (Fort Worth: Texas Christian University Press, 1969), 11.

8 Henderson, "Meals by Fred Harvey," *Arizona and the West* (Winter 1966): 314.

9 Lucius Beebe, "Purveyor to the West," *The American Heritage* (February 1967): 28.

10 Henderson, "Meals by Fred Harvey," 315.

11 Poling-Kempes, *The Harvey Girls*, 54. A vivid description of Harvey House dining was provided by novelist Edna Ferber in her 1924 short story, "Our Very Best People": "The meal marched as inevitably, as irresistibly as death itself. . . . It was a huge meal, hot, savory, appetizing. But the dining hundreds made a ghastly ceremony of it. Not a murmur of conversation; eyes on their plates. They were grimly merciless, thorough. No sounds but the clink of cutlery against china, the low voices of white starched waitresses murmuring a chant of 'Teacoffeemilk? Teacoffeemilk? Teacoffeemilk?'" Published originally in *The Kansas City Star* (July 27, 1924; reprint, June 6, 1943): 14.

12 Poling-Kempes, *The Harvey Girls*, xii.

13 Poling-Kempes, *The Harvey Girls*, xiii.

14 Frank Waters, *Masked Gods: Navaho and Pueblo Ceremonialism* (Chicago: Swallow Press, 1950), 109.

15 Sandra D'Emilio and Suzan Campbell, *Visions and Visionaries: The Art and Artists of the Santa Fe Railway* (Salt Lake City: Peregrine Smith Books, 1991), 1–2.

16 Bryant, *History of the Atchison, Topeka and Santa Fe Railway*, 111–12. Poling-Kempes, *The Harvey Girls*, 152–53. Kathleen L. Howard and Diana F. Pardue, *Inventing the Southwest: The Fred Harvey Company and Native American Art* (Flagstaff, AZ: Northland, 1996), 84.

17 Edward Hungerford, "A Study in Consistent Railroad Advertising," *The Santa Fe Magazine* (March 1923): 45. D'Emilio and Campbell, *Visions and Visionaries*, 9. The painting was hung in the new El Tovar Hotel (opened in 1905), the first of a number of locations.

18 Hungerford, "Consistent Railroad Advertising," 45.

19 Robert A. Trennert, "Fairs, Exhibitions, and the Changing Image of Southwestern Indians, 1876–1904," *New Mexico Historical Review* (April 1987): 136.

20 In addition to publications for public distribution, the railway also published *The Santa Fe Magazine*, a periodical for the company's employees.

21 Erna Fergusson, *Our Southwest* (New York and London: Alfred A. Knopf, 1940), 198.

22 Kathleen L. Howard, "A Most Remarkable Success: Herman Schweizer and the Fred Harvey Indian Department," in Weigle and Babcock, eds., *The Great Southwest of the Fred Harvey Company and the Santa Fe Railway*, 87–88.

23 Sandra D. Lynn, *Windows on the Past: Historic Lodgings of New Mexico* (Albuquerque: University of New Mexico Press, 1999), 15.

24 *Albuquerque Journal Democrat*, May 11, 1902. Albuquerque Public Library.

25 The depot portion survived until it, too, was destroyed by a fire in 1998.

26 Marta Weigle, "Mary Colter, Erna Fergusson, and the Santa Fe/Harvey Popularization of the Native Southwest, 1902–1940," *Frontiers*, vol. XII no. 3 (1992).

27 Virginia L. Grattan, *Mary Colter: Builder Upon the Red Earth* (Grand Canyon, AZ: Grand Canyon natural History Association, 1992), 6. In a letter to the author, Grattan states that Alvina Zimmerman, Colter's aide late in life, stated that Herman Schweizer sent the telegram.

28 Karen Bartlett, "In the House Made of the Dawn: The Mary Colter Story," *Craftsman Home Owner*, vol. 9 no. 1 (1997). Matilda McQuaid with Karen Bartlett, "Building an Image of the Southwest: Mary Colter, Fred Harvey Company Architect," in Weigle and Babcock, eds., *The Great Southwest of the Fred Harvey Company and the Santa Fe Railway*, 25, 34n. Howard and Pardue, *Inventing the Southwest: The Fred Harvey Company and Native American Art*, 103.

29 Grattan, *Mary Colter*, 8 (unattributed quote).

30 Elle and Tom were two of the few Indians that the companies identified by name. In one of many promotions, Elle wove a blanket that was given to President Theodore Roosevelt when he arrived in Albuquerque on May 5, 1903. Presentation of the white, red, and blue blanket provided the Harvey Company valuable publicity both within and outside the region. Elle subsequently wove a rug for President William Howard Taft. Howard and Pardue, *Inventing the Southwest: The Fred Harvey Company and Native American Art*, 58–60. Diana F. Pardue and Kathleen L. Howard, "Making Art, Making Money: The Fred Harvey Company and Indian Artisan," in Weigle and Babcock, eds., *The Great Southwest of the Fred Harvey Company and the Santa Fe Railway*, 168–71.

31 "The Alvarado, a New Hotel at Albuquerque, New Mexico," The Fred Harvey Company and the Santa Fe Railway, 1904. Kansas State Historical Society.

32 Leah Dilworth, *Imagining Indians in the Southwest: Persistent Visions of a Primitive Past* (Washington, D.C.: Smithsonian Institution Press, 1996), 87. The location of this room, shown on page tk of this book, is probably the most often published photo of the Indian Building, is not entirely certain. According to Byron Harvey III, who has written extensively on the Harvey collections, "this was the salesroom of the Alvarado Hotel complex, not the museum." (Weigle and Babcock, eds., *The Great Southwest of the Fred Harvey Company and the Santa Fe Railway*, 74 (emphasis his)). His use of "complex," however, clouds the issue, since that could be interpreted to still placing the room in the Indian Building (if not the museum per se).

33 Howard and Pardue, *Inventing the Southwest*, 12.

34 At the time, there were a number of gorges called "grand canyon," including the Grand Canyon of the Yellowstone and the Grand Canyon of the Arkansas, so the Arizona chasm was known as the Grand Canyon of the Arizona, sometimes spelled "Cañon" in the Spanish mode. Gordon Chappell, "Railroad at the Rim: The Origin and Growth of Grand Canyon Village," *The Journal of Arizona History*, Vol. 17, No. 1 (1976): 105–106n.

35 Stephen J. Pyne, *How the Canyon Became Grand* (New York: Penguin Books, 1998), 88.

36 Bryant, *History of the Atchison, Topeka and Santa Fe Railway*, 186. Chappell, "Railroad at the Rim: The Origin and Growth of Grand Canyon Village," 94.

37 Pyne, *How the Canyon Became Grand*, 6.

38 Parks historian Linda Flint McClelland traces both hotels' designs to "the frame-and-timber construction and romantic Swiss and Scandinavian style architecture of the camps and lodges of the Adirondacks," in which Andrew Jackson Downing played a role, as well as to naturalistic urban-park structures designed or inspired by Frederick Law Olmsted and H. H. Richardson. Linda Flint McClelland, *Building the National Parks*, 3–4.

39 *The Hotel Monthly* (June 1908): n.p. Hospitality Industry Library and Archives, University of Houston.

40 William H. Simpson, "El Tovar by Fred Harvey: A New Hotel at Grand Canyon of Arizona," Santa Fe Railway, 1905. Grand Canyon National Park Museum Collection.

41 Woodward Architectural Group, Phoenix, "Project Description: Use of Masonry in Design," 1997 (summary for award submission for Hopi House restoration). Author's interview, James Woodward, March 30, 2000.

42 William C. Tweed, Laura E. Soulliere, and Henry G. Law, *National Park Service Rustic Architecture: 1916–1942* (San Francisco: National Park Service Western Regional Office, 1977), 8.

43 Grattan, *Mary Colter*, 14–18.

44 George Wharton James, *The Grand Canyon of Arizona: How to See It* (Boston: Little, Brown, 1910), 126.

45 Howard and Pardue, *Inventing the Southwest*, 105–110. Dilworth, *Imagining Indians in the Southwest: Persistent Visions of a Primitive Past*, 89, 232n.

46 W. H. Simpson, "El Tovar by Fred Harvey: A New Hotel at Grand Canyon of Arizona," 23.

47 Fred Harvey Company, *The Great Southwest Along the Santa Fe*, brochure, sixth ed., 1921, n.p. La Posada Hotel files.

48 Miner R. Tillotson and Frank J. Taylor, *Grand Canyon Country* (Stanford: Stanford University Press, 1929), 27, as quoted in Mark Neumann, *On the Rim* (Minneapolis: University of Minnesota Press, 1999), 37.

49 Research in recent years suggests that Voth was on site more frequently than Colter, who still lived officially in St. Paul. Architect James Woodward cites, among other evidence, letters from Voth at the Grand Canyon to his superiors at the Field Museum in Chicago. Also, it is possible that since Colter at that time was not yet a permanent Harvey employee, she was not able to take complete charge of a project as she would later on. Author's interview with Woodward, March 30, 2000.

50 McQuaid with Bartlett, "Building an Image of the Southwest: Mary Colter, Fred Harvey Company Architect," in Weigle and Babcock, eds., *The Great Southwest of the Fred Harvey Company and the Santa Fe Railway*, 26, 34n.

51 Grattan, *Mary Colter*, 19. "Mary E. J. Colter," two-page typed autobiography, October 25, 1952. Robert Spector, *More Than a Store: Frederick and Nelson, 1890 to 1990* (Bellevue, Washington: Documentary Book Publishers, 1990), 1–25.

52 In 1896 Frederick and Nelson brought an exhibit of Japanese prints, costumes, and other wares to Seattle.

53 Michael Conforti, ed., *Art and Life on the Upper Mississippi, 1890–1915* (Newark: University of Delaware Press, 1994), 63–71.

54 In an interesting sidelight, Native Americans, encouraged by Frederick and Nelson's owners, sold handcrafted baskets and other wares on the sidewalk in front of the store. Given the tremendous appeal of Indian arts to Colter, one wonders what notice she took of these street vendors and whether she ever incorporated such crafts into store displays.

55 Grattan, *Mary Colter*, 19.

56 Grattan, *Mary Colter*, 21–22.

57 Mary N. Woods, *From Craft to Profession: The Practice of Architecture in Nineteenth-Century America* (Berkeley: The University of California Press, 1999), 80–81, 99.

58 Woods, *From Craft to Profession*, 76.

59 Lamy was named for the famous Catholic archbishop, Jean Baptiste Lamy (1814–1888) of Santa Fe.

60 Chris Wilson, "Pflueger General Merchandise Store and Annex Saloon," National Register of Historic Places nomination, (February 17, 1987), 3.

61 Wilda Sandy, *Stalking Louis Curtiss* (Kansas City: Ward Parkway Press, 1991), 11–12, 81, 87. Fred T. Comee, "Louis Curtiss of Kansas City," *Progressive Architecture* (August 1963): 128–134.

62 Byron Harvey, III, "The Fred Harvey Company Collects Indian Art: Selected Remarks," in Weigle and Babcock, eds., *The Great Southwest of the Fred Harvey Company and the Santa Fe Railway*, 74.

63 Diane H. Thomas, *The Southwestern Indian Detours* (Phoenix: Hunter Publishing, 1978), 298.

64 David Gebhard, "Architecture and the Fred Harvey Houses," *New Mexico Architect* (July/August 1962): 11–17.

65 "Lamy, the Town the Railroad Built," *The Atom* (April 1966): 18.

66 Harvey, "The Fred Harvey Company Collects Indian Art: Selected Remarks," 74.

67 "Lamy, the Town the Railroad Built," 19.

68 Owen Wister, "A Preface by Owen Wister," typed manuscript for the Architectural Book Publishing Company, November 1922. Fred Harvey Collection, Heard Museum. Wister wrote it for a book on houses designed by Philadelphia architects Mellor, Meigs, and Howe. It is curious but perhaps not surprising, given the purpose of the book, that Wister does not transfer any of his effusive praise for the hotel to either Curtiss or Colter, failing to mention either designer by name.

69 *Santa Fe New Mexican*, [n.d.]. Fred Harvey Collection, Heard Museum.

70 *Kansas City Star*, (August 9, 1943): n.p. Fred Harvey Collection, Heard Museum.

FOUR

1 "A Dream Come True," *The Santa Fe Magazine* (November 1914): 44. Santa Fe Railway Archives, Kansas State Historical Society.

2 "A Dream Come True," 48.

3 Lesley Poling-Kempes, *The Harvey Girls*, 116–17. Peter A. Hansen, "Give the People a Monument," *Trains* (April 1999): 62–72. Conover C. Smith, "Fred Harvey Closing Marks End of Era," *Kansas City Times* (December 28, 1968): 12C. "A Dream Come True," 40–44.

4 His brother Byron moved to Chicago to manage the dining-car division.

5 *Kansas City Star*, (March 28, 1915): n.p.

6 Mary Colter to Mary Colter Larkin, telegram, February 13, 1913. Courtesy Mary Colter Larkin Smith.

7 Mary Colter to Mary Colter Larkin, October 19, 1913. Courtesy Mary Colter Larkin Smith.

8 Mary Colter Larkin Smith, author's interview, December 10, 1999.

9 Patricia Smyth, author's interview, June 22, 2000.

10 *New York Sun* (May 7, 1903): 8. J. Donald Hughes, *In the House of Stone and Light* (Grand Canyon, AZ: Grand Canyon Natural History Association, 1978), 65–66.

11 Stephen J. Pyne, *How the Canyon Became Grand* (New York: Penguin Books, 1998), 116.

12 "Grand Canyon Village Historic District," National Register of Historic Places registration form (January 17, 1990): 17–20.

13 Mark Neumann, *On the Rim: Looking for the Grand Canyon* (Minneapolis: University of Minnesota Press, 1999), 39.

14 George Wharton James. Fred Harvey Company postcard.

15 Grattan, *Mary Colter*, 26.

16 Fred Harvey Company, *California and the Grand Canyon of Arizona* (Chicago and New York: American Colortype Press, 1914), n.p.

17 Fred Harvey Company, *The Lookout, Grand Canyon* (Arizona, 1915), n.p.

18 Marta Weigle with Kathleen L. Howard, "'To Experience the Real Grand Canyon': Santa Fe/Harvey Panopticism, 1901–1935," in Weigle and Babcock, eds., *The Great Southwest of the Fred Harvey Company and the Santa Fe Railway* (Phoenix: The Heard Museum, 1996), 19.

19 The first large fair exhibit that the Harvey Company prepared for the Santa Fe was at the St. Louis fair, the Louisiana Purchase Exposition. Displayed in the Anthropology Building, the exhibit won four awards, including two grand prizes— for the best ethnological exhibit and for the Navajo blanket exhibit. Kathleen L. Howard and Diana F. Pardue, *Inventing the Southwest: The Fred Harvey Company and Native American Art* (Flagstaff: Northland Publishing, 1996), 57, 62–63.

20 Howard and Pardue, *Inventing the Southwest*, 75. Matilda McQuaid with Karen Bartlett, "Building an Image of the Southwest: Mary Colter, Fred Harvey Company Architect," in Weigle and Babcock, eds., *The Great Southwest of the Fred Harvey Company and the Santa Fe Railway*, 34.

21 "Model of Indian Pueblo Shows Santa Fe Exhibit," *San Diego Union* (March 24, 1914): 1. Accompanying the article was a photo of the model being inspected by Schweizer, noted archaeologist Jesse Nusbaum, who oversaw construction of the village, and Santa Fe official Clifford Payson. San Diego Public Library.

22 Phoebe S. Kropp, "'There is a Little Sermon in That': Constructing the Native Southwest at the San Diego Panama-California Exposition of 1915," in Weigle and Babcock, eds., *The Great Southwest*, 36–46. Kropp analyzes the ways in which the exhibit's presentation of Native Americans furthered the interests of the Santa Fe Railroad and the Harvey Company, and also, by way of contrast with other exhibits at the fair, "cast regional progress in terms of conquest and racial succession."

23 Even the sheep were genuine, for Schweizer smuggled in a carload of the animals from Gallup, New Mexico, on the night before the fair opened, to avoid the official animal inspects. Howard and Pardue, *Inventing the Southwest*, 76.

24 "Santa Fe Railroad's Indian Pueblo Marvel of Primitive Craft," *San Diego Union* (January 1, 1915).

25 Ford Harvey, "The Public and the Grand Canyon," *Proceedings of the National Parks Conference* (Washington, D.C.: U.S. Government Printing Office, 1917), 323. Cited in Mark Neumann, *On the Rim: Looking for the Grand Canyon*, 135.

26 "Grand Canyon Village Historic District," National Register registration form, 21–22.

27 Most texts and many maps spell the site as "Indian Gardens," but historically it was known as "Indian Garden." Colter, however, used the plural.

28 Grattan, *Mary Colter: Builder Upon the Red Earth*, 32.

29 *Kansas City Times* (November 23, 1916). Fred Harvey Collection, Heard Museum.

30 Grattan, *Mary Colter*, 25. David Gebhard and Robert Winter, *Architecture in Los Angeles: A Complete Guide* (Salt Lake City: Peregrine Smith Books, 1985), 379–383.

31 National Park Service, "Report of the Director of the National Park Service" (Washington, D.C.: Government Printing Office, 1918), 274.

32 Linda Flint McClelland, *Building the National Parks: Historic Landscape Design and Construction* (Baltimore: The Johns Hopkins University Press, 1998), 153, 164.

33 "Grand Canyon Village Historic District," National Register registration form, 22–24.

34 Quoted in McQuaid with Bartlett, "Building an Image of the Southwest: Mary Colter, Fred Harvey Company Architect," in Weigle and Babcock, eds., *The Great Southwest of the Fred Harvey Company and the Santa Fe Railway*, 33.

35 William C. Tweed, Laura E. Soulliere, and Henry G. Law, *National Park Service Rustic Architecture: 1916–1942* (San Francisco: National Park Service Western Regional Office, 1977), 28.

36 McClelland, *Building the National Parks*, 165.

37 McClelland, *Building the National Parks*, 113–14.

38 "Mules could only carry six-foot sections of wood down. Thus, Colter had to design beams strong enough to hold up the roof out of six-foot sections bolted together in an offset manner." Keith B. Green to author, January 7, 2001.

39 Grattan, *Mary Colter*, 37. "Phantom Ranch," National Register of Historic Places nomination form [draft] (n.d.): 1–3. "Over New Kaibab Trail From Rim to Rim," *The Hotel Monthly* (September 1928): 70–71. Keith B. Green, "The Early History of Phantom Ranch," Arizona Historical Society (February 1987): 4–8.

40 Lewis R. Freeman, *The Colorado River: Yesterday, To-Day and Tomorrow* (1923), excerpt quoted from typed manuscript in Special Collections, Cline Library, Northern Arizona University.

41 Gale Burak worked many years at the canyon, including Phantom Ranch, and recalled Colter as "a very imaginative and intelligent person who was quick to get the romanticism and impact of a name that would lend intrigue to somebody. Certainly they wanted people to come down, and Phantom would be a very nice name for something down in the deep recesses, out of general sight on the rim of the Canyon." In Betty Leavengood, *Grand Canyon Women: Lives Shaped by Landscape* (Boulder, CO: Pruett Publishing Company, 1999), 38.

42 "The Alvarado of Albuquerque, New Mexico," *The Hotel Monthly* (October 1922): 50–51. "Enlarged Lunch Room of Alvarado Hotel to be Open Monday for Public Inspection," *The Albuquerque Herald* (December 3, 1922): n.p. New Mexico State Library.

43 "The Fred Harvey 'Santa Fe' Service," *The Hotel Monthly* (October 1928): 39–42.

44 J. F. Huckel to R. H. Clarkson, July 11, 1928. John Gaw Meem Collection, University of New Mexico. Marcia G. Anderson, "Art for Life's Sake: The Handicraft Guild of Minneapolis," in Michael Conforti, ed., *Art and Life on the Upper Mississippi, 1890–1915* (Newark: University of Delaware Press, 1994), 130–31.

45 "The Fred Harvey 'Santa Fe' Service," 42.

46 Erna Fergusson, *Our Southwest* (New York: Alfred Knopf, 1940): 203–204.

FIVE

1 *New Mexico State Tribune*, May 25, 1923.

2 Claire Shepherd-Lanier, "Trading on Tradition: Mary Jane Colter and the Romantic Appeal of Harvey House Architecture," *Journal of the Southwest*, vol. 38 no. 2 (Summer 1996): 179, 182.

3 David Gebhard, "Architecture and the Fred Harvey Houses," *New Mexico Architect* (July/August 1962): 16. Soon after El Navajo opened, *The Hotel Monthly* called it "the oddest modern hotel structure that we have ever printed," in "El Navajo Hotel Reflects the Painted Desert," *The Hotel Monthly* (July 1923): 42.

4 "Navajo Sand Paintings as Decorative Motive," *Albuquerque Daily Herald* (May 26, 1923) reprinted in *El Palacio*, vol. 14 no. 12 (June 15, 1923): 176.

5 Information provided by Gallup historian Sally Noe, author's interviews, March 30 and October 2, 2000.

6 "El Navajo Hotel Reflects the Painted Desert," 40.

7 Nancy J. Parezo, *Navajo Sandpainting: From Religious Act to Commercial Art* (Tucson: University of Arizona Press, 1983), 1–21.

8 Parezo, *Navajo Sandpainting*, 23, 51. Leland C. Wyman, *Navaho Sandpainting: The Huckel Collection* (Colorado Springs: The Taylor Museum, 1960), 25–27.

9 "Navajo Sand Paintings as Decorative Motive," 179–183.

10 Sam Day, Jr., Collection, correspondence of J. F. Huckel, et. al., Cline Library, Northern Arizona University. Kathleen L. Howard, "'A Most Remarkable Success': Herman Schweizer and the Fred Harvey Indian Department," in Weigle and Babcock, eds., *The Great Southwest*, 86.

11 Frank Waters, *Masked Gods: Navaho and Pueblo Ceremonialism* (Chicago: Swallow Press, 1950), 111.

12 Shepherd-Lanier, "Trading on Tradition," 189. James David Henderson, *"Meals by Fred Harvey": A Phenomenon of the American West* (Fort Worth: Texas Christian University, 1969), 31.

13 "Contract Awarded for Gallup Harvey House Addition," *Albuquerque Herald* (July 23, 1922): n.p. Fred Harvey Collection, Heard Museum. The article also mentioned that the addition's foundation would be designed to support a third story.

14 "A Remarkable Indian Ceremony," *The Santa Fe Magazine* (July 1923): 17–22.

15 "A Remarkable Indian Ceremony," 21.

16 Will C. Barnes, "Arizona Place Names," *University of Arizona Bulletin* vol. VI no. 1 (January 1, 1935). From the Mary Colter book collection, Mesa Verde National Park Library.

17 Bainbridge Bunting, *John Gaw Meem: Southwestern Architect* (Albuquerque: University of New Mexico Press, 1983), 7–8.

18 Shepherd-Lanier, "Trading on Tradition," 182, 184–85.

19 Parezo, *Navajo Sandpainting*, 52.

20 Virginia L. Grattan, *Mary Colter: Builder Upon the Red Earth* (Grand Canyon, AZ: Grand Canyon Natural History Association, 1992), 44.

21 "Fred Harvey, Caterer, Chicago Union Station," *The Hotel Monthly* (August 1925): 53. Fred Harvey Collection, Cline Library, Northern Arizona University.

22 "Fred Harvey, Caterer, Chicago Union Station," 57.

23 Sandra D. Lynn, *Windows on the Past: Historic Lodgings of New Mexico* (Albuquerque: University of New Mexico Press, 1999), 31–37.

24 Bunting, *John Gaw Meem*, 8–9.

25 Chris Wilson, *The Myth of Santa Fe: Creating a Modern Regional Tradition* (Albuquerque: University of New Mexico Press, 1997), 124. Sylvanus G. Morley, "Keeping a City Old," *Santa Fe Trail* (August 1913): 93–95.

26 The principals, Isaac Rapp, Jr., and his brother William, were older siblings of Cornelius and George, whose Chicago firm, Rapp and Rapp, became famous for its movie theater designs.

27 Quoted in Diane H. Thomas, *The Southwestern Indian Detours* (Phoenix: Hunter Publishing, 1978), 65.

28 It is easy to forget from our present-day perspective how important the subject of road building was in the Southwest of the 1920s, when links between towns were still crude, indirect, or nonexistent. Much in the same way that cities today fret over constructing, then brag about when finishing, new stadiums, cities of that time could be whipped into a chamber-of-commerce fever pitch over a new road.

29 Erna Fergusson was a New Mexico native who later became a well-known author of books on southwestern subjects, including the estimable *Our Southwest* (1940).

30 Bunting, *John Gaw Meem*, 73.

31 Wilson, *The Myth of Santa Fe*, 237–243.

32 Bunting, *John Gaw Meem*, 73.

33 Memorandum of conference [R. Hunter Clarkson, Louise (Mrs.) Clarkson, Mary Colter, and John Gaw Meem] in Clarkson's office, August 3, 1926. John Gaw Meem Collection, Center for Southwest Research, University of New Mexico.

34 Memorandum of conference at La Fonda [Colter, the Clarksons, Mr. Jacobs, Meem, C. D. McCormick], September 24, 1926. John Gaw Meem Collection.

35 John Gaw Meem to M.E.J. Colter, April 1, 1927. John Gaw Meem Collection.

36 John Gaw Meem to M. E. J. Colter, June 3, 1927. John Gaw Meem Collection.

37 John Gaw Meem to R. H. Clarkson. July 27, 1927. John Gaw Meem Collection.

38 John Gaw Meem to R. H. Clarkson. February 25, 1927. John Gaw Meem Collection.

39 M. E. J. Colter to Hunter Clarkson, January 17, 1929. John Gaw Meem Collection. In an earlier letter she showed disappointment that one of her requests was turned down: "I regret that you can't have the dimmer switches. . . . There are some compact and not greatly expensive rheostats. I used to use them in amateur theatricals." M. E. J. Colter to Hunter Clarkson, December 21, 1928. John Gaw Meem Collection.

40 R. H. Clarkson to M. E. J. Colter, October 6, 1926. John Gaw Meem Collection.

41 "Taxi Into Street Car," *Kansas City Star* (March 14, 1929): 17.

42 Lionel Benjamin to R. H. Clarkson, March 20, 1929. John Gaw Meem Collection.

43 Grattan, *Mary Colter*, 52.

44 "La Fonda, Tripled in Size Becomes Spanish Fairyland," *Santa Fe New Mexican* (May 18, 1929): 2. Fred Harvey Collection, Arizona State University Library.

45 Mary E. J. Colter to John Gaw Meem, March 28, 1929. John Gaw Meem Collection.

46 "La Fonda, Santa Fe, New Mexico," *The Hotel Monthly* (March 1932): 27.

47 M. E. J. Colter to R. H. Clarkson, October 4, 1926. John Gaw Meem Collection.

48 M. E. J. Colter to John Gaw Meem, September 28, 1928. John Gaw Meem Collection.

49 Sadie Rubins to John G. Meem, April 26, 1929. John Gaw Meem Collection.

50 Ernie Pyle, *Home Country* (New York: William Sloane, 1947), 76.

51 Simone de Beauvoir, *America Day by Day* (Berkeley: University of California Press, 1999), 185, 186.

52 Ford Harvey to Byron Harvey, February 21, 1927. Grattan, *Mary Colter*, 41–42.

53 "Harvey House Plans Announced," *Winslow Daily Mail* (January 27, 1929): 1, 5. "Harvey House Work Will Begin at Once," *Winslow Daily Mail* (April 16, 1929): 1, 3.

54 Colter's boss, J. F. Huckel, had trouble choosing a name for the hotel. La Fonda had already been used, so he chose El Ranchito. However, very soon after that choice was announced in press releases, the Winslow Chamber of Commerce sent Huckel a telegram informing him that that name "is widely used for houses of prostitution along the Mexican border." As Grattan described his response, "Huckel found a new name in a hurry." Grattan, *Mary Colter*, 67.

55 Elizabeth W. DeHuff, "Architecture and Furnishings of 'La Posada,'" Courier's Instructional Bulletin No. 52, The Santa Fe Transportation Company (April 1, 1930): 1. From the collections of the Raton Museum, Raton, New Mexico.

56 Gertrude Henson, "'La Posada,' a Typical Spanish Rancho," *Winslow Daily Mail*, special supplement (June 2, 1930): 1.

57 "The Furnishings of La Posada, Winslow, Arizona," undated Harvey Company brochure. Guests were supplied this twelve-page publication to explain the multitude of objects both within and on the grounds of La Posada. Colter's humorous ashtrays became somewhat of a trademark for her and were found also at La Fonda and other Fred Harvey locations. Grattan, *Mary Colter*, 60.

58 Henson, "'La Posada,' a Typical Spanish Rancho," 16.

59 "La Posada and Harveycars, Winslow," *The Hotel Monthly* (February 1931): 47–55.

60 Above this point rises the hotel's short tower, which Colter perforated with small openings, creating a current that siphons hot air up and out of the hotel and sucks in cool air from the watered south lawns. The holes in the ceiling were designed as a series of squares and crescent wedges.

61 Henson, "'La Posada,' a Typical Spanish Rancho," 16. Although La Posada was a luxury hotel, it followed the practice of the day in not supplying all guest rooms with full baths. A number of the rooms were only partially equipped, with baths, and in a few cases toilets also, down the hall. The Harvey Girls as well as the rest of the staff, except for the hotel manager, lived in the old Harvey House across the tracks.

62 Charles J. Smith to Frank Pinkley, May 28, 1930. Petrified Forest National Park Archives. In this letter, Smith, custodian of the monument, reported to Pinkley, superintendent of Southwestern National Monuments, that "during this month specimens have been furnished under permit from the National Park Service to Miss M. E. J. Colter of the Santa Fe R. R. for the hotel La Posada at Winslow, and to museums in Roanoke Ill., and Houston, Texas."

63 "La Posada Historic District," National Register of Historic Places registration form, Section 7, 2. Colter had a difficult time getting the stone cut and laid for the wall, but finally attracted a group of Italian immigrants to Winslow. She agreed to their desire to leave imbedded in the wall certain symbols—a five-pointed star, a ram's head, and other designs—that reminded them of their native towns. Winslow Historical Society.

64 DeHuff, "Architecture and Furnishings of 'La Posada,'" 2.

65 Henson, "'La Posada,' a Typical Spanish Rancho," 1.

66 Mary Colter book collection, Mesa Verde National Park Library. Among her many history books were some published by The Quivira Society, beautiful and exquisitely printed limited editions on the New World expeditions of Spanish explorers.

67 Winslow Historical Society files.

68 Gene Schmitz (son of Leon and Clara), author's interview, April 12, 2000.

69 Daggett Harvey to Fred A. Tipple, September 1, 1976. Courtesy of Virginia L. Grattan.

70 Patricia Smyth, author's interview, June 22, 2000.

71 Winslow Historical Society files.

72 "La Posada," *Winslow Daily Mail* supplement (June 2, 1930): 9–11, 14–15, 18, 20.

73 Grattan, *Mary Colter*, 67. Budgeted at $600,000, the hotel cost about $1 million to build.

SIX

1   J. Donald Hughes, *In the House of Stone and Light: A Human History of the Grand Canyon* (Grand Canyon, AZ: Grand Canyon Natural History Association, 1978), p. 87. Another source cites 1927 as the year that the automobile majority first occurred; Gordon Chappell, "Railroad at the Rim: The Origin and Growth of Grand Canyon Village," *The Journal of Arizona History*, vol. 17 no.1 (1976): 100, 102.

2   Virginia L. Grattan, *Mary Colter: Builder Upon the Red Earth* (Grand Canyon, AZ: Grand Canyon Natural History Association, 1992), 59.

3   After the Watchtower opened, a new park-entrance station was built nearby in 1934, and a new highway from the east was completed to that point in 1935. The 34-mile road connected the eastern boundary of the park to U.S. Route 89 in Cameron, AZ. "Grand Canyon Village Historic District," National Register of Historic Places registration form (January 17, 1990): 31.

4   Mary Colter, *Manual for Drivers and Guides Descriptive of the Indian Watchtower at Desert View and its Relation, Architecturally, to the Prehistoric Ruins of the Southwest* (Grand Canyon National Park, AZ: Fred Harvey Company, 1933), 11–12.

5   John Gaw Meem to M. E. J. Colter, July 28, 1927. John Gaw Meem Collection, Center for Southwest Research, University of New Mexico.

6   Colter, *Manual for Drivers and Guides*, 2.

7   "Desert View Watchtower Historic District," National Register of Historic Places registration form

(August 29, 1994). Grattan, *Mary Colter*, 67–80.

8   Colter, *Manual for Drivers and Guides*, 15.

9   Edwin D. McKee to Virginia L. Grattan, March 1, 1982. Letter supplied to author.

10   Colter, *Manual for Drivers and Guides*, 13.

11   Grattan, *Mary Colter*, 69. McQuaid with Bartlett, "Building an Image of the Southwest: Mary Colter, Fred Harvey Company Architect," in Weigle and Babcock, eds., *The Great Southwest of the Fred Harvey Company and the Santa Fe Railway*, 31.

12   Colter, *Manual for Drivers and Guides*, 16–17.

13   Sallie Saunders, "Indian Watchtower at Grand Cañon is Dedicated by Hopi Indians," *The Santa Fe Magazine* (July 1933): 30.

14   Colter, *Manual for Drivers and Guides*, 17.

15   Colter, *Manual for Drivers and Guides*, 21

16   Colter, *Manual for Drivers and Guides*, 18, 19.

17   The Antiquities Act of 1906, which aided in the establishment of Grand Canyon National Park, already prohibited such removal on federal lands. A similar prohibition became law in Arizona in 1927 for state lands. The Archaeological Resources Protection Act of 1979 further strengthened federal controls. New Mexico and Utah (1953) and Arizona and Colorado (1973) passed similar laws.

18   Colter, *Manual for Drivers and Guides*, 61.

19   Colter, *Manual for Drivers and Guides*, 23–24.

20   Colter, *Manual for Drivers and Guides*, 62–64. Colter described the painted wood ornaments used as a frieze in the women's restroom as "head-dresses worn for the last time by Hopi maidens in the Butterfly Dance at Chimopovy in 1932. It will be noticed that the colors have run a little which is indicative that the Butterfly Dance, which is an invocation for rain, was in this case successful." Letter to author from Jeanne Schick, November 2000.

21   Colter, *Manual for Drivers and Guides*, 28n.

22   Fred Kabotie with Bill Belknap, *Fred Kabotie: Hopi Indian Artist* (Flagstaff, AZ: Northland Press, 1977), 50.

23   Image # 16958, Grand Canyon National Park Museum Collection.

24   Parallels between Colter and Wright are intriguing. Their life spans were virtually coterminous, Colter (1869–1958) and Wright (1867–1959). Having grown up in the Midwest, they were both rooted in the Arts and Crafts philosophy and pioneered in American regional architecture that derived from the landscape and, to a lesser extent for Wright, cultural history. They both practiced heavily in the desert Southwest and used its stone and wood to masterful effect in walls. Colter certainly knew of the world-famous Wright, and it is likely that he knew of her, having visited the Grand Canyon and probably other locations of her works. Wright stayed at El Tovar and would have at least seen Hopi House across from its front entrance. Frank Lloyd Wright to V. Patrosso, November 17, 1928, Fred Harvey Collection, Cline Library, Northern Arizona University.

25 Kathleen L. Howard, "'A Most Remarkable Success': Herman Schweizer and the Fred Harvey Indian Department," in Weigle and Babcock, eds., *The Great Southwest*, 91.

26 Colter, *Manual for Drivers and Guides*, p. 52.

27 Frederick Doyle, "A Little Journey to the Indian Watchtower of the Grand Canyon," unpublished and undated (circa 1933) manuscript, Grand Canyon National Park Museum Collection.

28 Oral history of Michael Harrison, June 1, 1995, transcript. Special Collections, Cline Library, Northern Arizona University.

29 Frank Waters, *Masked Gods: Navaho and Pueblo Ceremonialism* (Chicago: The Swallow Press, 1950), 111.

30 "De-Ki-Veh," Harvey Company dedication booklet, May 13, 1933.

31 Colter named her structure the Indian Watchtower, and it is often called that, but later it was officially named simply the Watchtower.

32 Mary Colter to Grand Canyon Transportation Department, March 1933.

33 The Fred Harvey Auto Camp was started in 1926 at the west end of the village. Today known as the Maswick cabins, the camp included seventeen one-room cottages and ancillary buildings. "Grand Canyon Village Historic District," National Register, 28. Colter's role, if any, in the design of the camp is uncertain.

34 Grand Canyon Working Plan, 1917, n.p. As quoted in McQuaid with Bartlett, "Building an Image of the Southwest: Mary Colter, Fred Harvey Company Architect," 32.

35 J. Donald Hughes, *In the House of Stone and Light*, 94.

36 Chappell, "Railroad at the Rim: The Origin and Growth of Grand Canyon Village," 103–04.

37 "The New Bright Angel Lodge and Cabins," *The Hotel Monthly* (December 1936): 21.

38 "140,000 Visit Grand Canyon in 1934; $500,000 to be Spent on New Bright Angel Lodge," *Santa Fe New Mexican* (September 20, 1934): n.p.

39 The lodges were named for Grand Canyon pioneers Buckey O'Neill and John Wesley Powell.

40 Grand Canyon Village Historic District, National Register of Historic Places, registration form (January 17, 1990): 32.

41 "The New Bright Angel Lodge and Cabins," *The Hotel Monthly* (December 1936): 17.

42 Grand Canyon Village Historic District, National Register, 32.

43 Edwin D. McKee to Virginia L. Grattan, March 1, 1982. Letter supplied to author.

44 M. E. J. Colter to Eddie McKie [*sic*], April 1, 1935. Grand Canyon National Park Archives. Colter also wrote in the letter: "Apparently we are losing out on the fossil rock for the Lobby fireplace. It is too bad for it would have been a knockout."

45 "The New Bright Angel Lodge and Cabins," *The Hotel Monthly*, 17–18.

46 "The New Bright Angel Lodge and Cabins," *The Hotel Monthly*, 22.

47 Byron Harvey III, "The Fred Harvey Company Collects Indian Art: Selected Remarks," in Weigle and Babcock, eds., *The Great Southwest*, 74.

48 "Homely Epic Story of West Told in Bright Angel Lodge, Picturesque New Hotel," *Santa Fe New Mexican* (June 10, 1935): n.p.

49 Unidentified and undated newspaper clipping. Fred Harvey Collection, Heard Museum.

50 Grattan, *Mary Colter*, 90.

51 Betty Leavengood, *Grand Canyon Women: Lives Shaped by Landscape* (Boulder, Colorado: Pruett Publishing, 1999), 44.

52 Linda Flint McClelland, *Building the National Parks: Historic Landscape Design and Construction* (Baltimore: Johns Hopkins University Press: 1998), 245.

53 Albert H. Good, *Park and Recreation Structures, Part III, Overnight and Organized Camp Facilities* (Washington D.C.: National Park Service, 1938; reprint, New York: Princeton Architectural Press, 1999). The book also cited the lobby fireplace and the preservation of the Buckey O'Neill Cabin and the Cameron Hotel as worthy of emulation.

54 "Grand Canyon Village Historic District," National Register, 32.

55 "Grand Canyon Village Historic District," National Register, 33.

56 "Grand Canyon Village Historic District," National Register, 29.

57 Memoranda of conferences, May 11, 1934 [Meem, David Cole, and Colter present] and July 6, 1934 [Meem and Cole present]. John Gaw Meem to David L. Cole, July 31, 1934. John Gaw Meem Collection, University of New Mexico. "The matter of the fountain in the patio was also discussed [at the May meeting]. Mr. Cole said that he never liked the fountain. . . . Both Miss Colter and I said that we thought it was good looking, but the trouble was in the way it was arranged. . . . Miss Colter thought it would be wise to provide a more elaborate fountain in the center than the present small spout—something on the order of a series of Mexican Majolica tiles."

58 Information from Virginia L. Grattan to author.

59 Gale Burak to author, July 30, 2000.

60 Gale Burak to author, May 2000.

SEVEN

1 Keith L. Bryant, Jr., *History of the Atchison, Topeka and Santa Fe Railway* (New York City: Macmillan, 1974), 335–36.

2 Lesley Poling-Kempes, *The Harvey Girls: Women Who Opened the West* (New York City: Marlowe and Company, 1991), 182–83.

3 "Hold Services For J. F. Huckel Monday," *Colorado Springs Sunday Gazette*, n.d., n.p.

4 Grattan, *Mary Colter*, 91.

5 Bryant, *History of the Atchison, Topeka and Santa Fe Railway*, 338–340. Stephen E. Drew, "Atchison, Topeka and Santa Fe Diner No. 1474 'Cochiti,'" information sheet, California State Railroad Museum, n.d.

6 Fergusson, *Our Southwest*, 116.

7 Alfred Vincent Kidder, *An Introduction to the Study of Southwestern Archaeology* (New Have, CT: Yale University Press, 1924; reprint, 2000).

8 Both the Kidder book in note 7 and the Mimbres book, written by Harriet and C. B. Cosgrove and published by Harvard's Peabody Museum in 1932, are in the collection of volumes that Mary Colter donated to Mesa Verde National Park before she died. Harriet Cosgrove prepared hundreds of ink drawings of Mimbres ware. Colter had become a friend over the years with many archaeologists, including Cosgrove. Carolyn O'Bagy Davis, the author of a biography of Cosgrove, speculates that Colter first saw Mimbres pottery at an exhibition in Santa Fe.

9 Kidder, *An Introduction to the Study of Southwestern Archaeology*, 292.

10 Cleota Reed and Stan Skoczen, *Syracuse China* (Syracuse, N.Y.: Syracuse University Press, 1997), 112–13.

11 Richard W. Luckin, *Mimbres to Mimbreño: A Study of Santa Fe's Famous China Pattern* (Golden, Colorado: RK Publishing, 1992), 14–15.

12 Luckin, *Mimbres to Mimbreño*, 17.

13 "Food Service on the Santa Fe's New Streamlined Trains," *The Hotel Monthly* (September 1938): 17–19.

14 The Harvey Company also used Syracuse China for its Crossroads Room in Chicago's Dearborn Station (the Santa Fe's primary station) and its restaurants in Los Angeles' union station—designed by Colter in 1939—and for many of its other railroad dining cars. Reed and Scoczen, *Syracuse China*, 135–36.

15 Bryant, *History of the Atchison, Topeka and Santa Fe Railway*, 341–42.

16 Kenneth Force, "Kansas City Likes Westport Room," *Restaurant Management* (February 1938): 82–85.

17 *The Independent* (July 24, 1937): cover.

18 Untitled article in *Kansas City Journal Post* (July 25, 1937): n.p.

19 Bill Bradley, *The Last of the Great Stations* (Glendale, Calif.: Interurban Press, 1992), 56–69.

20 "Los Angeles Union Passenger Railway Station," *Architect and Engineer* (May 1939): 37.

21   A newspaper report on the type of building chosen by officials noted that "one has been selected which reflects Southern California architecture. In some quarters this has been variously described as Spanish mission, Mexican, Mediterranean, Moorish or Southern Californian design." "Design of Union Station to be California Style," *Los Angeles Times* (August 7, 1934): n.p

22   Officially, the station was designed by architects from each of the three railroads: H. L. Gilman of the Santa Fe, R. J. Wirth of the Union Pacific, and J. H. Christie of the Southern Pacific. The Parkinsons were called "consulting architects." "Los Angeles Union Passenger Railway Station," 37.

23   Irving S. Fritzen, "Streamlining a Pueblo," *The Santa Fe Magazine* (June 1939): 7.

24   "Open Union Passenger Terminal at Los Angeles, Cal.," *Railway Age* (May 6, 1939): 773. Steve Harvey, "Union Station," *Los Angeles Times* (March 1, 1987): Part 2, 1. Fritzen, "Streamlining," 10.

25   "Fred Harvey Welcomes You!," advertisement in the *Los Angeles Times* (May 3, 1939): 6.

26   "Hedda Hopper's Hollywood," column, *Los Angeles Times* (May 17, 1939): n.p. Fred Harvey Collection, Heard Museum Archives. The company kept up with celebrity visits, reporting their appearances in its *Hospitality* magazine. In 1955 it noted: "Movie stars at Fred Harvey's lunch counter in the station: Agnes Moorhead, Allen Jones, Irene Hervey and Pat O'Brien. In the Cocktail Lounge: Victor Mature and Pat Hogan. Ruby Brodigan, "Los Angeles," *Hospitality* (June 1955): 11.

Fred Harvey Collection, Cline Library, Northern Arizona University.

27   Bradley, *The Last of the Great Stations*, 8–19.

28   Grattan, *Mary Colter*, 95.

29   "Alvarado's Cocktail Lounge Opens to Display Spanish Atmosphere," *Albuquerque Tribune* (July 10, 1940): n.p. Albuquerque Public Library.

30   "Alvarado's Cocktail Lounge Opens." Grattan, *Mary Colter*, 99–100.

31   "Alvarado's Cocktail Lounge Opens."

32   Poling-Kempes, *The Harvey Girls*, 165.

33   Fred Harvey brochure, 1940. Dorothy Woodward Collection, New Mexico State Records and Archives. Cited in Poling-Kempes, *The Harvey Girls*, 158.

34   Ernie Pyle, "Why Albuquerque?", *New Mexico Magazine* (January 1942; reprint, July 1997): 103.

35   Jack Mullen, "America's Best-Fed Travelers," *The Santa Fe Magazine* (December 1943): 9.

36   Poling-Kempes, T*he Harvey Girls*, 192–96. The shortage of Harvey Girls to serve the troops was eased by the hiring of Hispanic and Native American women, who had rarely been employed before. At El Navajo, virtually the entire staff of waitresses was Navajos.

37   Kathleen L. Howard, "'A Most Remarkable Success': Herman Schweizer and the Fred Harvey Indian Department," in Weigle and Babcock, eds., *The Great Southwest*, 95.

38   Frank Waters to Kathleen L. Howard, April 8, 1990. Quoted in Howard, "'A Most Remarkable Success,'" 93.

39   Byron Harvey, III, "The Fred Harvey Company Collects Indian Art: Selected Remarks," in Weigle and Babcock, *The Great Southwest*, 73.

40   Byron Harvey to Herman Schweizer, June 30, 1939. Fred Harvey Collection, Heard Museum. Quoted in Howard, 98.

41   Harvey III, "The Fred Harvey Company Collects Indian Art," 85.

42   Although she worked officially for the Fred Harvey Company, part of Colter's salary had always been paid by the Santa Fe Railway. She retired from that arrangement in January 1944. Grattan, *Mary Colter*, 102.

43   "Lamy, the Town the Railroad Built," *The Atom* (April 1966): 19. Quoted in Poling-Kempes, *The Harvey Girls*, 205.

44   Gale Burak, author's interview, January 26, 2001.

45   "Painted Desert Inn," brochure, National Park Service, n.d. Fred Harvey Collection, Cline Library, Northern Arizona University.

46   The inn and land were added to the Petrified Forest National Monument to the south. Both were assembled in 1962 into the Petrified Forest National Park.

47 Harvey H. Kaiser, *Landmarks in the Landscape: Historic Architecture in the National Parks of the West* (San Francisco: Chronicle Books, 1997), 246–253. "Painted Desert Inn" brochure.

48 "Historic Structure Report: Painted Desert Inn, Petrified Forest National Park, AZ," U.S. Department of the Interior, National Park Service, October 1994, 34. Petrified Forest National Park Archives. "Superintendent's Monthly Report," Petrified Forest National Monument, December 1947, p. 2. "In company with [Harvey officials, the park superintendent, and a painter], a color scheme was decided upon, and the actual painting started that P.M." Petrified Forest National Park Archives.

49 "Superintendent's Monthly Report," Petrified Forest National Monument, May 1948. Petrified Forest National Park Archives.

50 From a recording of Fred Kabotie made at the dedication of the Kabotie Room at Painted Desert Inn, June 23, 1976. As quoted in "Historic Structure Report: Painted Desert Inn," 36. "But now they don't do that anymore," he added, "because they can get all their salt from the supermarket."

51 "Painted Desert Inn," Fred Harvey Company brochure, 1955. La Posada files.

52 Charles J. Smith, custodian of Petrified Forest National Monument, to Frank Pinkley, superintendent of Southwestern National Monuments, May 28, 1930. "During the month specimens have been furnished under permit from the National Park Service to Miss M. E. J. Colter of the Santa Fe R. R. for the hotel at La Posada at Winslow." Petrified Forest National Park Archives.

53 Colter also considered retiring in Sedona, Arizona, where she owned a parcel of land purchased years before as a possible retirement retreat. Grattan, *Mary Colter*, 103. The remoteness of the location and Santa Fe's greater attraction to her persuaded her to sell the ten-acre Sedona tract, which was bought by Jack Fry, president of TWA, and later by Bruce Babbitt, former secretary of the interior. Babbitt found Colter's name on the papers when he purchased the property. Virginia Grattan to author, August 8, 2000.

54 Mary E. J. Colter to Don Watson, April 12, 1947. Mary Colter papers, Mesa Verde National Park.

55 Mary E. J. Colter to Kenneth Ross, July 31, 1945. Mary Colter papers, Mesa Verde National Park.

56 Jesse L. Nusbaum to Mary E. J. Colter, September 4, 1945. Mary Colter papers, Mesa Verde National Park. Nusbaum designed many of the buildings at the park, including the Mesa Verde Museum of 1924 (now called Chapin Mesa Museum), where Colter's artifacts were put on display in 1957. He had been park superintendent from 1921 to 1931 and from 1936 to 1939 and served as acting superintendent from 1942 to 1946. Nusbaum's influence on southwestern archaeology and architecture and his role in the development of Mesa Verde National Park were both considerable.

57 Santa Fe City Directories, 1949 and 1951, Museum of New Mexico, History Division. Colter apparently rented the houses in which she lived in Santa Fe. Patricia Smyth, author's interview, June 22, 2000.

58 Smyth interview, June 22, 2000.

59 Amy Meadows, "Miss Colter Does it Again!" *Hospitality* (September 1949): 3. Fred Harvey Collection, Cline Library, Northern Arizona University.

60 Plaza Chamisal, Historic Building Inventory files, New Mexico State Historic Preservation Office.

61 Information sheets, Little Bighorn Battlefield National Monument.

62 Byron Harvey III, "The Fred Harvey Company Collects Indian Art: Selected Remarks," in Weigle and Babcock, eds., *The Great Southwest*, 74.

63 Notes made by Mary Colter and/or an assistant after 1950. Mary Colter papers, Mesa Verde National Park.

64 "Miss Colter's Indian Jewels on Public Exhibition at Lab," *The New Mexican* (April 20, 1952): n.p. Mary Colter papers, Mesa Verde National Park.

65 Kathleen L. Howard and Diana F. Pardue, "Mary Jane Colter: Designing the Dream of the West," *Cañon Journal* (Spring/Summer 1996): 43. Taken from a personal interview with Karen Bartlett.

66 Amy Meadows, "Santa Fe," *Hospitality* (June 1955): 11. Fred Harvey Collection, Cline Library, Northern Arizona University. Virginia Grattan to author, March 18, 2001.

67 Mary E. J. Colter to Don Watson, October 3, 1956. Mary Colter papers, Mesa Verde National Park.

68 Mary E. J. Colter to Kenneth Ross, July 31, 1945. Mary Colter papers, Mesa Verde National Park.

69 C. B. Wilson, Attorneys at Law, to Mesa Verde National Park Museum, March 4, 1959. Letter quoting portion of will of Mary E. J. Colter. Mary Colter papers, Mesa Verde National Park.

70 Carroll A. Burroughs to Mary Jane Colter, August 4 and November 29, 1957. Mary Colter papers, Mesa Verde National Park.

71 Mission 66 was the first major building program in the national parks since the heyday of public-works-program construction during the 1930s, when rustic architecture was the ruling mode. The shift to modernist design was, and in some quarters remains, controversial, although attempts to raze some of the more notable buildings of the newer group—such as the visitor centers at Gettysburg National Military Park and Wright Brothers National Memorial—have met with considerable opposition.

72 Mary Colter to Mary Colter Larkin Smith, January 31, 1952. Mary Colter Larkin Smith files.

73 Mary Colter to Mary Colter Larkin Smith, December 11, 1952. Mary Colter Larkin Smith files.

74 Grattan, *Mary Colter*, 110.

75 Grattan, *Mary Colter*, 111. Colter had kept up on some of her buildings and interiors. Patricia Smyth related Colter's reaction to "[an unspecified] hotel in Arizona" that the architect had visited in the early 1950s in the presence of her successor at Fred Harvey, who had just redone the rugs and the curtains. The new designer recalled that Colter came in, stomped on the floor with her cane, and declared, "ruined, absolutely *ruined*!" Smyth interview, June 22, 2000.

76 *Hospitality* (January 1958): 3. Fred Harvey Collection, Cline Library, Northern Arizona University.

77 Frank Waters, *Masked Gods: Navaho and Pueblo Ceremonialism* (Chicago: Swallow Press, 1950), 111.

EIGHT

1 *Hospitality* (May 1957): n.p. Fred Harvey Collection, Cline Library, Northern Arizona University.

2 John B. Hungerford, "Death of an Inn," *Los Angeles Times* (August 27, 1957): n.p.

3 Conover C. Smith, "Fred Harvey Closing Marks End of Era," *The Kansas City Times* (December 28, 1968): 12. Fred Harvey Collection, Cline Library, Northern Arizona University.

4 The station was finally restored and reopened in 1999 as a museum called Science City at Union Station. Included among its exhibits is a Fred Harvey soda fountain (not a restoration of the original), above which hang the three Meiere murals, linked in a continuous curve.

5 Doug Shuit, "Once-Bustling Union Station Loses Out to Jets, Freeways," *Los Angeles Times* (May 5, 1969): 1. By the turn of the twenty-first century, however, the station was enjoying a comeback as the focus of a regional multi-modal transportation center that includes Amtrak, commuter rail, subway, light rail, and bus service. The station and adjacent property are being redeveloped as this book goes to press by a descendent of the Santa Fe Railway, Catellus Development Corporation, which acquired the site in 1989.

6 Santa Fe president John S. Reed gave the following explanation: "The decision to close the hotel was a most difficult one, but the demonstrated preference of travelers for more modern motel facilities situated away from the Downtown area has made continued operation of the facility unduly burdensome." Quoted in W. Wilson Cliff, "Alvarado Hotel Will Close Doors," *Albuquerque Journal* (September 20, 1969): A-1.

7 The Fred Harvey Company ceased to exist as an independent firm in 1968, when it was purchased by Amfac, a Honolulu-based real estate development company. The Fred Harvey name continues to be used at Grand Canyon hotels and attractions, which are operated by the Amfac subsidiary, Grand Canyon National Park Lodges.

8 Ruth W. Armstrong, letter to the editor, *The New Mexican* [?], (December 1984): n.p.

9 Among the more debatable changes was the roofing over of the central patio, which John Gaw Meem and Colter had labored to infuse with southwestern open-air charm. A letter-to-the-editor complained: "I was filled with horror when I saw that the lovely outdoor dining area at La Fonda was torn down to make way for a dark, gloomy indoor dining room." Sally Reeder to *The New Mexican* (June 27, 1961): n.p. Fred Harvey Collection, Cline Library, Northern Arizona University.

10 Most of Colter's buildings are on the National Register; some also are National Historic Landmarks. Her remaining interiors are located in landmarked buildings. In recent decades, the scholarly study of buildings in the national parks has also helped illumine Colter's contributions. Two National Park Service reports, *National Park Service Rustic Architecture: 1916–1942* by William Tweed, Laura E. Soullière, and Henry G. Law (1977) and *Architecture in the Parks: National Historic Landmark Theme Study* (1986)

by Laura Soullière Harrison, have been especially helpful in this regard.

11 Jay C. Henry, "Virginia L. Grattan, *Mary Coulter* [*sic*]: *Builder Upon the Red Earth*," review in *Journal of the Society of Architectural Historians* (March 1982): 77–78.

12 Sara Holmes Boutelle, "Mary Colter: Builder Upon the Red Earth, Virginia L. Grattan," review in *AIA Journal* (June 1981): 59–60.

13 *The Watchtower Guide*, Fred Harvey/Amfac, n.d. The brochure explains Colter's role as Harvey architect, citing her public projects at the park: "In these structures, one may still catch the spirit of the remarkable Mary Elizabeth Jane Colter."

14 "Inventing the Southwest: The Fred Harvey Company and Native American Art," exhibit at the Heard Museum, Phoenix, 1996–97.

15 Jennifer Lee, producer/writer/ director, *Mary Jane Colter: The Desert View, 1996.* Karen Bartlett and Nemesis Productions, producer/ writer/director, *Mary Jane Colter: House Made of Dawn*, 1997. Broadcast on National Public Television, July 1999.

16 Woodward Architectural Group, Phoenix, "Project Description: Use of Masonry in Design," 1997 (summary for award submission for Hopi House restoration).

17 Amfac, like the Fred Harvey Company that preceded it, owns all of the Colter buildings, not on a complete or fee-simple basis, but rather as a possessory or leasehold interest. The Harvey Company acquired the buildings in 1954 from the Santa Fe Railway, which abandoned its passenger service to the canyon in 1969.

18 Design Collaborative Southwest, Albuquerque, "Gallup Multimodal Center Renovation," project description sheet, n.d.

19 Robert Hughes, *American Visions: The Epic History of Art in America* (New York: Alfred A. Knopf, 1997), p. 388.

20 Grand Canyon National Park Museum Collection. Colter titled the poem, "The Master Mason," possibly because it was the original title. Official compendiums of Kipling's works use "The Palace."

Bibliography

BOOKS

Berkeley, Ellen Perry and McQuaid, Matilda, eds. *Architecture: A Place for Women*. Washington, D.C.: Smithsonian Institution Press, 1989.

Blomberg, Nancy J. *Navajo Textiles: The William Randolph Hearst Collection*. Tucson: The University of Arizona Press, 1988.

Bradley, Bill. *The Last of the Great Stations*. Glendale, CA: Interurban Press, 1992.

Brown, Dee. *Hear That Lonesome Whistle Blow*. New York: Holt, Rinehart and Winston, 1977.

Bryant, Keith L., Jr. *History of the Atchison, Topeka and Santa Fe Railway*. New York: Macmillan Publishing, 1974.

Bunting, Bainbridge. *John Gaw Meem: Southwestern Architect*. Albuquerque: University of New Mexico Press, 1983.

Cole, Doris. *From Tipi to Skyscraper: A History of Women in Architecture*. Boston: i press incorporated, 1973.

Colter, Mary. *Manual for Drivers and Guides Descriptive of the Indian Watchtower at Desert View and its Relation, Architecturally, to the Prehistoric Ruins of the Southwest*. Grand Canyon National Park, AZ: Fred Harvey Company, 1933.

Conforti, Michael, ed. *Art and Life on the Upper Mississippi, 1890–1915*. Newark: University of Delaware Press, 1994.

De Beauvoir, Simone. *America Day by Day*. Berkeley: University of California Press, 1999.

D'Emilio, Sandra, and Campbell, Suzan. *Visions and Visionaries: The Art and Artists of the Santa Fe Railway*. Salt Lake City: Peregrine Smith, 1991.

Denker, Bert, ed. *The Substance of Style: Perspectives on the American Arts and Crafts Movement*. Hanover, NH: University Press of New England, 1996.

Dilworth, Leah. *Imagining Indians in the Southwest: Persistent Visions of a Primitive Past*. Washington, D.C.: Smithsonian Institution Press, 1996.

Ehrlich, George. *Kansas City, Missouri: An Architectural History, 1826–1990*. Columbia, MO: University of Missouri Press, 1992.

Fergusson, Erna. *Our Southwest*. New York: Alfred A. Knopf, 1940.

Gebhard, David, and Winter, Robert. *Architecture in Los Angeles: A Compleat Guide*. Salt Lake City: Peregrine Smith Books, 1985.

Good, Albert H. *Park and Recreation Structures, Part III, Overnight and Organized Camp Facilities*. Washington, D.C.: National Park Service, 1938; reprint, New York: Princeton Architectural Press, 1999.

Grattan, Virginia L. *Mary Colter: Builder Upon the Red Earth*. Grand Canyon, AZ: Grand Canyon Natural History Association, 1992.

Harrison, Laura Soullière. *Architecture in the Parks: National Historic Landmark Theme Study*. Washington, D.C.: National Park Service, 1986.

Hayes, Allan, and Blom, John. *Southwestern Pottery: Anasazi to Zuni*. Flagstaff, AZ: Northland Publishing, 1996.

Henderson, James David. *"Meals by Fred Harvey:" A Phenomenon of the American West*. Fort Worth: Texas Christian University Press, 1969.

Hjalmarson, Birgitta. *Artful Players: Artistic Life in Early San Francisco*. Los Angeles: Balcony Press, 1999.

Howard, Kathleen L., and Pardue, Diana F. *Inventing the Southwest: The Fred Harvey Company and Native American Art*. Flagstaff, AZ: Northland Publishing, 1996.

Hughes, J. Donald. *In the House of Stone and Light: A Human History of the Grand Canyon*. Grand Canyon, AZ: Grand Canyon Natural History Association, 1978.

Hughes, Robert. *American Visions: The Epic History of Art in America*. New York: Alfred A. Knopf, 1997.

Irish, Sharon. *Cass Gilbert, Architect: Modern Traditionalist*. New York: Monacelli Press, 1999.

James, George Wharton. *The Grand Canyon of Arizona: How to See It*. Boston: Little, Brown, 1910.

Jones, Harvey L. *Mathews: Masterpieces of the California Decorative Style*. Layton, UT: Peregrine Smith Books, 1985.

Kabotie, Fred, with Belknap, Bill. *Fred Kabotie: Hopi Indian Artist*. Flagstaff, AZ: Northland Press, 1977.

Kaiser, Harvey H. *Landmarks in the Landscape: Historic Architecture in the National Parks of the West*. San Francisco: Chronicle Books, 1997.

Kaplan, Wendy and others. *"The Art That Is Life": The Arts and Crafts Movement in America, 1875–1920*. Boston: Museum of Fine Arts, 1987.

Kidder, Alfred Vincent. *An Introduction to the Study of Southwestern Archaeology*. New Haven, CT: Yale University Press, 1924; reprint, 2000.

Kirker, Harold. *California's Architectural Frontier: Style and Tradition in the Nineteenth Century*. Salt Lake City: Peregrine Smith Books, 1986.

Kropp, Phoebe S. "'There is a Little Sermon in That': Constructing the Native Southwest at the San Diego Panama-California Exposition of 1915," in Weigel and Babcock, eds. *The Great Southwest of the Fred Harvey Company and the Santa Fe Railway*. Phoenix: The Heard Museum, 1996.

Kunz, Virginia Brainard. *St. Paul: Saga of an American City*. Woodland Hills, CA: Windsor Publications, 1977.

Lathrop, Alan K. "Architecture in Minnesota at the Turn of the Century," in Conforti, Michael, ed. *Art and Life on the Upper Mississippi, 1890–1915*. Newark: University of Delaware Press, 1994.

Leavengood, Betty. *Grand Canyon Women: Lives Shaped by Landscape*. Boulder, CO: Pruett Publishing Company, 1999.

Longstreth, Richard. *On the Edge of the World: Four Architects in San Francisco at the Turn of the Century*. Cambridge: MIT Press, 1983.

Luckin, Richard W. *Mimbres to Mimbreño: A Study of Santa Fe's Famous China Pattern*. Golden, CO: RK Publishing, 1992.

Lynn, Sandra D. *Windows on the Past: Historic Lodgings of New Mexico*. Albuquerque: University of New Mexico Press, 1999.

McClelland, Linda Flint, *Building the National Parks: Historic Landscape Design and Construction*. Baltimore: The Johns Hopkins University Press, 1998.

Meeks, Carroll L. V. *The Railroad Station: An Architectural History*. New Haven: Yale University Press, 1956.

Neumann, Mark. *On the Rim: Looking for the Grand Canyon*. Minneapolis: University of Minnesota Press, 1999.

Oliver, Richard. *Bertram Grosvenor Goodhue*. Cambridge, MA: The MIT Press, 1983.

Parezo, Nancy J. *Navajo Sandpainting: From Religious Act to Commercial Art*. Tucson: University of Arizona Press, 1983.

Poling-Kempes, Leslie. *The Harvey Girls: Women Who Opened the West*. New York: Marlowe and Company, 1991.

Pyle, Ernie. *Home Country*. New York: William Sloane, 1947.

Pyne, Steven J. *How the Canyon Became Grand*. New York: Penguin Books, 1998.

Reed, Cleota, and Skoczen, Stan. *Syracuse China*. Syracuse, NY: University of Syracuse Press, 1997.

Ripley, John W., and Richmond, Robert W., eds. *The Santa Fe in Topeka*. Shawnee, KS: The Shawnee County Historical Society, 1979.

Sandy, Wilda. *Stalking Louis Curtiss*. Kansas City, MO: Ward Parkway Press, 1991.

Spector, Robert. *More Than a Store: Frederick and Nelson, 1890 to 1990*. Bellevue, WA: Documentary Book Publishers, 1990.

Thomas, Diane H. *The Southwestern Indian Detours*. Phoenix: Hunter Publishing, 1978.

Thompson, Ian. The Towers of Hovenweep. Mesa Verde, CO: Mesa Verde Museum Association, 1993.

Tillotson, Miner R., and Taylor, Frank J. *Grand Canyon Country*. Stanford: Stanford University Press, 1929.

Tweed, William C., Soullière, Laura E., and Law, Henry G. *National Park Service Rustic Architecture: 1916–1942*. San Francisco: National Park Service, 1977.

Waters, Frank. *Masked Gods: Navaho and Pueblo Ceremonialism*. Chicago: The Swallow Press, 1950.

Weigle, Marta, and Babcock, Barbara A., eds. *The Great Southwest of the Fred Harvey Company and the Santa Fe Railway*. Phoenix: The Heard Museum, 1996.

Wilson, Chris. *The Myth of Santa Fe: Creating a Modern Regional Tradition*. Albuquerque: University of New Mexico Press, 1997.

Woods, Mary N. *From Craft to Profession: The Practice of Architecture in Nineteenth-Century America*. Berkeley: The University of California Press, 1999.

Wyman, Leland C. *Navaho Sandpainting: The Huckel Collection*. Colorado Springs, CO: The Taylor Museum, 1960.

ARTICLES, REPORTS, AND MEDIA

"A Dream Come True," *The Santa Fe Magazine* (November 1914): 39–44.

Albuquerque Journal Democrat (May 11, 1902): n.p.

"Alvarado's Cocktail Lounge Opens to Display Spanish Atmosphere," *Albuquerque Tribune* (July 10, 1940): n.p.

"The Alvarado of Albuquerque, New Mexico," *The Hotel Monthly* (October 1922): 50–51.

Amero, Richard W. "The Southwest on Display at the Panama-California Exposition," *Journal of San Diego History* (1990, Vol. 36): 186–219.

Armstrong, Ruth W. Letter to the editor, *The New Mexican* [?] (December 1984): n.p.

Art Workers' Guild of St. Paul, "Annual Report of Secretary, Year Ending May 1, 1906."

Balmer, J. E. "The Navajo is Becoming Civilized," *Winslow Daily Mail* (June 2, 1930, special supplement): 20.

Bartlett, Karen. "In the House Made of the Dawn: The Mary Colter Story," *Craftsman Home Owner* (1997, Vol. 9, No.1): 1–5.

Beebe, Lucius. "Purveyor to the West," *The American Heritage* (February 1967): 28–31, 99–102.

Berke, Arnold. "Drawing From the Desert," *Preservation* (July/August 1997): 34–43.

Boutelle, Sara Holmes. *"Mary Colter: Builder Upon the Red Earth, Virginia L. Grattan,"*

review, *AIA Journal*, (June 1981): 58, 60.

Chappell, Gordon. "Railroad at the Rim: The Origin and Growth of Grand Canyon Village," *The Journal of Arizona History* (1976, Vol. 17, No. 1): 89–107.

City of St. Paul Board of Education, "Report of Board of Education" (1899).

Cliff, W. Wilson. "Alvarado Hotel Will Close Doors," *Albuquerque Journal* (September 20, 1969): A-1.

Colter, Mary. "Mary E. J. Colter," typed manuscript (October 25, 1952).

Comee, Fred T., "Louis Curtiss of Kansas City," *Progressive Architecture* (August 1963): 128–134.

"Contract Awarded for Gallup Harvey House Addition," *Albuquerque Herald* (July 23, 1922): n.p.

DeHuff, Elizabeth W., "Architecture and Furnishings of 'La Posada,'" Courier's Instructional Bulletin No. 2, The Santa Fe Transportation Company (April 1, 1930).

Design Collaborative Southwest. "Gallup Multimodal Center Renovation," project description sheet, Albuquerque (n.d.).

"Design of Union Station to be California Style," *Los Angeles Times* (August 7, 1934): n.p.

Donahoe, James M. "Desert View Watchtower Historic District," National Register of Historic Places registration form (August 29, 1994).

Doyle, Frederick, "A Little Journery to the Indian Watchtower of the Grand Canyon," typed manuscript (n.d.).

Drew, Steven E. "Atchison, Topeka and Santa Fe Diner No. 1474, 'Cochiti,'" information sheet, California State Railroad Museum (n.d.).

"El Navajo Dedicated for Service to All Mankind With Religious Rites," *The Gallup Herald* (May 26, 1923): 1.

"El Navajo Hotel Reflects the Painted Desert," *The Hotel Monthly* (July 1923): 40–42.

"Enlarged Lunch Room of Alvarado Hotel to be Open Monday for Public Inspection," *The Albuquerque Herald* (December 3, 1922): n.p.

Ferber, Edna. "Our Very Best People," *The Kansas City Star* (June 6, 1943 reprint of July 27, 1924): 14.

"Food Service on the Santa Fe's New Streamlined Trains," *The Hotel Monthly* (September 1938): 17–19.

Force, Kenneth, "Kansas City Likes Westport Room," *Restaurant Management* (February 1938): 82–85.

"Fred Harvey, Caterer, Chicago Union Station," *The Hotel Monthly* (August 1925): 38–73.

Fred Harvey Company. "California and the Grand Canyon of Arizona," booklet (1914).

———. "De-Ki-Veh," booklet (May 13, 1933).

———. "The Furnishings of La Posada, Winslow, Arizona," brochure (undated).

———. "The Great Southwest Along the Santa Fe," booklet (1921).

———. *Hospitality* (June 1955): 11.

———. *Hospitality* (May 1957): n.p.

———. *Hospitality* (January 1958): 3.

———. "La Posada, Winslow, Arizona," brochure (n.d.).

———. "The Lookout, Grand Canyon," booklet (1915).

———. "Painted Desert Inn," brochure (1955).

———. "The Sand Paintings of the Navajo," booklet (1923).

Fred Harvey Company/Amfac. "The Watchtower Guide," brochure (various undated).

Fred Harvey Company and the Santa Fe Railway. "The Alvarado, a New Hotel at Albuquerque, New Mexico," booklet (1904).

"The Fred Harvey 'Santa Fe' Service," *The Hotel Monthly* (October 1928): 39–42.

"Fred Harvey Welcomes You!," advertisement, *Los Angeles Times* (May 3, 1939): 6.

Freeman, Lewis R. *The Colorado River: Yesterday, To-Day and Tomorrow* (afterword), typed manuscript (1923).

Fritzen, Irving S. "Streamlining a Pueblo," *The Santa Fe Magazine* (June 1939): 7–14.

Gebhard, David. "Architecture and the Fred Harvey Houses," *New Mexico Architect* (July/August 1962): 11–17; (January–February 1964): 18–25.

Graham, Robert G. "La Posada Historic District," National Register of Historic Places registration form (July 9, 1991).

Green, Keith B. "The Early History of Phantom Ranch," unpublished manuscript for Arizona Historical Society (February, 1987).

Hansen, Peter A. "Give the People a Monument," *Trains* (April 1999): 62–72.

Harrison, Michael, oral history transcript (June 1, 1995).

Harvey, Byron III. "The Fred Harvey Collection, 1899–1963," *Plateau* (Fall 1963): 33–53

Harvey, Ford. "The Public and the Grand Canyon," in *Proceedings of the National Parks Conference.* Washington, D.C.: U.S. Government Printing Office, 1917.

"Harvey House Plans Announced," *Winslow Daily Mail* (January 27, 1929): 1, 5.

"Harvey House Work Will Begin at Once," *Winslow Daily Mail* (April 16, 1929): 1, 3.

Harvey, Steve. "Union Station," *Los Angeles Times* (March 1, 1987): Part 2, 1–2.

Heard Museum. "Inventing the Southwest: The Fred Harvey Company and Native American Art," exhibit (1996–97).

"Hedda Hopper's Hollywood," column, *Los Angeles Times* (May 17, 1939): n.p.

Henderson, James D. "Meals by Fred Harvey," *Arizona and the West* (Winter 1966): 305–322.

Henry, Jay C. "Virginia L. Grattan, Mary Coulter [sic]: Builder Upon the Red Earth," review, *Journal of the Society of Architectural Historians* (March 1982): 77–78.

Henson, Gertrude. "'La Posada,' a Typical Spanish Rancho," *Winslow Daily Mail* (June 2, 1930, special supplement): 1, 16–17.

"Hold Services For J. F. Huckel Monday," *Colorado Springs Sunday Gazette* (n.d.): n.p.

"Homely Epic Story of West Told in Bright Angel Lodge, Picturesque New Hotel," *Santa Fe New Mexican* (June 10, 1935): n.p.

The Hotel Monthly (June 1908): n.p.

Howard, Kathleen L., and Pardue, Diana F. "Mary Jane Colter: Designing the Dream of the West," *Cañon Journal* (Spring/Summer 1996): 30–43.

Hungerford, Edward, "A Study in Consistent Railroad Advertising," *The Santa Fe Magazine* (March 1923): 43–48.

Hungerford, John B. "Death of an Inn," *Los Angeles Times* (August 27, 1957): n.p.

"Impressions of El Ortiz," *Santa Fe Employes' Magazine* (October 1910): 55–56.

The Independent (Kansas City) (July 24, 1937): cover.

"Indians Demand Privacy During Ritual in Hotel," *The Gallup Independent* (May 22, 1923): 1.

Johnson, Don P., and Leopold, Aldo. "Grand Canyon Working Plan" (U.S. Forest Service, April 1917).

Kansas City Journal Post (July 25, 1937): n.p.

Kansas City Star (August 9, 1943): n.p.

Kansas City Star (March 28, 1915): n.p.

Kansas City Times (November 23, 1916): n.p.

Kipling, Rudyard, "The Feet of the Young Men," 1897.

Kipling, Rudyard, "The Palace," 1902.

"La Fonda, Santa Fe, New Mexico," *The Hotel Monthly* (March 1932): 24–29.

"La Fonda, Tripled in Size Becomes Spanish Fairyland," *Santa Fe New Mexican* (May 18, 1929): n.p.

"Lamy, the Town the Railroad Built," *The Atom* (April 1966): 18.

"La Posada and Harveycars, Winslow," *The Hotel Monthly* (February 1931): 44–55.

Long, Lily A. "The New Century Club, 1887–1922," booklet (April 26, 1922).

"Los Angeles' New Union Station," *Los Angeles Times* (May 1, 1939): B.

"Los Angeles Union Passenger Railway Station," *Architect and Engineer* (May 1939): 37–41.

Lovret, Ruben. "Los Angeles Union Passenger Terminal," National Register of Historic Places nomination form (August 1978).

"Mary Colter Dies Here," *The New Mexican* (January 8, 1958): 2.

"Mary Jane Coulter [sic] Helps Canyon Library," *The Arizona Republic* (August 2, 1957): 12.

Mary Jane Colter: House Made of Dawn. producer/writer/director Karen Bartlett. Nemesis Productions, 1997.

Mary Jane Colter: The Desert View, producer/writer/director Jennifer Lee. Catskill Films, 1996.

Mather, Christine. "Mexican Artifacts Collected by the Fred Harvey Company," *The Magazine Antiques* (December 1983): 1206–1211.

Meadows, Amy. "Miss Colter Does it Again!," *Hospitality* (September 1949): 3.

Meadows, Amy. "Santa Fe," *Hospitality* (June 1955): 11.

"Mechanic Arts High School," typed manuscript (February 23, 1932).

Mechanic Arts [High School] Literary Society. "M," booklet (April 1916).

"Miss Colter Dies in Santa Fe," *Hospitality* (January/February 1958): 3.

"Miss Colter's Indian Jewels on Public Exhibition at Lab," *The New Mexican* (April 20, 1952): n.p.

Mitchell, Harold D., "Architecture in America: Its History up to the Present Time," *California Architect and Building News*, (February 1882): 29–30.

"Model of Indian Pueblo Shows Santa Fe Exhibit," *San Diego Union* (March 24, 1914): 1.

Morley, Sylvanus G. "Keeping a City Old," *Santa Fe Trail* (August 1913): 93–95.

Mullen, Jack. "America's Best-Fed Travelers," *The Santa Fe Magazine* (December 1943): 9.

National Park Service. "Historic Structure Report: Painted Desert Inn, Petrified Forest National Park, AZ" (October 1994).

National Park Service. "Painted Desert Inn," brochure, n.d.

National Park Service, Petrified Forest National Monument. "Superintendent's Monthly Report" (December 1947).

National Park Service, Petrified Forest National Monument. "Superintendent's Monthly Report" (May 1948).

National Park Service. "Report of the Director of the National Park Service" (1918).

"Navajo Medicine Men Will Officiate at El Navajo Opening Here May 25," *The Gallup Herald* (May 19, 1923): 1.

"Navajo Sand Paintings as Decorative Motive," *El Palacio* (June 15, 1923): 175–188.

"The New Bright Angel Lodge and Cabins," *The Hotel Monthly* (December 1936): 13–22.

New Mexico State Tribune (May 25, 1923): n.p.

New York Sun (May 7, 1903): n.p.

"140,000 Visit Grand Canyon in 1934; $500,000 to be Spent on New Bright Angel Lodge," *Santa Fe New Mexican* (September 20, 1934): n.p.

"Open Union Passenger Terminal at Los Angeles, Cal.," *Railway Age* (May 6, 1939): 768–778, 786.

"Over New Kaibab Trail From Rim to Rim," *The Hotel Monthly* (September 1928): 65–72.

"Phantom Ranch," National Register of Historic Places nomination form (draft) (n.d.).

"Plan Rite for Each Indian Sacred Painting in Hotel," *The Gallup Independent* (May 15, 1923): 1.

Pyle, Ernie. "Why Albuquerque?", *New Mexico Magazine* (July 1997 reprint of January 1942): 102–05.

Reeder, Sally. Letter to the editor, *The New Mexican* (June 27, 1961): n.p.

"A Remarkable Indian Ceremony," *The Santa Fe Magazine* (July 1923): 17–22.

"The San Francisco Art Association, 1871–1906," exhibition brochure, California Historical Society (1906).

"Santa Fe Railroad's Indian Pueblo Marvel of Primitive Craft," *San Diego Union* (January 1, 1915): n.p.

Saunders, Sallie. "Indian Watchtower at Grand Cañon is Dedicated by Hopi Indians," *The Santa Fe Magazine* (July 1933): 27–31.

Shepherd-Lanier, Claire. "Trading on Tradition: Mary Jane Colter and the Romantic Appeal of Harvey House Architecture," *Journal of the Southwest* (Summer 1996, Vol. 38, No.2): 163–195.

Shuit, Doug. "Once-Bustling Union Station Loses Out to Jets, Freeways," *Los Angeles Times* (May 5, 1969): 1.

Simpson, William H. "El Tovar by Fred Harvey: A New Hotel at Grand Canyon of Arizona," Santa Fe Railway (1905).

Smith, Conover C. "Fred Harvey Closing Marks End of Era," *The Kansas City Times* (December 28, 1968): 12C.

"Taxi Into Streetcar," *Kansas City Star* (March 14, 1929): 17.

Tisdale, Shelby J. "Railroads, Tourism and Native Americans in the Greater Southwest," *Journal of the Southwest* (Vol. 38, No. 4, 1996): 433–462.

Trennert, Robert A. "Fairs, Exhibitions, and the Changing Image of Southwestern Indians, 1876–1904," *New Mexico Historical Review* (April 1987): 127–150.

Van Slyck, Abigail A. "Women in Architecture and the Problems of Biography," review, *Design Book Review* (Summer 1992): 19–22.

Weber, Herbert Y. "The Story of the *St. Paul Globe*," *Minnesota History* (Winter 1965): 327–334.

Weigle, Marta. "Exposition and Mediation: Mary Colter, Erna Fergusson, and the Santa Fe/Harvey Popularization of the Native Southwest, 1902–1940," *Frontiers* (1992, Vol. 12, No. 3): 117–50.

Wilson, Chris. "Pflueger General Merchandise Store and Annex Saloon," National Register of Historic Places nomination form (February 17, 1987).

Wister, Owen. "A Preface by Owen Wister," typed manuscript for Architectural Book Publishing Company (November 1922).

Woodward Architectural Group. "Project Description: Use of Masonry in Design," summary for award submission for Hopi House restoration (1997).

Woodward, James W., Jr. "Grand Canyon Village Historic District," National Register of Historic Places registration form (January 17, 1990).

ARCHIVAL SOURCES

American Institute of Architects Archives, Washington, D.C.

Arizona Historical Society/Northern Arizona Division/Flagstaff, Arizona.

Center for Southwest Research, John Gaw Meem Archives, University of New Mexico, Albuquerque, New Mexico.

Cline Library, Special Collections, Northern Arizona University, Flagstaff, Arizona.

La Fonda Hotel files, Santa Fe, New Mexico.

La Posada Hotel files, Winslow, Arizona.

Heard Museum Archives, Heard Museum, Phoenix, Arizona.

Mesa Verde National Park Archives, Mesa Verde National Park, Colorado.

Minnesota Historical Society, Special Collections, St. Paul, Minnesota.

Museum of Northern Arizona, Harold S. Colton Research Center, Flagstaff, Arizona.

Museum of New Mexico, Palace of the Governors, Photographic Archives, Santa Fe, New Mexico.

Grand Canyon National Park Museum Collection, Grand Canyon National Park, Arizona.

Grand Canyon National Park Research Library, Grand Canyon National Park, Arizona.

National Trust for Historic Preservation Library, University of Maryland, College Park, Maryland.

New Mexico Office of Cultural Affairs, Historic Preservation Division files, Santa Fe, New Mexico.

Octavia Fellin Public Library, Gallup, New Mexico.

Winslow Historical Society, Old Trails Museum, Winslow, Arizona.

Illustration Credits

The Albuquerque Museum 53

Amon Carter Museum, Fort Worth, Texas 267

Arizona Historical Society/Northern Arizona Division 27

Autry Museum of Western Heritage 151

Berke, Arnold 95, 142, 263 (top left)

Burlington Northern Santa Fe Railroad 129, 165

California Historical Society 29

California State Railroad Museum 47

Center for Southwest Research, University of New Mexico 155, 157

Chicago Historical Society 145

Cline Library, Northern Arizona University 76, 86, 210, 213, 239

Crawford, Grey 203 (right)

Dilworth, Leah 49

Grand Canyon National Park Museum Collection 12, 16, 60, 68, 93, 97, 101, 102, 109, 110, 114, 118, 120, 136, 138, 173, 177, 190, 191, 194 (right), 196, 197, 201, 203 (left), 205, 206, 209, 213 (bottom right), 214, 216, 221, 222 (top), 230, 250, 263, 273

Grand Canyon National Park, Mary Larkin Smith Collection 34, 36

Heard Museum 39, 150, 151

Hight, George C. 274

Kansas State Historical Society 41, 44, 58, 61, 126, 130, 131, 135, 193

Lake County (IL) Discovery Museum, Curt Teich Postcard Archives 48, 94, 97, 119, 119, 128, 158, 162 (left), 226

La Posada Hotel Archives 51, 62, 74, 122, 178

Library of Congress 167, 210, 215, 237, 236

Little Bighorn Battlefield National Monument 26

Los Angeles Public Library/Photo Collection 245 (bottom)

Luckin, Richard 13, 232

Mesa Verde National Park Archives 187, 188, 189, 258, 266

Minneapolis Public Library 71

Minnesota Historical Society 22, 32, 33, 37

Museum of New Mexico 21, 45, 52, 75, 79, 149, 261, 263 (bottom left)

Museum of Northern Arizona 89, 120, 213 (right), 222 (bottom)

Philadelphia Museum of Art 46

San Diego Historical Society, Photograph Collection 106, 107

Schick, Jeanne 223

Seattle Museum of History and Industry 70

Smalling, Walter 82

Union Station Kansas City, Inc. 236

University of Arizona Library, Special Collections 11, 38, 54, 55, 65, 125, 128, 132, 133, 146, 159, 162 (right), 168, 172, 175 (bottom), 199, 271

University of Kansas, Kansas Collection, Kansas City Terminal Railway Company Collection 84, 85

University of Southern California, Whittington Collection 241, 242,

Vertikoff, Alexander © 1, 10, 14, 18, 63, 90, 91, 98, 99, 102, 170, 171, 174, 175, 179, 182, 186, 194 (left), 195, 197 (top left), 202, 211, 215 (right), 262, 279 (right), 282, 283, 286, 287, 290, 291

Winslow Historical Society, Old Trials Museum 44, 165, 185

Acknowledgments

Just as the Fred Harvey Company and Santa Fe Railway enticed travelers to the Southwest, so did the remarkable story of Mary Colter lure me into writing this book. The project proved to be an expedition of many months and miles in pursuit of Colter and her works amid southwestern cultures and landscapes. A host of people have helped and inspired me along the way, beginning with the germ for the book, the cover story I wrote in 1997 for *Preservation* magazine.

Gathering information and images for the project was smoothed by research staff at a number of institutions, certain of whom stand out for their unflagging professionalism, on site and over the miles: Colleen Hyde and Michael Quinn at the Grand Canyon National Park Museum Collection; Bradford Cole at Northern Arizona University's Cline Library; and Carolyn Landes and Paul Rogers at the Mesa Verde National Park Archives. Other archivists and curators include Marilyn Fletcher and staff at the University of New Mexico's Center for Southwest Research; Tracey Baker, Tino Avaloz, and Marcia Anderson, Minnesota Historical Society; Michael O'Hara and Tony Marinella, Museum of Northern Arizona; Mo Palmer, Albuquerque Museum; Sarah Stebbins, former director of the Grand Canyon National Park Research Library; Janice Griffith, Old Trails Museum; Nancy Hanks, New Mexico Historic Preservation Division; Janet Russell, Jackson County (Missouri) Historical Society; Rita Garcia, Petrified Forest National Park; Jan Kathy Davis and Roger Myers, University of Arizona's Special Collections; Cathleen Baird, Hospitality Industry Library and Archives, University of Houston; Susan Wilcox, Arizona Historical Society/Flagstaff; and LaRee Bates, Heard Museum. Thanks also go to Faye Phillips, whose photo research uncovered gems and saved me untold hours, and to Sally Sims Stokes, who directs the National Trust Library of the University of Maryland, for her help in skillfully guiding my first forays into the research for the book.

My explorations brought me in contact with a most delightful assortment of people who knew about Mary Colter or related topics, all of them generous in sharing information, memories, or contacts. Karen Bartlett, creator of a radiant documentary on Colter, helped early on to initiate my trip. Among the others are Claire Shepherd-Lanier, Sally Noe, Jeanne Schick, Gale Burak, Patricia Smyth, James Woodward, Marie LaMar, Jere Krakow, Carol Naille, J. Stewart Harvey, Cleota Reed, Betty Leavengood, Harvey Jones, Nancy Meem Wirth, Scott Field, Andrew Gulliford, Brenda Thowe, Octavia Fellin, John Fowler, James Garrison, Robert Frankeberger, Barbara Cooke, Robert Hallwachs, Kathleen Howard, Juti Winchester, Barbara Waters, Jennifer Hall Lee, and Colter's namesake, Mary Colter Larkin Smith. For Chapter Seven's fetching images of Colter's jewelry, kudos to professional photographer and Mesa Verde volunteer James Goff. Special thanks are due to Virginia Grattan, author of the first book on Colter, who went beyond that path-breaking work to graciously share information and photos with me.

Through the hospitality of Bill Johnston, Grand Canyon National Park Lodges (successor to the Harvey Company) kindly provided accommodations during one of my research trips. Jerry Schadt at the Painted Desert Inn was equally gracious. Other Lodges staff, especially Dennis Reason and Henry Karpinski, offered invaluable information about and tours of buildings that Colter designed at the canyon. Author Michael Anderson's encyclopedic knowledge of the park's human history proved more than once to be invaluable. As always, National Park Service staff members were a delight to work with. I thank especially Keith Green for sharing his expansive knowledge of Phantom Ranch, Lisa Collins for my second tour of the Watchtower, and Joanne Wilkins for hosting my inspection of the Bright Angel complex and other structures by Colter.

For their tireless hospitality, help, and friendship from the very beginning, I offer the warmest of thanks to Allan Affeldt, Dan Lutzick, and Tina Mion, who have worked wonders to revive and reopen their Colter charmer in Winslow, La Posada. Thank you, too, to the folks at La Fonda in Santa Fe: owner Sam Ballen, concierge Steven Wimmer, and Lisa Bertelli. Back home in Washington, I extend my appreciation to Bob Wilson and other associates at Preservation and the National Trust for their support and encouragement.

Books are written but they also must be edited and produced. Gina Bell, an editor formerly at Princeton Architectural Press, gets the credit for first floating past me the notion of writing this book. My editor through the many months of detail-laden finish and publication of the book, Jan Cigliano, deserves a special award for keeping it all moving forward with aplomb. To art director Deb Wood and designer Angela Voulangas go many thanks for bringing Mary Colter to life in the book's design.

Finally, deep gratitude to my partner, Jake Pearce, for sharing this long journey with me, for offering encouragement and advice, and for being patient—not once throwing me out of the house, even during the worst of computer calamity.